Bell, S. Tuten

Nashat, Middle Eastern History

Selected Reading Lists and Course Outlines from American Colleges and Universities

Middle Eastern History

edited by Guity Nashat
University of Illinois at Chicago

Library of Congress Cataloging-in-Publication Data

Middle Eastern history / edited with an introduction by Guity Nashat.
p. cm. -- (Selected course outlines and reading lists from leading American colleges and universities ; 16)
Bibliography: p.
ISBN 0-910129-70-3 :
1. Middle East--Study and teaching (Higher)--Curricula. 2. Middle East--Study and teaching (Higher)--United States--Curricula. I. Nashat, Guity, 1937- . II. Series: Selected reading lists and course outlines from American colleges and universities ; vol. 16.
DS61.9.M628M53 1987
956'.007'1173--dc19 87-33409
CIP

Printed in America

INTRODUCTION

The term Middle East is of recent vintage; it was coined in 1902 by an American naval historian. But the interest of the West in this region goes back to Herodotus, the father of history. Yet despite the millennia of contact and some shared heritage, the relationship between the West and the Middle East has been colored more by misunderstanding and conflict than by friendly interchange. Since the rise of Islam in the 7th century, religious controversy added a new dimension to the hostility between the two sides. The failure of the Crusades to establish a permanent foothold in the region only intensified animosity to the new religion and reduced any meaningful exchange between the two sides to a minimum for several centuries.

The anti-Islamic polemic that characterized medieval church-sponsored writing on Islam continued, and has survived to our day. But beginning with the Renaissance, interest in a better understanding of Islam, the West's closest neighbor, began to emerge. Some of the reasons for this new attitude were: the revival of classical studies, curiosity stimulated by the Reformation in Islam, the Ottoman Empire's expansion into the heart of Europe, and the need for more accurate information generated by Europe's economic and political expansion into many regions.

During the 19th century, "Oriental Studies," as the study of the region began to be called, entered a new phase. Under this vague rubric, amateurs and scholars began to apply critical historical methodology to the study of classical Islam - dealing mainly with theological or philological issues. Some of these studies resulted in works of lasting importance. But many of the products of the orientalists, like the growing body of private Western travel accounts and official studies, were marred by a sense of superiority that 19th century Westerners felt towards non-Western societies. Even worse, some of these studies were prepared by officials, who were promoting and justifying the colonial or imperialist policies of their governments.

The study of the Middle East has finally come of age since World War II. The scope of scholarship about the Middle East has widened, and the number of scholars interested in the region has increased vastly. This trend is particularly true of the United States, where major universities have developed degree programs on Middle Eastern fields and smaller universities offer elective courses on the region. A greater effort to study the region and its civilization in a more objective fashion seems to be underway. The present volume of more than sixty course syllabi offered at different institutions of higher education throughout the United States is important evidence of this new trend.

In preparing this volume I have tried to cover a broad range of topics and periods. I received many more excellent course outlines than could be used. Therefore, to help make the difficult choice among a large number of outstanding course syllabi, I gave preference to those that arrived earliest when considering syllabi of equal merit on similar subjects.

I would like to thank all the colleagues who generously sent me their outlines. I hope to include some of those not used in this volume in the new edition, in-sha'allah. I would also like to thank Markus Wiener, the publisher of this series, for his inspiration and assistance.

University of Illinois, Chicago
December 1987

SELECTED COURSE OUTLINES: MIDDLE EASTERN HISTORY

TABLE OF CONTENTS

D. Historiography

E. Regional History

Documents were reproduced from originals as submitted.

NEW YORK INSTITUTE OF TECHNOLOGY
(Dept. of Soc. & Pol. Sci.)

Prof. A. J. Abraham
(212 399-8387/ Rm. 401 B)

An Introduction To Islamic Civilization And Institutions

This course will survey the civilization and institutions of Islam. The intended audience for the course is college-wide; and there is no prerequisite.

Course requirements include a term paper and a comprehensive final exam. Reading assignments will be selected from the reading list, and the books on reserve.

On Reserve:

Gaudefroy-Desmombynes, M., Muslim Institutions, N.Y.: Barnes and Noble, 1961.

Hitti, Philip K., History of the Arabs, 10th. ed., N.Y.: St. Martin's Press, 1974.

COURSE OUTLINE

1. Introduction: Pre-Islamic Arabia and the Superpowers of the ancient Near East in the 6th. century A.D.
2. The life and times of Muhammad.
3. The Book and the faith.
4. The Arab kingdom: the Umayyads of Damascus.
5. The Arab Empire: the Abbasids of Baghdad.
6. The era of petty states.
7. Islam and Christianity, Crossroads in Faith.
8. The Islamic State, from Caliphate to modern times.
9. The Law (Shari'ah).
10. The Social Structure of Islam.
11. Islamic Economics, the new alternative.
12. "Islam and the isms," Arab/Islamic Socialism, Islamic Marxism/ Communism, Arab/Islamic Nationalism, etc..
13. Paper and comprehensive final exam (2 hr.).

READING LIST

An Introduction To Islamic Civilization And Institutions

Required Reading:

Abraham, A.J., Islam and Christianity: Crossroads in Faith, IN.: Wyndham Hall Press, 1986.

Gaudefroy-Desmombynes, M., Muslim Institutions, N.Y.: Barnes and Noble, 1961.

Hitti, P.K., History of the Arabs, 10th. ed., N.Y.: St. Martin's Press, 1974.

Islamic Law:

Anderson, J.N.D., Islamic Law in the Modern World, N.Y.: NYU Press, 1959.

Coulson, N.J., History of Islamic Law, Edinburgh: Edinburgh Univ. Press, 1964.

__________, Conflicts and Tensions in Islamic Jurisprudence, Chicago: Univ. of Chicago Press, 1969.

Doi, A.R.I., Non-Muslims Under Shari'ah (Islamic Law), U.S.A.: International Graphics, 1976.

Fyzee, A.A.A., Outlines of Muhammadan Law, Gt. Brit., Oxford Univ. Press, 1960.

Khadduri, M., War and Peace in the Law of Islam, Baltimore: Johns Hopkins Univ. Press, 1955.

__________, Islamic Jurisprudence, Shafi'i's Risala, Baltimore: Johns Hopkins Press, 1961.

__________ and Liebesny, H.J., Law In The Middle East, Wash.: The Middle East Institute, 1955.

Mayer, A.E. (ed.), Property, Social Structure, and Law in the Middle East, N.Y.: St. Univ. of N.Y. Press, 1985.

Ramadan, S., Islamic Law: Its Scope and Equity, London: Macmillam, 1961.

Schacht, J., The Origins of Muhammadan Jurisprudence, Oxford: The Clarendon Press, 1950.

The Social Structure of Islam:

Abraham, A.J., Khoumani, Islamic Fundamentalists And The Contributions of Islamic Sciences To Modern Civilization, IN.: Foundations Press of Notre Dame, 1983.

Beck, L. and Keddie, N., Women in the Moslem World, MA.: Harvard Univ. Press, 1984.

Berger, M., The Arab World Today, N.Y.: Anchor Books, 1964.

________, Islam in Egypt Today, Cambridge: Cambridge Univ. Press, 1970.

Esposito, J.L., Women in Muslim Family Law, N.Y.: Syracuse Univ. Press.

Hanifi, M.J., Islam And The Transformation of Culture, N.Y.: Asia Pub. House, 1970.

Gellner, E., Muslim Society, London: Cambridge Univ. Press, 1981.

Lerner, D., The Passing of Traditional Society, N.Y.: The Free Press, 1965.

Levy, R., The Social Structure of Islam, Cambridge: The Univ. Press, 1969.

Said, A.M., Arab Socialism, N.Y.: Barnes and Noble, 1972.

Taleghani, M., Society and Economics in Islam, Berkely: Mizan Press, 1982.

Islamic Economics:

Ahmad, M., Economics of Islam, Pakistan: Ashraf Pub. House, 1958.

Ahmad, K. (ed.), Studies in Islamic Economics, U.K.: The Islamic Foundation, 1980.

Amin, S., The Arab Economy Today, London: Zed Press, 1982.

Bonne, A., State and Economy in the Middle East: A Society in Transition, London: Routledge & Kegen, 1955.

Chapra, M., Objectives of the Islamic Economic Order, U.K.: The Islamic Foundation, 1979.

__________, The Islamic Welfare State and its Role in the Economy, U.K.: The Islamic Foundation, 1979.

Issawi, C.P., The Economic History of The Middle East, 1800-1914, N.Y.: Columbia Univ. Press, 1984.

Kermani, T.T., Economic Development in Action: Theory, Problems, and Procedures as Applied to the Middle East, Cleveland: World Pub. Co., 1967.

Naqvi, N.H., Ethics and Economics, U.K., The Islamic Foundation, 1981.

Rodinson, M., Islam and Capitalism, N.Y.: Pantheon, 1973.

Sayigh, Y.A., The Arab Economy: Past Performance and Future Prospects, N.Y.: Oxford Univ. Press, 1982.

Siddiqi, M.N., Muslim Economic Thinking, U.K.: The Islamic Foundation, 1981.

_____________, Issues in Islamic Banking, U.K.: The Islamic Foundation, 1983.

Taleghani, M., Society and Economics in Islam, Berkely: Mizan Press, 1982.

The Islamic State:

Abdel-Malek, A. (ed.), Contemporary Arab Political Thought, London: Zed Pub., 1983.

Abraham, A.J., Khoumani, Islamic Fundamentalists And The Contributions of Islamic Sciences To Modern Civilization, IN.: Foundations Press of Notre Dame, 1983.

Afshar, H. (ed.), Iran: A Revolution in Termoil, N.Y.: St. Univ. of N.Y. Press.

Ajami, F., The Arab Predicament, Cambridge: Cambridge Univ. Press, 1981.

Azzam, S. (ed.), Concepts of The Islamic State, London: Islamic Council of Europe, 1979.

Bill, J.A. and Lieden, C., The Middle East, Politics and Power, Boston: Allyn and Bacon, 1974.

Dekmejian, R.H., Islam in Revolution: Fundamentalism in the Arab World, N.Y.: Syracuse Univ. Press, 1985.

Dessouki, A.E.H., Islamic Resurgence in the Arab World, N.Y.: Praeger, 1982.

Enayat, H., Modern Islamic Political Thought, TX.: Univ. of Texas Press.

Esposito, J.L., Islam and Politics, N.Y.: Syracuse Univ. Press, 1984.

Hudson, M.C., Arab Politics, N.H.: Yale Univ. Press, 1977.

Irfani, S., Revolutionary Islam in Iran, London: Zed Press, 1984.

Ismael, T.Y., The Arab Left, N.Y.: Syracuse Univ. Press, 1984.

Jensen, G., Militant Islam, N.Y.: Harper and Row, 1979.

Keddi, N.R., Roots of Revolution, New Haven: Yale Univ. Press, 1981.

Khadduri, M., War and Peace in The Law of Islam, N.Y.: AMS Press, 1955.

Voll, J.O., Islam: Continuity and Change in The Modern World, Colorado: Westview Press, 1982.

HISTORY 354: INTRODUCTION TO ISLAM

Course Syllabus
Fall, 1986

Instructor: Elton L. Daniel
Sakamaki B-205
Phone: ext. 6759

Textbooks and Required Readings:

F. M. Denny, *An Introduction to Islam*

(Short excerpts from other works will be provided in labs or during lectures)

Course Requirements: Attendance at scheduled lectures; completion of assigned readings; participation in classroom discussions and other work; completion of a midterm exam and a final, one-hour, non-comprehensive final examination. Grades will be determined on the following basis: midterm exam (35%); final exam (35%); book report (15%); attendance and participation (15%)

Office Hours: I will be available for consultations with students during my regular office hours, MWF 8:00-9:00 a.m., in Sakamaki B-205 or by appointment.

LECTURE SCHEDULE

Date		*Topic*	*Suggested Reading*
Sept.	3	Introduction	
	5	The Pre-Islamic Middle East	3-15
	8	Hebrew Religion	17-30
	10	Eastern Christianity	32-44
	12	Iranian Religions	
	15	The Arabs Before Islam	46-59
	17	Muhammad in Mecca	65-80
	19	Muhammad in Madina	80-90
	22	The Koran	153-166
	24	The Concepts of the Koran	92-98
	26	Interpreting the Koran	166-173
	29	Islamic Rituals	99-117
Oct.	1	Pilgrimage	117-124
	3	The Muslim Conquests	125-130
	6	The Early Caliphate	130-135
	8	The Umayyads	135-140
	10	Umayyad Civilization	
	13	The Abbasids	140-148
	15	Abbasid Secular Culture: Science	
	17	Abbasid Secular Culture: Philosophy	212-214
	20	Abbasid Secular Culture: Literature	
	22	Abbasid Secular Culture: Art	
	24	MIDTERM EXAM	

	27	The Study of Hadith	174-188
	29	Scholastic and Dogmatic Theology	190-212
	31	Islamic Legal Theory	216-222
Nov.	3	Islamic Schools of Law	222-226
	5	Islamic Political Theory	228-238
	7	Shi'ism	226-228
	10	The Shi'ite Dynasties	
	12	Early Sufism	241-254
	14	Esoteric Sufism	254-264
	17	Al-Ghazzali	265-267
	19	The Sufi Orders	270-291
	21	Muslim Ethics and Social Customs	295-321
	24	Sunni Folk Islam	323-343
	26	Shi'i Folk Islam	343-346
	28	Wahhabi Revivalism	351-357
Dec.	1	Early Muslim Reformers	358-360
	3	Islamic "Modernism"	360-366
	5	Islam and Nationalism	366-376
	8	The Muslim Brotherhood	
	10	Khomeini and Contemporary Shi'ism	
Dec.	15:	FINAL EXAMINATION	

History 181 INTRODUCTION TO THE MIDDLE EAST Dr. Goldschmidt

Schedule of Lectures and Reading Assignments (Fall 1986)

The texts for this course are A Concise History of the Middle East (2nd ed.) and the Middle Eastern news from the Monday through Friday issues of The New York Times. Plan to complete all reading assignments on time.

Date	Topic	Reading
27 Aug.	Introduction to the study of the Middle East	
28	Geographical and social background	Intro. & ch. 1
3 Sep.	The Middle East before Islam	ch. 2
4	discussion	
8	Muhammad and the beginnings of Islam	chs. 3-4
10	Arab conquests	ch. 5
11	discussion **map quiz #1**	
15	Early Muslim dynasties	ch. 6
17	Islamic institutions and culture	ch. 8
18	discussion and review	
22	**FIRST EXAM** (bring 16 page bluebook and pen)	
24	Muslim sects and the Turkish takeover	pp. 77-86
25	discussion	
29	Crusader and Mongol conquests	pp. 86-92
1 Oct.	Slaves on horseback	pp. 111-118
2	discussion	
6	The Ottoman and Safavid empires	pp. 118-134
8	The Eastern Question	ch. 10
9	discussion **map quiz #2**	
13	Westernizing reform	ch. 11
15	Beginnings of nationalism	ch. 12
16	discussion and review	
20	**SECOND EXAM**	
22	The Arab awakening	ch. 13
23	discussion	
27	Ataturk and Reza Shah	ch. 14
29	Saudi Arabia and Egypt	ch. 15
30	discussion	
3 Nov.	The origins of Zionism	pp. 227-240
5	From Palestine to Israel	pp. 241-252
6	discussion **map quiz #3**	
10	Emergence of the Arab states	pp. 252-262
12	Nasserism vs. the West	ch. 18
13	discussion and review	
17	**THIRD EXAM**	
19	The June 1967 ("Six Day") War	ch. 19
20	discussion	
24	The October 1973 ("Yom Kippur") War	pp. 297-308
26	class cancelled for Thanksgiving vacation	
1 Dec.	The road to Camp David	pp. 308-315
3	The Iranian revolution (**BOOK CRITIQUE**)	pp. 317-331
4	discussion	
8	The crisis in Lebanon	pp. 331-339
10	The Current Situation	
11	discussion and review (**FINAL EXAM** during finals period)	

Instructor: Arthur Goldschmidt, 614 Oswald Tower, MW 2-3:15 PM, Th 8:30-9:30 AM or by appointment. Section Leaders: Mike Arlen, Andy Gross, Jeff Laubach, Mike O'Connor, Chris Pacilio, Mark Saba

M.I.T.

SYLLABUS

21.480. THE MIDDLE EAST: FROM THE RISE OF ISLAM TO WORLD WAR I

Prof. Philip S. Khoury
E51-207
253-2601
Office Hours: (Tues., 2:30-3:30)
or by appointment)

Fall 1986
T,Th. 10:30-12:00
Room: 66-168
3-0-6
HUM-D

This course is a survey of Middle Eastern History. We begin with an examination of the classical age of Islam (622-1300) through the themes of Arab expansion and adaptation and by stressing nomadic-urban encounters, sociopolitical institutions, religious sects, cultural-scientific achievements, and their transmission to Europe. We then turn to the later Islamic empires and states (post 1300), especially the Ottoman Empire and its background to the modern Middle East. Particular attention will be devoted to the dramatic expansion of Europe after 1800 and the various Middle Eastern reactions and responses to this European challenge, including the rise of modern nationalisms: Turkish, Arab, and Iranian.

I. INTRODUCTION

T. Sept. 9 THE DESERT AND THE SOWN: INTRODUCING THE MIDDLE EAST
Th. Sept. 11 THE PROPHET AND THE EARLY WORLD OF ISLAM

Readings: J.J. Saunders, *A History of Medieval Islam*, 1-76
Bernard Lewis, "Islamic Movements"

T. Sept. 16 FILM AND DISCUSSION: WHAT IS ISLAM?

Readings: *Sourcebook*, Part I.

II. THE CLASSICAL AGE (650-1300)

Th. Sept. 18 THE ARAB EMPIRE
T. Sept. 23 THE ABBASID REVOLUTION AND ISMA^{c}ILI SCHISM

Readings: Saunders, 76-186

Th. Sept. 25 DISCUSSION: URBAN LIFE AND SOCIAL INSTITUTIONS

Readings: *Sourcebook*, Part II.
Saunders, 187-204

III. THE OTTOMAN EMPIRE: ITS RISE AND DECLINE (1300-1800)

T.	Sept. 30	THE TURKS: FROM THE STEPPES TO THE GATES OF ISTANBUL
Th.	Oct. 2	STRUCTURE OF OTTOMAN RULE

FIRST PAPER DUE

Readings: Norman Itzkowitz, Ottoman Empire and Islamic Tradition, 1-61
Raphaella Lewis, Everyday Life in Ottoman Turkey, 41-89

T.	Oct. 7	SOCIAL AND RELIGIOUS LIFE
Th.	Oct. 9	CHALLENGES FROM THE PROVINCES
T.	Oct. 14	HOLIDAY
Th.	Oct. 16	THE GROWTH OF EUROPEAN INFLUENCE IN THE MIDDLE EAST

Readings: Itzkowitz, 62-109
Raphaella Lewis, 90-161
P.M. Holt, Egypt and the Fertile Crescent, 71-133
Bernard Lewis, The Emergence of Modern Turkey, 21-39
Charles Issawi, The Economic History of the Middle East, 1800-1914, 24-29, 359-366.

T. Oct. 21 DISCUSSION: WHY DID THE OTTOMAN EMPIRE DECLINE?

Sourcebook, Part III.

IV. MIDDLE EASTERN RESPONSES TO THE EUROPEAN CHALLENGE (1800-1882)

Th.	Oct. 23	THE WORLD RE-ORDERED: TRIUMPH OF EUROPEAN IMPERIALISM
T.	Oct. 28	REFORM IN THE OTTOMAN EMPIRE TO 1871
Th.	OCT. 30	EGYPT: THE LEGACIES OF NAPOLEON AND MUHAMMAD ALI
T.	Nov. 4	REFORM IN THE ARAB AND BALKAN PROVINCES TO 1861

Readings: R. Owen, and B. Sutcliffe, Studies in the Theory of Imperialism, 117-140.
Bernard Lewis, 74-128.
Holt, 155-163, 176-192, 193-230, 231-246.

Th. Nov. 6 DISCUSSION: HOW EFFECTIVE WAS OTTOMAN/EGYPTIAN REFORM?

SECOND PAPER DUE

Readings: Sourcebook, Part IV.

T.	Nov. 11	HOLIDAY
Th.	Nov. 13	CRISIS OF THE 1870s: CAIRO
T.	Nov. 18	CRISIS OF THE 1870s: ISTANBUL
Th.	Nov. 20	NO CLASS
T.	Nov. 25	OVERVIEW: CHANGE IN THE MIDDLE EAST IN THE 19th CENTURY

Readings: Janet Abu-Lughod, Cairo: 1001 Years of the City Victorious, 98-117
Gabriel Baer, Studies in the Social History of Modern Egypt, 210-229.
W.R. Polk and R.L. Chambers, eds., Beginnings of Modernization in the Middle East, 41-68.

Th. Nov. 27 THANKSGIVING HOLIDAY

T. Dec. 2 DISCUSSION: POPULAR PROTEST AND REBELLION

Readings: Sourcebook, Part V.

V. THE LAST YEARS OF EMPIRE: RUMBLINGS OF NATIONALISM (TO WORLD WAR I)

Th. Dec. 4 THE REIGN OF SULTAN ABDULHAMID II
T. Dec. 9 TURKISH AND ARABIC POLITICAL & SOCIAL THOUGHT
Th. Dec. 11 END OF EMPIRE: THE OTTOMAN LEGACY

Readings: Bernard Lewis, 129-238.
M.S. Anderson, The Eastern Question, 178-219
Albert Hourani, Arabic Thought in the Liberal Age, 103-221, 260-291

Fri. Dec. 12 DISCUSSION: WHAT IS MODERN NATIONALISM?

Readings: Sourcebook, Part VI.

THIRD PAPER DUE

21.480 COURSE MECHANICS
(READ CAREFULLY!!)

1. **READINGS:** There are two kinds:

a) books and articles which complement my lectures and serve as a background for Discussion Sections.

b) primary materials (all in translation): These sources and documents will form the basis of our Discussion Sections. These are bound in a single volume, called the Middle East Sourcebook, which you must purchase. The Sourcebook is offered to you "at cost" and can only be acquired in the History Faculty Office (E51-210, tel: 253-4965).

All syllabus readings (with the exception of the Sourcebook) are located in the Reserve Book Room of the Humanities Library (Building 14). Many, though not all, of the readings can be done in the comfort of your own room without having to visit the library! Simply purchase at the MIT Coop the following paperbacks in the textbook section under 21.480.

J. Bacharach, A Near East Studies Handbook, 570-1974
J.J. Saunders, A History of Medieval Islam
N. Itzkowitz, Ottoman Empire and Islamic Tradition
P.M. Holt, Egypt and the Fertile Crescent, 1516-1922
Bernard Lewis, The Emergence of Modern Turkey
Albert Hourani, Arabic Thought in the Liberal Age
Charles Issawi, The Economic History of the Middle East, 1800-1914

2. **REQUIREMENTS:**

a) Since this is a HUM-D subject, you are required to write three 8-9 page papers. Each will address a specific question or issue raised in my lectures, the required readings, and our Discussion Sections. For each paper, I shall offer you a choice of questions on which to write and will do so at least two weeks before each paper is due. I will help you pick your topics and will discuss each essay with you individually, if you wish.

Essays due: Thurs., Oct. 2
Thurs., Nov. 6
Fri. Dec. 12

b) Your grade will be based on your three essays (weighted equally) and your participation in Discussion Sections.

THERE ARE NO MIDTERM OR FINAL EXAMINATIONS!!

SYLLABUS

Political Science 144
Introduction to the Middle East
Autumn Quarter 1986

Instructor: K. Mostofi
Office: 256E OSH
Phone: 581-6223

Office Hours:
M & W, 10-11
or by appointment

The Course: The primary objective of the course is to provide background information for more advanced study of the history, geography, politics, religions, cultures and the civilizations of the Middle East. The main emphasis will be on pre-Islamic Arabia; Muhammad and his teachings; the establishment of the first Islamic state; the rise, decline and fall of Islamic empires; and the impact of the West on political, social and economic institutions of the region since the nineteenth century.

Texts:

Farah, Caesar E. Islam: Beliefs and Observances. New York: Baron's Educational Services, Inc., 1970.

Lewis, Bernard. The Arabs in History. New York: Harper and Row, 1966.

Watt, W. Montgomery. Islamic Political Thought: The Basic Concepts. Edinburgh: The University Press, 1968.*

LECTURES

Dates	Topics	Reading Assignments
Sept. 29 - Oct. 6	The scope of the course; requirements; definition of technical terms; major ethnic/linguistic groups in the Middle East; pre-Islamic Arabia: the land and the people; political, social and economic institutions before the advent of Islam; the Persian Empire; Iranian religions; the Byzantine Empire.	Required: Farah, Chap. 1; Lewis, Chap. 1 Recommended: Farah, Chap. 2; Lewis, Introduction
Oct. 8-22	Muhammad's life and teachings; the Qur'an; the Hadith; the establishment of the first Islamic state and the unification of Arabia A.D. 622-632; the Constitution of Medina; the political crisis caused by Muhammad's death in A.D. 632; the Caliphate; the four orthodox Caliphs; the Shari'ah (Islamic Law); the Wars of Conquest,	Required: Farah, Chaps. 3, 5, 9, & 10; Lewis, Chaps. 2 & 3; Watt, Chaps. 1, 3, 5, & 10 Recommended: Farah, Chaps. 4, 6, & 7; Lewis, Chap. 7; Watt, Chap. 2

* Seven copies of Watt's book are on reserve.

	A.D. 633-644; heterodoxy and orthodoxy; the orthodox schools of jurisprudence; Sufism.	
Oct. 24	FIRST MIDTERM EXAMINATION	
Oct. 27 - Nov. 17	The Umayyads, A.D. 661-750; from theocracy to monarchy; resumption of expansionist policies; Yazid ibn Muawiya, A.D. 680-683; Abdul Malik, A.D. 685-705; Omar ibn Abdul Aziz, A.D. 717-720; revolt in Khorasan, A.D. 747; the fall of the Umayyads, A.D. 750; the Abbasids, A.D. 750-1258; from monarchy to divine kingship; the Golden Age of Islam, A.D. 750-847; the emergence of autonomous Persian and Turkish principalities/kingdoms/empires; economic, political, and industrial developments under the early Abbasids.	<u>Required</u>: Lewis, Chaps. 4, 5, 6, & 8; Watt, Chaps. 7 & 9 <u>Recommended</u>: Farah, Chap. 8; Watt, Chap. 8
Nov. 14	SECOND MIDTERM EXAMINATION	
Nov. 17-28	Stagnation and decline; the Mongols and the Tatars, A.D. 1219-1406; the Ottoman Empire, A.D. 1453-1517; the Safavid Empire, A.D. 1501-1736.	<u>Required</u>: Lewis, Chap. 9; to be assigned
Dec. 1-12	The impact of the West; the beginning of reform movements in Turkey, Egypt, and Iran.	<u>Required</u>: Farah, Chap. 11; Lewis, Chap. 10; Watt, Chap. 11 <u>Recommended</u>: Farah, Chap. 12
Dec. 15	FINAL EXAMINATION	

Political Science 144
Introduction to the Middle East

A Selected Bibliography

Arberry, A. J. Aspects of Islamic Civilization. Ann Arbor: The University of Michigan Press, 1967.

Arnold, Sir Thomas and Guillaume, Alfred, eds. The Legacy of Islam. Oxford: The University Press, 1965.

Arnold, Sir Thomas. The Caliphate. Oxford: The Clarendon Press, 1924.

Atiya, Aziz S. Crusade, Commerce and Culture. Bloomington: Indiana University Press, 1962.

Brockelman, Carl. History of the Islamic Peoples. New York: Capricorn Books, 1947.

Cressey, George B. Crossroads: Land and Life in Southwest Asia. New York: J.B. Lippincott Co., 1960.

Daniel, N. Islam and the West: The Making of an Image. Edinburgh: The University Press, 1966.

Findley, C.V. Bureaucratic Reform in the Ottoman Empire: The Sublime Porte, 1789-1922. Princeton: The University Press, 1980.

Fisher, Sydney N. The Middle East: A History. New York: Alfred A. Knopf, 1959.

Fyzee, A. A. A. Outlines of Muhammadan Law. Oxford: The University Press, 1964.

Gibb, A. R. Studies on the Civilization of Islam. Princeton: The University Press, 1962.

Glubb, John Bagot. The Life and Times of Muhammad. New York: Stein and Day, 1970.

Guillaume, Alfred. Islam. Baltimore: Penguin Books, 1961.

Hanna, Sami A. ed. Arab Socialism. Salt Lake City and Leiden: E.J. Brill, 1969.

Hitti, Phillip K. History of the Arabs. New York: St. Martin's Press, 1966.

____________. The Near East in History. New York: D. Van Nostrand & Company, Inc., 1961.

____________. Islam and the West. New York: D. Van Nostrand & Company, Inc., 1962.

____________. Islam, A Way of Life. Minneapolis: University of Minnesota Press, 1970.

____________. Makers of Arab History. New York: St. Martin's Press, 1968.

Jeffrey, Arthur. Islam: Muhammad and His Religion. New York: The Liberal Arts Press, 1968.

Levy, Reuben. The Social Structure of Islam. Cambridge: The University Press, 1969.

Lewis, Bernard. The Emergence of Modern Turkey. Oxford: The University Press, 1969.

Mostofi, Khosrow. Aspects of Nationalism. Salt Lake City: Institute of Government, University of Utah, 1964.

Nasr, S. H. Science and Civilization in Islam. Cambridge: Harvard University Press, 1968.

____________. Sufi Essays. Albany: SUNY Press, 1972.

____________. Islamic Life and Thought. Albany: SUNY Press, 1981.

Rosenthal, E. I. J. Political Thought in Medieval Islam. Cambridge: The University Press, 1962.

Runciman, Steven. A History of the Crusades. 3 vols. New York: Harper & Row, 1965.

Setton, Kenneth M. ed. A History of the Crusades. 2 vols. Madison: The University of Wisconsin Press, 1969.

Sykes, Sir Percy. A History of Persia. 2 vols. 3rd ed. London: MacMillan, 1951.

Tabataba'i, A. S. M. H. The Shi'ite Islam. Translated by S. H. Nasr. Albany: SUNY Press, 1975.

Watt, W. Mongomery. Mohammad at Mecca. Oxford: The Clarendon Press, 1953.

________________. Mohammad at Medina. Oxford: The Clarendon Press, 1956.

________________. Mohammad: Prophet and Statesman. Oxford: The University Press, 1961.

GENERAL REFERENCES

Encyclopaedia of Islam. 2nd ed. Leiden: E.J. Brill, 1960-.

The Middle East and North Africa: 1986. 32nd ed. London: Europa Publications Ltd., 1983.

Gibb, H.A. and Kramers, J.H., eds. Shorter Encyclpaedia of Islam. Ithaca: Cornell University Press, 1961.

History B70
Islam in History
Fall Quarter, 1986

Prof. Carl Petry
Office 103-b
Office hours:
W & F 1 and by appointment

Required Texts (available at SBX):

G. Perry, The Middle East: Fourteen Islamic Centuries (Prentice-Hall)
J. Gulick, The Middle East, An Anthropoligical Perspective (Prentice-Hall)
A. J. Arberry, Aspects of Islamic Civilization (Ann Arbor) (on reserve also)
F. W. Denny, An Introduction to Islam (MacMillan)

Required Texts on Reserve:

C. Coon, Caravan
E. Fernea, Middle Eastern Women Speak
P. Hitti, Makers of Arab History
A. Jeffrey, Reader on Islam

E. Schroeder, Muhammad's People

Recommended Text (also on Reserve):

E. Fernea, Guest of the Sheikh (Doubleday)

Course Description: The course will focus on the historical impact of Islam as a religion and cultural tradition on the three major social elements in the Middle East: nomads, peasants and townspeople. Lectures will raise the question of how the course of historical development, as measured by changes in these groups, was altered by the establishment of Islam and the extent to which Islam itself reflects the characteristics of the Middle Eastern environment.

Course Procedures: Readings are assigned according to broad lecture subjects. Note that assignments are topical and do not necessarily include the full contents of each work. For works available only on reserve, several xeroxed copies of assigned readings are provided.

The student's grade will be determined according to his/her performance on a mid-term and a final examination, the format to be discussed in class. Several brief essays analyzing assigned readings, will supplement the examinations.

In addition to lecture and discussions, films from the series "World of Islam" will be shown during the course.

HISTORY B70

Lecture and Discussion Topics

1) Introductory Remarks

Rec. Hodgson I 3-70 (for fun)

2) Religion and the Issue of Historical Causality
Hodgson I, 71-100; Denny 3-16

3) Ecology of the Middle East

Perry 1-16, Gulick 1-29, rec. Coon, 10-26

4) The Components of Middle Eastern Society: Nomads, Peasants, Townspeople

Gulick 30-100, 203-237; Denny 295-350; rec. Coon 47-85, 171-190, 211-225; Fernea, 127-134

5) The Ideological Climate of the Region before Islam

Perry 16-33; Denny 17-45; Jeffrey, 161-196, rec. 197-252; rec. Hodgson, I, 103-142.

6) Bedouin Culture before Islam
Coon, 191-210; Denny 46-64; Fernea, 3-6; Schroeder, 1-22; rec. Arberry 19-31

7) The Advent of Islam
Perry 34-59; Denny 65-124; rec. Coon, 86-119; rec. Hodgson I, 146-186; Hitti, 3-21; Fernea, XVII-XXXV, 7-36; Jeffrey, 283-289, 333-338, rec. 621-634.

8) The Classical Islamic Age

Perry 60-94; Denny 125-152; Schroeder, 165-180, 203-262; Hodgson I, 187-240 (and 241-358 background, not required); rec. Hitti, 21-58; rec Arberry, 72-118.

9) Emergence of a Mature Civilization, 9th-13th Centuries

Political Realities, the social Order, the Cultural Tradition

Coon, 226-259; Gulick 163-202; Denny 153-240; rec. Hodgson I, 473-497, 359-409; Hodgson II, 1-151 (skim over political narrative pp. 22-61), 329-368; rec. Hitti, 76-94, 116-166; rec. Arberry, 155-190, 279-307; rec. Fernea, 67-86; rec. Jeffrey, 347-365; rec. Schroeder 357-396, 445-520, 679-690, 781-816.

HISTORY B70

10) <u>The Invasion Era, 13th-15th Centuries</u>
Hodgson II, 369-385; Schroeder, 645-666.

11) <u>The Impact of Alien Conquest</u>
Hodgson II, 386-500, rec. 501-531.

12) <u>Heirs of the Invasion Era: The Military Empires</u>
1) The Mamluk Sultanate, Institutionalized Inertia?
2) The Safavid Monarchy, Institutionalized Charisma?
3) The Ottoman Sultanate, A Roman Revival?

Perry 95-132; Hodgson II, 532-574, III 18-58, 99-133.

13) <u>Islam and Middle Eastern Society during the Later Traditional Period, 15th-18th Centuries</u>

Hodgson III, 13-162; Hitti, 238-256.

14) <u>The Major Components during the Later Period</u>

Gulick 101-150; Denny 291-294; rec. Fernea 201-230, 263-272

15) <u>Concluding Remarks</u>

Perry 133-166

<u>Xeroxed Readings in Jeffrey</u>:

Traditions on Beginnings--161-252
Creation Story from al-Kisa'i--161-188
Fall of Adam--189-196

Traditions About the End
Death and the Hereafter--197-247
Repentance of Iblis (Satan)--248-252

The Sira--283-338 (Biography of the Prophet Muhammad)
Introduction
Commencement of the Prophet's Revelations--283-289
Prophet's Farewell Sermon--306-308
Muhammad among the prophets--333-338

Creeds and Confessions--339-374
Introduction--339-340
Credal Statement of al-Nasafi--347-352
Credal Statement of Ibn Tumart--353-365
ᶜAli's Statement to ᶜAbbad b. Qais--368-374

Practical Piety--519-668
Introduction--519

HISTORY B70

Prayers--521-529
Litany and Blessings on the Prophet--530-536
Friday Prayers--537-549
Litany of the Beautiful Names of God--553-555
On the Virtue of Piety--550-552
Story of the Prophet's Night Journey--621-639

Xeroxed Readings in Schroeder

The Desert: Arab Chivalry of the Ignorance before Muhammad--1-22

The Caliphate of Conquest (Career of ^{c}Umar)--165-180

The World and the Flesh (Mu^{c}awiya and the Martyrdom of Husayn)--203-262

Intelligence (the career of Caliph Ma'mun)--357-380

Restlessness (the career of Caliph Mu'tasim)--381-396 (introduction of Turkish Mamluk troops)

Life and Death of a Vizier--445-520

Passing of the Age of Reason (anecdotes about al-Ash^{c}ari)--569-580

The Sophisticated (salon culture during the ^{c}Abbasid period)--611-644

The Sword and the Pen: Prince and Clerks-645-666 (anecdotes from the Invasion Era)

Comedies--679-690

The Public Road (definitions of Orthodoxy)--769-780

Muslim Science: the Body and the Doctor--781-816

HISTORY 187A

The Middle East, 570-1718

Joel Beinin
328 History Corner
Office hours: Mon. 2:30-4:30
497-9270

Autumn 1985
MTWTh
1:15-2:05

Week 1

[Sept. 25] Introduction to the Course
[Sept. 26] International Situation Prior to the Rise of Islam

<u>Reading</u>
Bernard Lewis. <u>The Arabs in History</u>, pp. 9-48
*<u>Qur'an</u> selections

Week 2

[Sept. 30] Conditions in Mecca and the Hijaz
[Oct. 1] The Career of Muhammad
[Oct. 2] The Religion of Islam
Evening: Movie--"Muhammad, Messenger of God"
[Oct. 3] Discussion

<u>Reading</u>
Maxime Rodinson, <u>Muhammad</u> (all)

Week 3

[Oct. 7] The Early Islamic Community
Map exercise due.
[Oct. 8] The Islamic Conquests and the Early Caliphate
[Oct. 9] The Umayyad/Marwanid Caliphate
[Oct. 10] Discussion

<u>Reading</u>
Bernard Lewis, <u>The Arabs in History</u>, pp. 49-79
Marshall Hodgson, <u>The Venture of Islam</u> v.1, pp.1-145

Week 4

[Oct. 14] The Abbasid Revolution
[Oct. 15] Abbasid State and Society
[Oct. 16] The Pirenne Thesis and Economic Aspects of the Islamic Conquests
[Oct. 17] Discussion

<u>Reading</u>
Bernard Lewis, pp. 80-98
Alfred Havighurst, <u>The Pirenne Thesis: Analysis, Criticism, and Revision</u>, sections by Pirenne, Lopez, Dennett, Riising

Week 5

[Oct. 21] The Islamic Cultural Synthesis: Hellenic and Irano-Semitic Traditions Arabized and Islamicized
[Oct. 22] The Formation of Islamic Orthodoxy
[Oct. 23] Abbasid Disintegration
[Oct. 24] Discussion

Reading
Bernard Lewis, pp. 99-114
Marshall Hodgson v.1, pp. 315-358, 410-443
*al-Jahiz, selection

Week 6

[Oct. 28] Origins of the Turco-Persian Ascendency
[Oct. 29] The Fatimids
[Oct. 30] The Arabs in Europe: Sicily and Spain
[Oct. 31] Midterm exam

Reading
Bernard Lewis, pp. 111-130
Marshall Hodgson, v. 2, pp. 1-151

Week 7

[Nov. 4] The Seljuks and the Post-High Caliphal Social and Political Order
[Nov. 5] The Crusades and Saladin
[Nov. 6] Early Middle High Culture
[Nov. 7] Discussion

Reading
Marshall Hodgson, v. 2, pp. 152-200, 255-268, 315-323
*Francesco Gabrielli, Arab Historians of the Crusades, pp. 1-11, 76-80
*al-Ghazzali, Deliverance from Error (excerpt)

Week 8

[Nov. 11] The Mongol Challenge
[Nov. 12] The Egyptian Mamluks
[Nov. 13] The Timurid Invasion and the Military-Patronage State
[Nov. 14] Discussion

Reading
Marshall Hodgson v. 2, pp. 279-292, 371-419, 424-436

Week 9

[Nov. 18] Late Middle High Culture: Ibn Taymiyyah and Ibn Khaldun
[Nov. 19] Origins of the Ottoman State to 1402
[Nov. 20] The Ottoman Empire: 1402- 1520

[Nov. 21] Discussion

Reading
Marshall Hodgson, v.2, pp. 437-500
*Ibn Khaldun, al-Muqaddimah (excerpt)
Norman Itzkowitz, Ottoman Empire and Islamic Tradition pp.1-63

Week 10

[Nov. 25] No Class--Middle East Studies Association meeting
[Nov. 26] No class--Middle East Studies Association meeting
[Nov. 27] Slides: Islamic Art and Architecture
[Nov. 28] No class--Thanksgiving

Week 11

[Dec. 2] The Safavids: 1501-1722
[Dec. 3] The Absolutist State and its Transformation
[Dec. 4] The Ottoman Empire and the World Economy
[Dec. 5] Discussion

Reading
Marshall Hodgson, v.3, pp.3-58, 99-133
Norman Itzkowitz, pp. 63-109

COURSE REQUIREMENTS

A map exercise is due on Monday, October 7. This exercise will be ungraded; but it is a requirement and if your map contains more than minimal errors or omissions it will be handed back for you to do over.

There will be an in class mid-term examination on Thursday, October 31. The exam will be part objective and part essay.

On Monday, December 2 a 4-6 page typed essay is due. The essay should compare the historical point of view of Lewis, Rodinson, Hodgson, Itzkowitz and the film "Muhammad, Messenger of God." You can also include remarks about other readings if you wish. Your essay should address questions of historical periodization, Orientalist vs. anti-Orientalist approaches, the kind of history the various authors emphasize, the contribution of social and economic history, attitudes toward the role of God in history, etc. This is meant to be an open ended assignment in which you should demonstrate that you can not only learn the "facts" of history, but think about what they mean and how to interpret them. In order to help you think about Hodgson, which is by far the most difficult and complex text, I will place copies of the following articles on reserve. You should not, however, simply repeat their discussions of Hodson, but rather use them to stimulate your own thinking.

Edmund Burke III, "Islamic History as World History: 'Marshall Hodgson, The Venture of Islam,'" International Journal of Middle Eastern Studies 10(1979): 241-264

Bryan S. Turner, "Conscience in the Construction of Religion: A Critique of Marshall G.S. Hodgson's 'The Venture of Islam', Review of Middle Eastern Studies 2(1976): 95-112

There will be a final examination.

The essay and exams each count for 30% of the final grade. Class participation in discussion section counts 10%.

TEXTS

The following texts are available for purchase in the bookstore.

Marshall Hodgson, The Venture of Islam, Vols 1, 2, and 3
Maxime Rodinson, Muhammad
Bernard Lewis, The Arabs in History
Norman Itzkowitz, Ottoman Empire and Islamic Tradition
Alfred Havighurst, The Pirenne Thesis

All of the above are also on reserve at Meyer Library.

Items marked * in the weekly readings are available for purchase as a course reader. These items are not on library reserve.

History 207
Spring 1976

Austen, Chambers, Madelung

The Western Islamic World: Formation to Christian Conquest

Readings

Abun-Nasr, J. History of the Maghrib
Ajayi, J. A. and Crowder, M. History of West Africa (2 volumes)
Bel, A. La religion musulmane en Berberie
Dozy, R. Spanish Islam
Fage, J. and Oliver, R. Cambridge History of Africa IV (RR 2)
Hasan, Y. F. The Arabs and the Sudan
Hiskett, M. The Sword of Truth...Usuman dan Fodio
Holt, P. M. Modern History of the Sudan
Holt, P. M. et al. Cambridge History of Islam (RR 5)
Julien, Ch.-A. Histoire de l'Afrique du Nord, II (also in English)
Levi-Provencal, E. Histoire de l'Espagne musulmane
Levtzion, N. Ancient Ghana and Mali
Marcais, G. La Berberie musulmane et l'Orient au Moyen Age
O'Fahey, R. S. and Spaulding, J. L. Kingdoms of the Sudan

Schedule of Lectures (all at 11:30, Pick 218)

Week of March 29

1.	Introduction	
2.	Muslim conquest of the Maghreb	Madelung
3.	Muslim conquest of al-Andalus	Madelung

Week of April 5

4.	Separation of West from Caliphate	Chambers
5.	The Spanish Umayyads	Madelung
6.	Muluk at-Tawa'if in Spain	Madelung

Week of April 12

7.	The Almoravids	Chambers
8.	The Almohades	Chambers
9.	Ibadite and other sectarian communities	Madelung

Week of April 19

10.	Tunisian dynasties (Aghlabids to Hafsids)	Madelung
11.	Ottoman entry into the Maghreb	Andrew Hess
12.	Ottoman control of the Maghreb	Chambers

Week of April 26

13.	Moroccan empires since 1500	Chambers
14.	Medieval Western Sudan	Austen
15.	Western Sudan: 17th-19th centuries	Austen

Week of May 3

16.	Central Sudan to 19th century	Austen
17.	Nilotic Sudan to 1820	Austen
18.	Nilotic Sudan: Turkiyya and Mahdiyya	Austen

Week of May 10

19.	Urban society and economy of Mahgreb and al-Andalus	Chambers
20.	Rural society and economy of the Maghreb and Sahara	Chambers
21.	Transsaharan trade	Austen

Week of May 17

22.	Kharijism and other dissident sects	Madelung
23.	Malikite jurisprudence	Madelung
24.	Philosophers and poets of the Muslim West	Madelung

Week of May 24

25.	Maghrebian ulema and madrases	Chambers
26.	Maghrebian Sufism	Chambers
27.	Sudanic tariqas: the quietist mode	Austen/Hunter

Week of May 31 (begins June 2)

28.	Sudanic tariqus and jihad	Austen
29.	Architecture and the arts: the Western Islamic style(s)	Austen

Requirements for grade

Either term paper (to be discussed in advance with one of the instructors) or examination (to be arranged at end of quarter).

Office hours

Austen, Pick 214: Monday, Wednesday, Friday 10:30-11:30
Chambers, Kelly 408:
Madelung, OI 305:

THE UNIVERSITY OF CHICAGO

Social Science 220

INTRODUCTION TO ISLAMIC CIVILIZATION I

Fall Quarter, 1986 Fred M. Donner

Course Requirements

The Course consists of lectures, class discussions, a paper, and identification tests. Attendance at all scheduled classes and lectures is expected; lectures will frequently include material not covered in the assigned readings, and for which you will be held responsible on tests.

Readings for each week are given on the attached schedule of lectures. Weekly assignments normally consist of readings in various secondary works (particularly Marshall Hodgson's The Venture of Islam, volume I, which forms the basic text for the course), plus a selection of primary sources in translation. Make an effort to think especially carefully about the latter, and try to see what they can tell you about the people who wrote them, about the society in which they lived, and about the values and beliefs they held.

Paper: One paper (five page maximum) on a set topic will be assigned. This stands in lieu of essay questions on an examination. The purpose of the paper is two-fold: (1) to stimulate you to think more carefully about certain pivotal issues covered during the course and to help you clarify your own thinking on these issues, and (2) to exercise your skills in writing an historical essay. Emphasis in grading will be placed on clarity of thought (logical organization of the essay), clarity of expression, and effective support of points in your argument with available evidence. It is expected that assigned source and textbook readings will provide sufficient material for you to respond to the paper topic adequately. Use of additional materials is permitted, but receives no extra credit. About one week will be allowed for you to consider the assignment and write the essay. Papers must be handed in punctually. Taking extra time complicates grading and is unfair to others who make the effort to complete the assignment on time. For this reason, penalties will be assessed for lateness.

Examinations and Tests: There will be no examinations. Instead there will be two tests consisting of short identifications of names and terms, plus the paper described above.

Class Discussion: Several times during the quarter you will be divided into discussion sections, which will meet with one of the instructors in the course to talk about materials covered in reading and lectures.

Grading: The final course grade will be determined on the basis of your paper (roughly 40%), your tests (roughly 25% each), and your performance in discussion (roughly 10%).

Lecture Handouts: Most lectures will be accompanied by a handout providing a sketch outline, some basic bibliography to guide you in further reading on the subject, and a list of names and terms that occur during the lecture that are not common knowledge (e.g.: "Tihama" will be in the list; "Arabia" will not). These lists, while they do not include all terms on which you might be tested, and while they do contain many names and terms of lesser importance on which you will not be tested, nonetheless constitute a convenient way to begin reviewing terms for the identification tests. Please keep them!

INTRODUCTION TO ISLAMIC CIVILIZATION, I

Study Groups: In order to facilitate discussion of the material covered in the course, and to help provide continuity between this segment of the Islamic Civilization sequence and the segments offered in the Winter and Spring quarters, all students will be organized into study groups of 8-10 members. Each study group will decide on its own what activities, if any, it wishes to undertake. Further information will be forthcoming when you receive your study group assignments early in the quarter. Please note that the study groups are not the same as the discussion sections, which are a required part of the course.

* * *

A selection of basic reference works dealing with Islamic history and civilization can be found in the fifth floor reserve reading room (RR5) of Regenstein Library. They include the Encyclopaedia of Islam (first edition, 1913-1942; second edition, 1954-continuing), doubtless the most important single reference work for the study of Islamic civilization, which you should use as frequently as possible; The Cambridge History of Islam and The Cambridge History of Iran, both useful surveys; Clifford E. Bosworth's helpful The Islamic Dynasties; historical atlases; etc.

* * *

Required and Recommended Textbooks and Materials.

1) Marshall G. S. Hodgson, The Venture of Islam, volume 1. (**required**). Available at Chicago Theological Seminary Co-Op Bookstore (at CTS, corner of 58th and University, in cellar). The basic textbook for this course.
2) Collection of primary source readings (**required**). Available for purchase at Kinko's (1309 E. 57th Street). The basis for class discussions.
3) Marmaduke Pickthall, The Meaning of the Glorious Koran. (**required**). Available at CTS.
4) Bartholemew Map of the Middle East. (**strongly recommended**). Available at CTS.
5) W. Montgomery Watt, The Majesty that was Islam. (**recommended**). Available at CTS. Much less demanding (but also less rewarding) than Hodgson; it may help you to get your bearings in the subject matter if read before corresponding sections of Hodgson.

All readings are available in Regenstein Reserve.
Readings marked with an asterisk (*) in the following Syllabus are found in the packet of material available from Kinko's.

* * *

"To them belongs what they earned, and to you will belong what you will earn."
-Qur'ân, 2:134

"It is not enough to have a good mind. The main thing is to use it well."
-Descartes

INTRODUCTION TO ISLAMIC CIVILIZATION, I

LECTURE AND READING SCHEDULE -- FALL 1986

Mon Sep 29 I. Organizational Meeting; Geographical Overview
Wed Oct 1 II. Linguistic and Human Geography of the Middle East
Fri 3 III. The Byzantine and Sasanian Empires

Mon Oct 6 DISCUSSION
Wed 8 IV. The Arabian Peninsula; Pre-Islamic Arabia
Fri 10 V. The Problem of Muhammad

Reading for Class Discussion, Oct. 6:

Hodgson, pp. 71-99, 103-145. (If you are feeling very ambitious, you may try reading pp. 1-69, or parts of it. Otherwise, wait several weeks and come back to it.)

W. B. Fisher, The Middle East--A Physical, Social, and Regional Geography, pp. 11-65.

*Peter Brown, The World of Late Antiquity, pp. 137-187.

*Pre-Islamic Iran.

*The Martyrdom of Three Christian Women.

Mon Oct 13 VI. The Qur'ân and Early Islam
Wed 15 DISCUSSION
Fri 17 VII. Expansion of the Islamic State: Ridda and Conquests

Reading for Class Discussion, Oct. 15:

Hodgson, pp. 146-196.

*Traditional Muslim Names.

*Alois Musil, Manners and Customs of the Rwala Bedouins, selections (xerox YM 3473).

*From the Hamasa. Poems nos. I, XII, XIV, XXXI, XLIX.

*Ibn al-Kalbi, The Book of Idols, selections.

*The Constitution of Medina (xerox YC 3345)

*Ibn Hisham (Ibn Ishaq), The Life of Muhammad (Sira), pp. 104-114, 117-121, 212-216, 221-231, 450-460, 540-556.

Marmaduke Pickthall, The Meaning of the Glorious Koran:
sura 93 ("The Morning Hours", pp. 443-444);
sura 81 ("The Overthrowing", p. 431);
sura 4 ("Women"), verses 1-39 (pp. 78-83);
sura 12 ("Joseph", pp. 174-182);
Genesis 37ff, (Joseph story), compare with Qur'ânic account.

INTRODUCTION TO ISLAMIC CIVILIZATION, I

Mon Oct 20 VIII. The New Social and Political Order
Wed 22 IX. Pilgrimage in Islam
Fri 24 DISCUSSION

Reading for Class Discussion, Oct. 24:
Hodgson, pp. 197-211.
*The Conquerors and the Conquered.

Mon Oct 27 **TEST I**
Wed 29 X. The Fertile Crescent and Iran. Agricultural Technology
Fri 31 XI. The First Civil War; Emergence of the Umayyads

Mon Nov 3 XII. The Umayyads and their Rivals
Wed 5 XIII. The Abbasids: Themes and Methods of Rule
Fri 7 DISCUSSION

Reading for Class Discussion, Nov. 7:
Hodgson, pp. 212-314.
*The Account of the Killing of 'Uthman (xerox YA 2273)
*Al-Hasan al-Basri's Letter to 'Abd al-Malik (xerox YB 4192)
*The Fiscal Rescript of 'Umar II (xerox YG 2753)
*The Shu'ûbî Controversy
*A Letter to Secretaries (from Bernard Lewis, Islam I/186-191).
*An Attack on Secretaries (from Charles Pellat, Life and Work of Jâhiz, pp. 273-275)

Mon Nov 10 XIV. The Evolution of Islamic Law
Wed 12 XV. Early Islamic Art
Fri 14 DISCUSSION

Reading for Class Discussion, Nov. 14:
Hodgson, pp. 315-358.
*Shâfi'î's Risâla
*From the Muwatta'.

Mon Nov 17 XVI. The Development of Islamic Theology **[Paper Assigned]**
Wed 19 DISCUSSION
Fri 21 NO CLASS

Reading for Class Discussion, Nov. 19:
Hodgson, pp. 359-443.
*Four Professions of Faith.
*A Mu'tazilite View of Theology.
*Charles Pellat, The Life and Works of Jahiz, pp. 48-50, 62-82.

Mon Nov	24	XVII. Arabic Literature
Wed	26	DISCUSSION **[Paper Assignment Due]**
Fri	28	HAPPY THANKSGIVING

Reading for Class Discussion, Nov. 26:

*Ibn Qutayba, The Book of Government, selections.
*Charles Pellat, The Life and Works of Jahiz:
pp. 178-179 (a tiresome slave);
pp. 192-195 (Basra and Kufa);
pp. 205-206 (friends);
pp. 221-222 (on envy);
pp. 241-247 (on tenants and landlords).

Mon Dec	1	XVIII. Autonomy Movements and the Decline of Abbasid Power
Wed	2	DISCUSSION
Fri	5	READING PERIOD

Reading for Class Discussion, Dec. 2:

Hodgson, pp. 444-495.
*Miskawaih, The Experiences of the Nations, pp. 165-184 (xerox YM 3499).

* * *

SOC SCI 220: INTRODUCTION TO ISLAMIC CIVILIZATION, I

MAP ASSIGNMENT

On the first of the two maps provided, indicate the principal topographical features listed in section I. On the second map, locate the general regions and major urban centers detailed in section II. The regional toponyms should show geographical units, not modern political entities; it is thus not necessary to draw specific boundaries around the regions you locate, but it must be clear what areas you intend to include.

I. Major Topographical Features

A. Mountain Ranges

Atlas
Balkans
Caucasus
Elburz
Himalyas
Hindu Kush-Pamirs
Lebanon
Pyrenees
Taurus
Tien Shan
Zagros

B. Deserts

Dasht-i Kavir
Dasht-i Lut
Kara Kum
Kyzyl Kum
Nafud
Rub' al-Khali
Sahara
Takla Makan

C. Rivers

Araxes (Aras)
Don
Euphrates
Indus
Jaxartes (Syr-Darya)
Jordan
Kizilirmak
Nile
Orontes
Oxus (Amu-Darya)
Tigris
Volga

D. Bodies of Water

Aegean Sea
Arabian Sea
Aral Sea
Black Sea
Caspian Sea
Indian Ocean
Mediterranean Sea
Persian Gulf
Red Sea

E. Straits

Bab el-Mandeb
Bosporus
Dardanelles
Gibraltar
Hormuz
Suez

II. Regions of Settlement

A. General Regions

Anatolia
Arabian Peninsula
Azerbaijan
Fars
Hijaz
Iberian Peninsula
Iranian Plateau
Iraq (Mesopotamia)
Jazira
Khorasan
Khwarazm
Maghreb
Nejd
Nile Valley
Punjab
Sind
Sudan
Syria
Transoxiana
Yemen

B. Traditional Urban Centers (* = modern importance only)

Aleppo
Alexandria
Algiers*
Ankara*
Baghdad
Balkh (Mazar-i Shafif)
Basra
Beirut*
Bukhara
Cairo (Fustat)
Cordoba
Damascus
Delhi
Derbent
Fez
Granada
Hamadan
Herat
Isfahan
Istanbul (Constantinople)
Izmir
Jerusalem
Qayrawan (Kairouan)
Kashghar
Konya
Kufa
Lahore
Marrakesh
Marv (Mary)
Mashhad
Mecca
Medina
Mosul
Multan
Nishapur
Ray
Samarqand
Seville
Shiraz
Sijilmasa
Tabriz
Tangier*
Tashkent*
Tehran*
Tiflis (Tbilisi)
Timbuktu
Toledo
Trabzon (Trebizond)
Tunis
Urgench (Khiva)

The University of Chicago
Department of Near Eastern Languages & Civilizations

INTRODUCTION TO EARLY ISLAMIC HISTORY
(NEHIST 301, 302, 303)

Fred M. Donner
305 Oriental Institute

1986-87

Purpose of the Course.

The course is a three-quarter sequence designed to prepare for the field examination in early Islamic history, and to provide basic training in the methods and materials needed to embark upon a career as a professional historian of the early Islamic period.

The main objectives of the course are (1) to survey the contours of early Islamic history, (2) to familiarize you with interpretive issues that are currently the focus of debate within the profession, (3) to familiarize you with the most important sources for the period, and (4) to teach analytical methods that are of particular importance to the study of the period. Objectives (1) and (2) are mainly dealt with during the fall and winter quarters; (3) is covered throughout the course; and (4) occupies mainly the spring quarter.

Students preparing for the field exam only may limit themselves to taking the first two quarters if they wish; those expecting to do research in the earlier period should also take the third quarter of the course.

Prerequisites.

A good reading knowledge of Arabic is required for the spring quarter; it is helpful throughout the course. Reading knowledge of German, French, Italian, and/or Spanish is helpful throughout the course.

Structure and Requirements.

The course meets twice weekly for discussion of readings and assignments. The following requirements are imposed:

1. Attendance at, and participation in, all discussions.
2. Completion of assigned readings; be ready to discuss them on the dates due.
3. Several short written assignments and exercises. (Dates to be assigned)
4. At least one oral presentation in class will be required in each of the fall and winter quarters (Dates and topics to be selected early in course). In the spring quarter, these will be replaced by "workshops", in which all will participate, focusing on specific textual problems. The presentations during fall and winter quarters should, if possible, be linked to the topics on which you wish to write papers.
5. As part of your oral presentations you are asked to compile and distribute to the class a select bibliography on the subject you have chosen to present.
6. For students taking only the fall and winter quarters, two papers--one short paper (5-10 pages) and another longer paper (up to 15-25 pages) will be required. The short paper should make a special effort to utilize published documentary sources to the topic chosen. The long paper can be on any topic. Ideally, paper topics will be related to the subject of your class presentations. Students taking the third quarter of the course will be asked to prepare a third paper dealing with

the earliest Islamic period (Jâhiliyya-Second Civil War). The formal due date for these papers is at the end of each quarter. Please note that no classes are scheduled to meet in week nine of each quarter, in order to provide some time for writing up your papers.

DISCUSSION TOPICS SCHEDULE

FALL QUARTER, 1986

week of	
Sep 29	1. Organizational Meeting 2. Pre-Islamic Arabia, I
Oct 6	3. Pre-Islamic Arabia, II 4. Muḥammad and the Qur'ān, I
Oct 13	5. Muḥammad and the Qur'ān, II 6. Muḥammad and the Qur'ān, III
Oct 20	7. Muḥammad and the Qur'ān, IV 8. Ridda Wars/Early Conquests
Oct 27	9. First and Second Civil Wars, Early Umayyads, I 10. First and Second Civil Wars, Early Umayyads, II
Nov 3	11. First and Second Civil Wars, Early Umayyads, III 12. Later Umayyads, Abbasid Movement, Early Shi'ism, I
Nov 10	13. Later Umayyads, Abbasid Movement, Early Shi'ism, II 14. Later Umayyads, Abbasid Movement, Early Shi'ism, III
Nov 17	15. Abbasids to 945, I 16. Abbasids to 945, II
Nov 24	THANKSGIVING AND PAPER-WRITING WEEK. NO CLASSES.
Dec 1	17. Buyids and Later Shi'ism, I 18. Buyids and Later Shi'ism, II

WINTER QUARTER, 1987

Jan 5	19. The Fatimids and Ismā'īlism, I 20. The Fatimids and Ismā'īlism, II
Jan 12	21. North Africa and Spain, I 22. North Africa and Spain, II
Jan 19	23. North Africa and Spain, III 24. Minor Dynasties in the East, Yemen, etc. I
Jan 26	25. Minor Dynasties in the East, Yemen, etc. II 26. Saljuqs

INTRODUCTION TO EARLY ISLAMIC HISTORY

Feb 2 27. Zangids, Ayyūbids, Crusades, I
28. Zangids, Ayyūbids, Crusades, II

Feb 9 29. Zangids, Ayyūbids, Crusades, III
30. Revisionist Views of Rise of Islam, I

Feb 16 31. Revisionist Views of Rise of Islam, II
32. Revisionist Views of Rise of Islam, III

Feb 23 33. Documentary Sources for Rise of Islam, I
34. Documentary Sources for Rise of Islam, II

Mar 2 PAPER-WRITING WEEK. NO CLASSES

Mar 9 35. Narrative Sources for Rise of Islam, I
36. Narrative Sources for Rise of Islam, II

SPRING QUARTER, 1987

Exact schedule and topics to be arranged. The main concern will be to examine historiographical problems posed by the sources about the rise of Islam, types of sources for this period, problems of later interpolation, form criticism, problems of transmission and redaction, tradition analysis, etc.

PRE-ISLAMIC ARABIA
READING LIST

General Works

Encyclopaedia of Islam (2nd ed.), article "Al-'Arab", sec. (1) "Ancient History of the Arabs", and article "Djazīrat al-'ARAB," sec. (vii.) "History", subsection (1), "Pre-Islamic" (pp. 547-549)

Irfān Shahīd, "Pre-Islamic Arabia," Cambridge History of Islam, vol. 1, pp. 3-29.

Giorgio Levi della Vida, "Pre-Islamic Arabia," in Nabih Amin Faris (ed.), The Arab Heritage (Princeton, 1944), pp. 24-57.

Adolf Grohmann, Arabien (Munich: C. H. Beck, 1963) [=Handbuch der Altertumswissenschaften, III.1.3.4]

Fred M. Donner, The Early Islamic Conquests (Princeton, 1981), ch. 1 (pp. 11-49).

DeLacy O'Leary, Arabia before Muhammad (London, 1927).

South Arabian Kingdoms

Jacques Ryckmans, L'Institution monarchique en Arabie méridionale avant l'Islām (Ma'īn et Saba) (Louvain: Publications Universitaires, 1951). Chapter 4 (pp. 257-325) gives a chronological overview of historical developments. Pp. 317-325 covers 370 C.E. to rise of Islam.

Brian Doe, Southern Arabia (London: Thames & Hudson, 1971). Overview with emphasis on archaeological finds.

Hermann von Wissman, "Ḥimyar, Ancient History," Le Muséon 77 (1964), pp. 429-499.

Maria Höfner, "Die Kultur des vorislamischen Südarabien," ZDMG 99 (1945-49), pp. 15-28.

Maria Höfner, "War der sabäische Mukarrib ein 'Priesterfürst'?", WZKM 54 (1957), pp. 77-85.

Albert Jamme, "Le panthéon sud-arabe préislamique d'apres les sources épigraphiques," Le Muséon 60 (1947), pp. 55-147.

Client Kingdoms, relations with Great Powers

Gustav Rothstein, Die Dynastie der Laḫmiden in al-Hīra (Berlin: Reuther, 1899).

M. J. Kister, "Al-Ḥīra--Some Notes on its Relations with Arabia," Arabica 15 (1968), pp. 143-169.

Fred M. Donner, "The Bakr ibn Wā'il Tribes and Politics in Northeastern Arabia on the Eve of Islam," Studia Islamica 29 (1980), pp. 5-38.

Isma'il R. Khalidi, "The Arab Kingdom of Ghassān: its origins, rise, and fall," Moslem World 46 (1956), pp. 193-206.

Theodor Nöldeke, "Die Ghassānischen Fürsten aus dem Hause Gafna's," Abhandlungen der königlichen Akademie der Wissenschaften zu Berlin 1887, 2, pp. 1-63.

Irfan Kawar [I. Shahid], "The Arabs in the Peace Treaty of A. D. 561," Arabica 3 (1957), pp. 181-213.

Irfan Kawar, "Ghassān and Byzantium: A New terminus a quo," Der Islam 33 (1958), pp. 145-158.

Irfan Kawar, "The Last Days of Salīḥ," Arabica 5 (1958), pp. 145-158.

Irfan Kawar, "Procopius on the Ghassānids," JAOS 77 (1957), pp. 79-87.

Maurice Sartre, Trois Études sur l'Arabie Romaine et Byzantine (Bruxelles, 1982).

Irfan Shahid, Rome and the Arabs (Washington, 1984).

Irfan Shahid, Byzantium and the Arabs in the Fourth Century (Washington, 1984).

PRE-ISLAMIC ARABIA READING LIST

Gunnar Olinder, The Kings of Kinda of the Family of Ākil al-Murār (Lund, 1927).
John C. Wilkinson, "The Julandā of Oman," Journal of Oman Studies 1 (1975), pp. 97-108.
René Dussaud, La Pénétration des Arabes en Syrie avant l'Islam (2nd ed., Paris, 1955).
Franz Altheim and Ruth Stiehl, Die Araber in der alten Welt, 5 vols. (Berlin, 1964-69).
Edmond Rabbath, L'Orient chrétien à la veille de l'Islam (Beirut, 1980).

Religion, Society, Culture

Robert B. Serjeant, "Ḥaram and Ḥawṭah, the Sacred Enclave in Arabia," in Abdurrahman Badawi (ed.), Mélanges Taha Husain (Cairo, 1962), pp. 41-58.
Gonzague Ryckmans, "Les religions arabes pré-islamiques," Histoire Générale des Réligions, vol. 4 (Paris, 1947), pp. 307-332. Reprinted separately (Louvain, 1951).
Toufic Fahd, Le Panthéon de l'Arabie centrale à la Veille de l'Hégire (Paris, 1968).
Werner Caskel, "Die alten semitischen Gottheiten in Arabien," in Sabatino Moscati (ed.), Le Antiche Divinità Semitiche (Rome, 1958), pp. 95-117.
Meir M. Bravmann, The Spiritual Background of Early Islam (Leiden: Brill, 1972).
Henri Charles, Le Christianisme des arabes nomades sur le limes et dans le désert syro-mésopotamien aux alentours de l'Hégire (Paris, 1936).
J. Spencer Trimingham, Christianity among the Arabs in Pre-Islamic Times (London & Beirut, 1979).
Anton Baumstark, "Das Problem eines vorislamischen christlichkirchlichen Schrifttums in arabischer Sprache," Islamica 4 (1931), pp. 562-575.

Walter Dostal, "Zur Frage der Entwicklung des Beduinentums," Archiv für Völkerkunde 13 (1958), pp. 1-14.
Werner Caskel, Die Bedeutung der Beduinen in der Geschichte der Araber (Köln & Opladen, 1953).
Francesco Gabrieli (ed.), L'Antica Società Beduina (Rome, 1959). (Most articles in English or French).
Erich Bräunlich, "Beiträge zur Gesellschaftsordnung der arabischen Beduinenstämme," Islamica 6 (1934), pp. 68-111 and 182-229.
C. A. Nallino, "Sulla costituzione delle tribù arabe prima dell'islamismo," in Raccolta di scritti editi e inediti 3 (Rome, 1941), pp. 64-86 (written in 1893).
Édouard Farès, L'Honneur chez les Arabes avant l'Islam (Paris, 1932).
Siegmund Fraenkel, "Das Schutzrecht der Araber," in Carl Bezold (ed.), Orientalische Studien Theodor Nöldeke vol. I (Giessen, 1906), pp. 293-301.

Werner Caskel, "Aijām al-'Arab. Studien zur altarabischen Epik," Islamica 3 (1930), fascicule 5 (Ergänzungsheft), pp. 1-99.
Gustave von Grunebaum, "The Nature of Arab Unity before Islam," Arabica 10 (1963), pp. 5-23.
Abdulla El Tayib, "Pre-Islamic Poetry," The Cambridge History of Arabic Literature, I (Cambridge, 1983), pp. 27-113.
David S. Margoliouth, "The Origins of Arabic Poetry," JRAS (1925), pp. 417-449.
Arthur J. Arberry, The Seven Odes (London, 1957), "Epilogue," pp. 228-254.

Pre-Islamic Mecca and Hijāz

W. Montgomery Watt, Muhammad at Mecca (Oxford, 1953), pp. 1-29, 154-164.
W. Montgomery Watt, Muhammad at Medina(Oxford, 1956), pp. 151-174, 373-388.
W. Montgomery Watt, "Belief in a High God in Pre-Islamic Mecca," JSS 16 (1971), pp. 35-40.

PRE-ISLAMIC ARABIA READING LIST

W. Montgomery Watt, "The Qur'ān and Belief in a High God," Der Islam 55 (1979), pp. 205-211.

Muhammad Hamidullah, "Les 'Aḥābīsh' de la Mecque," Studi Orientalistici in Onore di Giorgio Levi della Vida, vol. I (Rome, 1956), pp. 434-447.

M. J. Kister, "Mecca and Tamīm--Aspects of their Relations," JESHO 8 (1965), pp. 113-165.

M. J. Kister, "Some Reports concerning Mecca from Jāhiliyya to Islam," JESHO 15 (1972), pp. 61-93.

M. J. Kister, "The Campaign of Ḥulubān," Le Muséon 78 (1965), pp. 425-436.

Henri Lammens, "La Mecque à la veille de l'Hégire," Mélanges de l'Université Saint-Joseph (Beirut) 9 (1924), pp. 97-439.

Henri Lammens, "La République marchande de la Mecaue vers l'an 600 de notre ère," Bulletin de l'Institut Égyptien, 5e serie, 4 (1910), pp. 23-54.

Henri Lammens, L'Arabie occidentale avant l'Hégire (Beirut, 1928).

Henri Lammens, Le Berceau de l'Islam. L'Arabie occidentale à la veille de l'Hégire (Rome, 1914)

Henri Lammens, La Cité arabe de Ṭāif à la veille de l'Hégire (Beirut, 1922).

Roger Paret, "Les Villes de Syrie du Sud et les routes commerciales d'Arabie à la fin du VIe siecle," Acts of XI. International Byzantine Congress, Munich, 1958 (München, 1960), pp. 438-444.

Werner Caskel, Liḥyān und Liḥyānisch (Köln & Opladen, 1954).

Sources for Pre-Islamic Arabian History

Werner Caskel, "Die einheimischen Quellen zur Geschichte Nord-Arabiens vor dem Islam," Islamica 3 (1927), pp. 331-341.

Nāṣir al-Dīn al-Asad, Maṣādir al-Shi'r al-Jāhilī (Cairo, 1962).

MUHAMMAD AND THE QUR'AN

READING LIST

Biographies

Maxime Rodinson, "A Critical Survey of Modern Studies on Muhammad," in Merlin L. Swartz (ed/transl), Studies on Islam (Oxford, 1981), pp. 23-85.

W. Montgomery Watt, Muhammad, Prophet and Statesman (Oxford, 1961).
W. Montgomery Watt, Muhammad at Mecca (Oxford, 1953).
W. Montgomery Watt, Muhammad at Medina (Oxford, 1956).
Maxime Rodinson, Mohammed (New York, 1974).
Frants Buhl, Das Leben Muhammeds (Leipzig, 1930).
Tor Andrae, Mohammed. The Man and His Faith (New York, 1960) (German orig. 1932).
Régis Blachère, Le Problème de Mahomet (Paris, 1952).
M. Gaudefroy-Demombynes, Mahomet (Paris, 1957).
Michael Cook, Muhammad (Oxford, 1983).

Leone Caetani, Annali dell'Islam (10 vols., Milan, 1905-1926).
Nabia Abbot, 'A'isha, The Beloved of Muhammad (Chicago, 1942).

Specific Problems

Robert B. Serjeant, "The Constitution of Medina," Islamic Quarterly 8 (1964), pp. 3-16.

D. Z. H. Baneth, "What did Muḥammad mean when he called his religion "Islam"?--The Original Meaning of Aslama and its derivatives," Israel Oriental Studies 1 (1971), pp. 183-190.

Fred M. Donner, "Mecca's Food Supplies and Muḥammad's Boycott," JESHO 20 (1977), pp. 249-266.

Fred M. Donner, "Muḥammad's Political Consolidation in Arabia up to the Conquest of Mecca: A Reassessment," Muslim World 69 (1979), pp. 229-247.

Fred M. Donner, The Early Islamic Conquests (Princeton, 1981), pp. 51-82.

M. J. Kister, "The Market of the Prophet," JESHO 8 (1965), pp. 272-276.

M. J. Kister, "The Expedition of Bi'r Ma'ūna," in G. Makdisi (ed.), Arabic and Islamic Studies in Honor of Hamilton A. R. Gibb (Leiden, 1965), 1pp. 337-357.

M. J. Kister, "A Bag of Meat," BSOAS 33 (1970), pp. 267-275.

M. J. Kister, "Al-taḥannuth: an Inquiry into the Meaning of a Term," BSOAS 31 (1968), pp. 223-236.

Theodor Nöldeke, "Die Traditionen über das Leben Muhammeds," Der Islam 5 (1914), pp. 160-170.

Maxime Rodinson, "The Life of Muhmmad and the Sociological Problem of the Beginnings of Islam," Diogenes 20 (1957), pp. 28-51.

Eric Wolf, "The Social Organization of Mecca and the Origins of Islam," Southwestern Journal of Anthropology 7 (1951), pp. 329-356.

Arent Jan Wensinck, Muhammad and the Jews of Medina (Freiburg, 1975) (Dutch original 1908).

Geo Widengren, Muḥammad, the Apostle of God, and his Ascension (Uppsala, 1955).

Richard Bell, The Origin of Islam in its Christian Environment (London, 1926).

Charles C. Torrey, The Jewish Foundation of Islam (New York, 1933).

I. Katsh, Judaism in Islam

J. C. Archer, Mystical Elements in Mohammed (New Haven, 1924).

Qur'ān

Muḥammad 'Abd al-Bāqī, Al-Mu'jam al-mufahras li-alfāẓ al-Qur'ān al-karīm (Cairo, 1378). (Concordance, permits user to locate places where any word or phrase is used in Q.)

Rudi Paret, Der Koran 2 vols (Stuttgart, 1962, 1971). The translation (vol. 1) has the merit of stating openly where the translation is uncertain; the commentary (vol. 2), keyed to the translation, will lead user to all discussion of the verses in question by modern scholarship.

Theodor Nöldeke, Geschichte des Qor'āns, new ed. by F. Schwally, G. Bergsträsser, and O. Pretzl (Leipzig, 1909-1938). The classic western treatment of the history of the Q. text.

W. Montgomery Watt, Bell's Introduction to the Qur'ān (Edinburgh, 1970). Very useful introduction to issues and problems.

Régis Blachère, Introduction au Coran (Paris, 1947).

Cambridge History of Arabic Literature I (Cambridge, 1983), chaps. 6-8 on Qur'ān (pp. 186-259).

Arthur Jeffery, The Foreign Vocabulary of the Qur'ān

Arthur Jeffery, The Qur'ān as Scripture

Josef Horovitz, Koranische Untersuchungen (Berlin, 1926).

H. Hirschfeld, New Researches into the Composition and Exegesis of the Qoran (London, 1902).

H. U. W. Stanton, The Teaching of the Qur'ān (London, 1919).

Toshihiku Izutsu, Ethico-Religious Concepts in the Qur'ān (Montreal, 1966).

K. Wagtendonk, Fasting in the Koran (Leiden, 1968).

Uri Rubin, "Al-Ṣamad and the High God. An Interpretation of Sūra CXII," Der Islam 61 (1984), pp. 197-217.

John MacDonald, "Joseph in the Qur'ān and Muslim Commentary," Muslim World 10 (1956), pp. 113-131, 207-224.

RIDDA AND EARLY ISLAMIC CONQUESTS

READING LIST

Ridda Wars

Elias Shoufani, Al-Riddah and the Muslim Conquest of Arabia (Beirut and Toronto, 1972)
Fred M. Donner, The Early Islamic Conquests (Princeton, 1981), pp. 82-90.
Fred M. Donner, "The Bakr b. Wā'il Tribes and Politics in Northeastern Arabia on the eve of Islam," Studia Islamica 29 (1980), pp. 5-38.
Ella Landau-Tasseron, "The Participation of Ṭayyi' in the Ridda," Jerusalem Studies in Arabic and Islam 5 (1984), pp. 53-71.
Ella Landau-Tasseron, "Asad from Jāhiliyya to Islām," Jerusalem Studies in Arabic and Islam 6 (1985), pp. 1-28.
Dale F. Eickelman, "Musaylima," JESHO 10 (1967), pp. 17-52.
Eduard Sachau, "Der erste Chalife Abu Bekr," Sitzungsberichte der königlichen Preussischen Akademie der Wissenschaften 43 (1903), pp. 16-37.

Early Islamic Conquests: Origins and Causes

Fred M. Donner, The Early Islamic Conquests (Princeton 1981), infra.
Georges H. Bousquet, "Observations sur la nature et les causes de la conquête arabe," Studia Islamica 6 (1956), pp. 37-52.
Georges H. Bousquet, "Quelques remarques critiques et sociologiques sur la conquête arabe et les théories émises à ce sujet," in Studi Orientalistici in Onore de Giorgio Levi della Vida, vol. I (Rome, 1956), pp. 52-60.
Karl W. Butzer, "Der Umweltfaktor in der grossen arabischen Expansion," Saeculum 8 (1957), pp. 359-371.
Marius Canard, "L'expansion arabe: le problème militaire," in L'Occidente e l'Islam nell'Alto Medioevo, vol. I (Spoleto, 1965), pp. 37-63.
Leone Caetani, Annali dell'Islam (Milan, 1905-1928).
John Joseph Saunders, "The Nomad as Empire Builder: A Comparison of the Arab and Mongol Conquests," Diogenes 52 (1965), pp. 79-103.
Gustave E. von Grunebaum, "The First Expansion of Islam: Factors of Thrust and Containment," Diogenes 53 (1966), pp. 64-72.
P. Donini, "Validità e limiti di un'interpretazione geodeterministica dell'espansione islamica," Oriente Moderno 1-6 (Jan.-June 1980), pp. 139-146.

Early Islamic Conquests: Surveys and Studies

Carl Heinrich Becker, "The Expansion of the Saracens," Cambridge Medieval History, vol. 2, chapters 11-12 (Cambridge, 1913).
Fred M. Donner, The Early Islamic Conquests (Princeton, 1981), pp. 91-278 (Syria, Iraq).
Michael Jan De Goeje, Mémoire sur la conquête de la Syrie, 2nd ed. (Leiden, 1900).
Philip Mayerson, "The First Muslim Attacks on Southern Palestine (A.D. 633-634)," Transactions and Proceedings of the American Philological Association 95 (1964), pp. 155-199.
Albrecht Noth, "Iṣfahān-Nihāwand. Eine quellenkritische Studie zur frühislamischen Historiographie," ZDMG 118 (1968), pp. 274-296.
Julius Wellhausen, Prolegomena zur ältesten Geschichte des Islams (Berlin, 1899)[=Skizzen und Vorarbeiten, 6:1].
Abd al-Husayn Zarrinkub, "The Arab Conquest of Iran and its Aftermath," Cambridge History of Iran, vol. 4, pp. 1-56.
H. Mandanean, "Les invasions arabes en Arménie," Byzantion 18 (1948), pp. 163-195.

THE FIRST TWO CIVIL WARS & EARLY UMAYYADS
READING LIST

General

Michael Morony, "Bayn al-Fitnatayn: Problems in the Periodization of Early Islamic History," JNES 40 (1981), pp. 247-251.
Julius Wellhausen, The religio-political factions in early Islam (Amsterdam & New York, 1975)(German original 1901)
M. A. Shaban, Islamic History, 600-750/132 A. H., A New Interpretation (Cambridge, 1971).
Julius Wellhausen, The Arab Kingdom and its Fall (Eng. transl. Calcutta, 1927).
Werner Caskel, Ǧamharat an-Nasab. Das Genealogische Werk des Hišām b. Muḥammad al-Kalbī (Leiden, 1966).

First Civil War

Laura Veccia-Vaglieri, "Il conflitto ʿAlī-Muʿāwiya e la secessione khārijita riesaminati alla luce di fonti ibāḍite," Annali (Istituto Universitario Orientale di Napoli), N.S. 4 (1952), pp. 1-94.
Laura Veccia-Vagliere, "ʿAlī b. Abī Ṭālib," Encyclopaedia of Islam (2nd ed.).
Martin Hinds, "The Murder of the Caliph ʿUthmān," IJMES 3 (1972), pp. 450-469.
Martin Hinds, "Kūfan Political Alignments and their Background in the Mid-seventh Century A.D.," IJMES 2 (1971), pp. 346-367.
Martin Hinds, "The Ṣiffīn Arbitration Agreement," JSS 17 (1972), pp. 93-129.
Rudolf Vesely, "Die Anṣār im ersten Bürgerkriege," Archiv Orientální 26 (1958), pp. 36-58.
Erling Ladewig Petersen, "ʿAlī and Muʿāwiya. The Rise of the Umayyad Caliphate," Acta Orientalia 23 (1959), 157-196.
G. R. Hawting, "The signficance of the slogan lā ḥukma illā li-llāh," BSOAS 41 (1978), pp. 453-463.
Giorgio Levi della Vida, "Il califatto di ʿAlī secondo il Kitāb ansāb al-ašrāf di al-Balāḏurī," Rivista degli Studi Orientali 6 (1914-1915), pp. 427-507.

Second Civil War

Gernot Rotter, Die Umayyaden und der Zweite Bürgerkrieg (680-692) (Wiesbaden, 1982).
Abd Ameer Abd Dixon, The Umayyad Caliphate, 65-86/664-705 (London, 1971).
Rudolf Sellheim, "Der zweite Bürgerkrieg im Islam," Sitzungsberichte der Wissenschaftliche Gesellschaft an der Johann Wolfgang Goethe-Universität Frankfurt/Main 8 (1969), no. 4, pp. 87-111.
Wilferd Madelung, "ʿAbdullāh b. al-Zubayr and the Mahdī," JNES 40 (1981), pp. 291-305.
M. J. Kister, "The Battle of the Ḥarra," in M. Rosen-Ayalon (ed.), Studies in Memory of Gaston Wiet (Jerusalem, 1977), pp. 33-49.

Early Umayyads

W. Montgomery Watt, "God's Caliph. Qur'ānic Interpretations and Umayyad Claims," in C. E. Bosworth (ed.), Iran and Islam. In memory of the late Vladimir Minorsky (Edinburgh, 1971), pp. 565-574.
Henri Lammens, Études sur le règne du Calife Omaiade Moāwiya Ier (Beirut, 1906).
Henri Lammens, "Le Califat de Yazīd Ier," in Mélanges de l'Université Saint-Joseph (Beirut) 4 (1910), pp. 233-312; 5 (1911), pp. 79-267, 589-724; 6 (1913), pp. 401-492; 7 (1914-1921), pp. 211-244.
Henri Lammens, "Moʿāwiya II," in Rivista degli Studi Orientali 7 (1915), pp. 1-49.
Henri Lammens, "Ziad b. Abīhī," in Rivista degli Studi Orientali (1912)
Henri Lammens, "L'avènement des Marwānides et le Califat de Marwān Ier," Mélanges de l'Université Saint-Joseph (Beirut) 12 (1927).

RIDDA AND EARLY ISLAMIC CONQUESTS READING LIST

Alfred J. Butler, The Arab Conquest of Egypt and the Last Thirty Years of the Roman Dominion (Oxford, 1902).

Jacques Jarry, "L'Égypte et l'invasion musulmane," Annales Islamologiques 6 (1966), pp. 1-29.

Robert Brunschvig, "Ibn 'Abdalh'akam et la conquête de l'Afrique du Nord par les Arabes," Annales de l'Institut d'Etudes Orientales (Algiers) 6 (1942-47), pp. 108-155.

E. Levi-Provençal, "Un nouveau récit de la conquête de l'Afrique du Nord par les Arabes," Arabica 1 (1954), pp. 17-43.

Islamic Conquests: Impact

Hugh Kennedy, "The Last Century of Byzantine Syria: A Reinterpretation," Byzantinische Forschungen 10 (1985), pp. 141-183.

Hugh Kennedy, "From Polis to Madina: Urban Change in Late Antique and Early Islamic Syria," Past and Present 106 (Feb., 1985), pp. 3-27.

Benjamin Z. Kedar, "The Arab Conquests and Agriculture," Asian and African Studies 19 (1985), pp. 1-16.

Ignaz Goldziher, "Muruwwa and Dīn," in his Muslim Studies, I (London, 1967).

Michael Morony, Iraq after the Muslim Conquest (Princeton, 1983).

Henri Pirenne, Mohammed and Charlemagne (New York, 1977) (first publ. 1939)

A. S. Ehrenkreutz, "Another Orientalist's Remarks concerning the Pirenne Thesis," JESHO 15 (1972), pp.

Richard Hodges and David Whitehouse, Muhammad, Charlemagne, and the Origins of Europe

THE ABBASIDS to 945 C. E.

General Works

Hugh Kennedy, The Early Abbasid Caliphate. A Political History (London, 1981).

Jacob Lassner, The Shaping of Abbasid Rule (Princeton, 1980).

Farouk Omar, The Abbasid Caliphate

Elton Daniel, The Political and Social History of Khurasan under Abbasid Rule, 747-820 (Chicago, 1979).

Farouk Omar, 'Abbâsiyât. Studies in the History of the Early 'Abbâsids (Baghdad, 1976).

Theodor Nöldeke, Sketches from Eastern History (Edinburgh, 1892).

Specific Problems

Nabia Abbott, Two Queens of Baghdad (Chicago, 1946).

Dominique Sourdel, Le Vizirat Abbaside, 2 vv. (Damascus, 1959-60).

Harold Bowen, The Life and Times of 'Alî b. 'Isâ, 'The Good Vizier' (Cambridge, 1928).

Clifford E. Bosworth, 'A pioneer Arabic encyclopaedia of the sciences: al-Khwârizmî's "Keys of the Sciences",' Isis 54 (1963), pp. 97-111. [Repr. in his Medieval Arabic Culture and Administration]

Heribert Busse, "Das Hofbudget des Chalifen al-Mu'tadid billâh," Der Islam 43 (1967), pp. 11-36.

Hugh Kennedy, "Central Government and Provincial Elites in the Early Abbasid Caliphate," BSOAS 44 (1981), pp. 26-38.

Helmut Töllner, Die türkischen Garden am Kalifenhof von Samarra (Walldorf-Hessen, 1971).

O. S. A. Ismail, "Mu'tasim and the Turks," BSOAS 29 (1966), pp. 12-24.

Ernst Herzfeld, Geschichte der Stadt Samarra (Berlin, 1948).

Claude Cahen, "Fiscalité, propriété, antagonismes sociaux en haute Mésopotamie au temps des premiers 'abbâsides, " Arabica 1 (1954), pp. 136-152.

David Waines, "The Third Century Internal Crisis of the Abbasids," JESHO 20 (1977), pp. 282-306.

Alexandre Popovic, La révolte des esclaves en Iraq au IIIe/IXe siècle (Paris, 1976).

S. Sabari, Mouvements populaires à Baghdad à l'époque 'Abbaside, IXe-XIe siècles (Paris, 1981).

Dominique Sourdel, "La politique religieuse du calife 'abbaside al-Ma'mûn," REI 30 (1962), pp. 27-48.

Francesco Gabrieli, Al-Ma'mûn e gli 'Alidi (Rome, 19__).

Henri Laoust, "Le Hanbalisme sous le califat de Bagdad (241/855-656/1258)," REI 27 (1959), pp. 67-128.

Laura Veccia-Vaglieri, "Abbasidi e Kharijiti," Rivista degli Studi Orientali 24 (1949), pp.

C. E. Bosworth, "The Tahirids and Arabic Culture," Journal of Semitic Studies 14 (1969), pp. 45-79. [repr. in his Medieval Arabic Culture and Administration].

J. B. Chabot, "Notes d'épigraphie et d'archéologie orientale," JA 16 (1900), pp. 249-288.

Nabia Abbott, "Arabic Papyri of the Reign of Ga'far al-Mutawakkil 'alâ-llâh (A.H. 232-247, A.D. 847-861)," ZDMG 92 (1938), pp.

THE ISLAMIC WEST
(8th - 12th centuries)
READING LIST

General

R. Le Tourneau, "L'Occident Musulman du milieu du VIIe siècle à la fin du XVe siècle," Annales de l'Institut d'Etudes Orientales (Algiers) 16 (1958), pp. 147-176.

North Africa, Sicily

[see also relevant entries on Fatimids]

R. Le Tourneau, "North Africa to the Sixteenth Century," Cambridge History of Islam 2, pp. 211-237.

Charles-André Julien, A History of North Africa

G. Marcais, La Berberie musulmane et l'Orient au Moyen Age (Paris, 1946)

C. Bekri, "Le Kharidjisme berbere, quelques aspects du royaume rustamide," Annales de l'Institut d'Etudes Orientales (Algiers) 15 (1957), pp. 55-108.

H. R. Idris, La Berbérie Orientale sous les Zirides (Paris,)

M. Solignac, "Recherches sur les installations hydraliques de Kairouan et des steppes tunisiennes du VIIe au XIe siecle," Annales de l'Institut d'Etudes Orientales (Algiers) 10-11 (1952-53),

Roger Le Tourneau, The Almohad Movement in North Africa in the Twelfth and Thirteenth Centuries (Princeton, 1969)

Michele Amari, Storia dei Musulmani di Sicilia (3 vv., rev. ed. 1933-39)

EI (2), "Aghlabids", "Hammudids", "Idrîs I," "Idrîs II".

Spain

Rachel Arié, España Musulmana (Siglos VIII-XV)(Madrid, 1983)[=Manuel Tuñon de Lara (ed.), Historia de España, vol. 3]

W. M. Watt and Pierre Cachia, A History of Islamic Spain (New York, 1967)

E. Lévi-Provencal, Histoire de l'Espagne Musulmane (3 vv., Paris, 1950-53)

R. Dozy, Histoire des Musulmans d'Espagne jusqu'à la conquête de l'Andalousie par les Almoravides (711-1110), 2nd ed. revised by Lévi-Provencal, vol. 3 (on Reyes de Taifas)(Paris, 1932)

J. Bosch Vilá, Los Almorávides (Tetuán, 1956)

H. Monès, "Les Almoravides. Esquisse historique," Revista del Instituto de Estudios Islámicos de Madrid 14 (1967-68), pp. 49-102.

H. Monès, "La división político-administrativa de la España musulmana," Revista del Instituto de Estudios Islámicos de Madrid 5 (1957), pp. 79-135.

C. Sánchez Albornoz, "Espagne préislamique et Espagne musulmane," Révue Historique 237 (1967), pp. 295-338.

E. Lévi-Provencal, "Le Cid de l'histoire," Révue Historique 180 (1937), pp. 58-74.

L. Torres Balbás, "Extensión y demografia de las ciudades hispano-musulmanas," Studia Islamica 3 (1955), pp. 36-59.

L. Torres Balbás, Ciudades hispano-musulmanas (2vv., Madrid, 1972)

C. Dubler, "Über das Wirtschaftsleben auf der iberischen Halbinsel vom XI. zum XIII. Jahrhundert," Romanica Helvetica 22 (1943), pp.

Karl Butzer et al., "Irrigation Agrosystems in Eastern Spain: Roman or Islamic Origins?", Annals of the Association of American Geographers 75 (1985), pp. 479-509.

EI, "Al-Andalus", "Abbadids", "Aftasids", Dhu l-Nunids", "Dhahwarids", "Almoravids", "Tudjib, Banu"

LATER UMAYYADS, ABBASID MOVEMENT, EARLY SHI'ISM
READING LIST

General Works

Julius Wellhausen, The Arab Kingdom and its Fall
M. A. Shaban, Islamic History, 600-750 A.D./132 A.H., A New Interpretation
Francesco Gabrieli, "Considerazioni sul califfato omayyade," Annali dell Istituto Orientali di Napoli 34 (1974), pp. 507-521.
Henri Lammens, Etudes sur le siècle des Omayyades (Beirut, 1930).

Umayyad Period: Specific Problems

Redwan Sayed, Die Revolte des Ibn al-Aš'at und die Koranleser: ein Beitrag zur Religions- und Sozialgeschichte der frühen Umayyadenzeit (Freiburg, 1977).
C. E. Bosworth, "Rajā' ibn Ḥaywa al-Kindī and the Umayyad Caliphs," Islamic Quarterly 16 (1972), pp. 36-80. [repr. in his Studies in Medieval Arabic Culture and Administration].
C. E. Bosworth, "'Ubaidallah b. Abī Bakra and the 'Army of Destruction' in Zabulistan (79/698)," Der Islam (1973), pp. 268-283.
W. W. Barthold, "The Caliph 'Umar II and the conflicting reports on his personality," Islamic Quarterly 15 (1977), 69-95.
C. H. Becker, "Studien zur Omejjadengeschichte. A. 'Omar II," Zeitschrift für Assyriologie 15 (1900), pp. 1-36.
Hamilton A. R. Gibb, The Arab Conquests in Central Asia (London, 1923).
Francesco Gabrieli, Il Califfato di Hishâm (Alexandria, 1935).

Administration; Mawālī and Arab Settlers

H. I. Bell, "The Administration of Egypt under the Umayyad Caliphs," Byzantinische Zeitschrift 28 (1928), pp. 278-286.
Henri Lammens, "Un gouverneur Omaiyade d'Egypte: Qorra ibn Šarīk, d'après les papyrus arabes," Bulletin de l'Institut égyptien, ser. 5, no. 2 (________), pp. 99-115.
Kosei Morimoto, The Fiscal Administration of Egypt in the Early Islamic Period (Kyoto, 1981).
A. A. Duri, "Notes on Taxation in Early Islam," JESHO 17 (1974), pp. 136-144.
Daniel C. Dennett, Conversion and the Poll-Tax in Early Islam (Cambridge, MA, 1950).
Naji Hasan, The Role of the Arab Tribes in the East during the period of the Umayyads, 40/660-132/749 (Baghdad, 1978).
Hichem Djaït, "Les Yamanites à Kufa au Ier siècle de l'Hégire," JESHO 19 (1976), pp. 148-181.
H. A. R. Gibb, "The Fiscal Rescript of 'Umar II," Arabica 2 (1955), pp. 3-16.
H. A. R. Gibb, "The Evolution of Government in Early Islam," Studia Islamica 4 (1955), pp. 1-17. [Repr. in his Studies on the Civilization of Islam].

Intellectual Movements; Proto-Shi'ism, Khavârij, Qadariyya

Julian Obermann, "Political Theology in early Islam: al-Ḥasan al-Baṣrī's treatise on qadar," JAOS 55 (1935), pp. 138-162.
M. Schwarz, "The Letter of al-Ḥasan al-Baṣrī," Oriens 20 (1967), pp. 15-30.
Josef van Ess, "The Beginnings of Islamic Theology," in J. E. Murdoch and E. D. Sylla (eds.), The Cultural Context of Medieval Learning (Dordrecht and Boston, 1975), pp.
Josef van Ess, "The Early Development of Kalām," in G. H. A. Juynboll (ed.), Studies on the First

LATER UMAYYADS READING LIST

Century of Islamic Society (Carbondale and Edwardsville, 1982), pp. 109-123.
Josef van Ess, "ʿUmar II and his Epistle against the Qadarīya," Abr-Nahrain 12 (1971), pp. 19-26.
W. Montgomery Watt, Free Will and Predestination in Early Islam (London, 1948).

Julius Wellhausen, The Religio-Political Factions in Early Islam (Amsterdam, 1975).
W. Montgomery Watt, "Khārijite Thought in the Umayyad Period," Der Islam 36 (1961), pp. 215-231.
R. Rubinacci, "Il califfo ʿAbd al-Malik b. Marwān e gli Ibāḍiti," Annali dell' Istituto Orientale di Napoli 5 (1952), pp. 99-121.

William F. Tucker, "Rebels and Gnostics: al-Mughīra ibn Saʿīd and the Mughīriyya," Arabica 22 (1975), pp. 33-47.
William F. Tucker, "Bayān b. Samʿān and the Bayāniyya: Shiʿite Extremists of Umayyad Iraq," Muslim World 65 (1975), pp. 241-253.
William F. Tucker, "Abū Manṣūr al-ʿIjlī and the Manṣūriyya: a study in medieval terrorism," Der Islam 54 (1977), pp. 66-76.
William F. Tucker, "ʿAbd Allāh b. Muʿāwiya and the Janāḥiyya: rebels and ideologues of the late Umayyad period," Studia Islamica 51 (1980), pp. 39-57.
S. H. M. Jafri, The Origins and Early Development of Shiʿa Islam (London, 1979).

Economics, Land Use, "Desert Palaces"

Jean Sauvaget, "Observations sur les monuments omeyyades, 1: Châteaux de Syrie," Journal Asiatique 231 (1939), pp.
Oleg Grabar, "Umayyad 'Palace' and the ʿAbbāsid 'Revolution'," Studia Islamica 18 (1963), pp. 5-18.

The Abbasid Movement

Moshe Sharon, Black Banners from the East (Jerusalem and Leiden, 1983).
Claude Cahen, "Points de vue sur la 'Revolution abbaside' ", Revue Historique (1963), pp. 295-335.
Tilman Nagel, Untersuchungen zur Entstehung des abbasidischen Kalifates (Bonn, 1972).

THE ABBASIDS to 945 C. E.

General Works

Hugh Kennedy, The Early Abbasid Caliphate. A Political History (London, 1981).
Jacob Lassner, The Shaping of Abbasid Rule (Princeton, 1980).
Farouk Omar, The Abbasid Caliphate
Elton Daniel, The Political and Social History of Khurasan under Abbasid Rule, 747-820 (Chicago, 1979).
Farouk Omar, 'Abbâsiyât. Studies in the History of the Early 'Abbâsids (Baghdad, 1976).
Theodor Nöldeke, Sketches from Eastern History (Edinburgh, 1892).

Specific Problems

Nabia Abbott, Two Queens of Baghdad (Chicago, 1946).
Dominique Sourdel, Le Vizirat Abbaside, 2 vv. (Damascus, 1959-60).
Harold Bowen, The Life and Times of 'Alî b. 'Isâ, 'The Good Vizier' (Cambridge, 1928).
Clifford E. Bosworth, 'A pioneer Arabic encyclopaedia of the sciences: al-Khwârizmî's "Keys of the Sciences",' Isis 54 (1963), pp. 97-111. [Repr. in his Medieval Arabic Culture and Administration]
Heribert Busse, "Das Hofbudget des Chalifen al-Mu'tadid billâh," Der Islam 43 (1967), pp. 11-36.
Hugh Kennedy, "Central Government and Provincial Elites in the Early Abbasid Caliphate," BSOAS 44 (1981), pp. 26-38.
Helmut Töllner, Die türkischen Garden am Kalifenhof von Samarra (Walldorf-Hessen, 1971).
O. S. A. Ismail, "Mu'tasim and the Turks," BSOAS 29 (1966), pp. 12-24.
Ernst Herzfeld, Geschichte der Stadt Samarra (Berlin, 1948).
Claude Cahen, "Fiscalité, propriété, antagonismes sociaux en haute Mésopotamie au temps des premiers 'abbâsides," Arabica 1 (1954), pp. 136-152.
David Waines, "The Third Century Internal Crisis of the Abbasids," JESHO 20 (1977), pp. 282-306.
Alexandre Popovic, La révolte des esclaves en Iraq au IIIe/IXe siècle (Paris, 1976).
S. Sabari, Mouvements populaires à Baghdad à l'époque 'Abbaside, IXe-XIe siècles (Paris, 1981).
Dominique Sourdel, "La politique religieuse du calife 'abbaside al-Ma'mûn," REI 30 (1962), pp. 27-48.
Francesco Gabrieli, Al-Ma'mûn e gli 'Alidi (Rome, 19__).
Henri Laoust, "Le Hanbalisme sous le califat de Bagdad (241/855-656/1258)," REI 27 (1959), pp. 67-128.
Laura Veccia-Vaglieri, "Abbasidi e Kharijiti," Rivista degli Studi Orientali 24 (1949), pp.
C. E. Bosworth, "The Tahirids and Arabic Culture," Journal of Semitic Studies 14 (1969), pp. 45-79. [repr. in his Medieval Arabic Culture and Administration].
J. B. Chabot, "Notes d'épigraphie et d'archéologie orientale," JA 16 (1900), pp. 249-288.
Nabia Abbott, "Arabic Papyri of the Reign of Ga'far al-Mutawakkil 'alâ-llâh (A.H. 232-247, A.D. 847-861)," ZDMG 92 (1938), pp.

THE BUYIDS (Buwayhids)

READING LIST

General Works

Heribert Busse, Chalif und Grosskönig. Die Buyiden im Iraq (945-1055) (Beirut, 1969).
Heribert Busse, "The Buyids in Iran," in Cambridge History of Iran, vol. 4.
Mafizullah Kabir, The Buwayhid Dynasty of Baghdad (Calcutta, 1964).
V. Minorsky, La Domination des Dailamites (Paris, 1932).
Encyclopaedia of Islam, article "Būyids" and articles on various amîrs, e.g. "'Adud al-Dawla", "Mu'izz al-Dawla", etc.
Roy Mottahedeh, Loyalty and Leadership in an early Islamic society (Princeton, 1980).
D. S. Richards (ed.), Islamic Civilization, 950-1150 (Oxford, 1973).

Specific Problems

J. C. Bürgel, Die Hofkorrespondenz 'Adud ad-Daulas und ihr Verhältnis zu anderen historischen Quellen der frühen Buyiden (Wiesbaden, 1965).
H. F. Amedroz, "Three Years of Buwayhid Rule in Baghdad, A.H. 389-93," JRAS (1901), pp. 501-536, 749-786.
H. F. Amedroz, "The Vizier Abu-Fadl b. al-'Amîd from the 'Tajârib al-Umam' of Abu 'Ali Miskawaih," Der Islam 3 (1912), pp. 323-351.
C. E. Bosworth, "Military Organization under the Buyids of Persia and Iraq," Oriens 18-19 (1965-66), pp. 143-167.
Harold Bowen, "The Last Buwayhids," JRAS (1929), pp. 225-245.
Claude Cahen, "L'Evolution de l'iqtā' du IXe au XIIIe siècle," Annales 8 (1953), pp. 25-52.
Claude Cahen, "Note pour l'histoire de la ḥimāya," Mélanges Louis Massignon (Damascus, 1956), pp. 287-303.
Wilferd Madelung, "The assumption of the title shāhanshāh by the Būyids," JNES 28 (1969), pp. 84-105, 168-183.
C. E. Bosworth, "The Banū Ilyās of Kirmān (320-57/932-68)," in Iran and Islam (V. Minorsky Festschrift) (Edinburgh, 1971), pp. 107-124.

SHI'ISM

INTRODUCTORY MATERIAL; GENERAL DESCRIPTIONS; RITUAL

Momen, Moojan, An Introduction to Shi'i Islam (New Haven, 1985).
Donaldson, Dwight M., The Shi'ite Religion (London, 1933).
Lewis, Bernard, "Some observations on the significance of heresy in the history of Islam," Studia Islamica 1 (1953), pp. 43-63.
Strothmann, W., "Shi'a," EI (old ed.).
Watt, W. Montgomery, "The Concept of the Charismatic Community in Islam," Numen 7 (1960), pp. 85-98.
Chelkowski, Peter J. (ed.), Ta'ziyeh: Ritual and Drama in Iran (New York, 1979)
Wach, Joachim, Sociology of Religion (Chicago, 1944).

EARLY HISTORY

Jafri, S. H. M., The Origin and Early Development of Shi'i Islam (London, 1979)
Lewis, Bernard, "'Alids," EI (new ed.).
Moscati, Sabatino, "Per una Storia dell'antica Si'a," Rivista degli Studi Orientali 30 (1955), pp. 252-267.
Tucker, William F., "Rebels and Gnostics: al-Mugira ibn Sa'id and the Mugiriyya," Arabica 22 (1975), pp. 33-47.
Tucker, William F., "Bayan b. Sam'an and the Bayaniyya: Shi'ite Extremists of Umayyad Iraq," Muslim World 65 (1975), pp. 241-253.
Tucker, William F., "Abu Mansur al-'Ijli and the Mansuriyya: a study in medieval terrorism," Der Islam 54 (1977), pp.66-76.
Veccia Vaglieri, L., "'Ali," EI (new ed.).
Watt, W. Montgomery, "Shi'ism under the Umayyads," JRAS (1960), pp. 158-172.

ABBASID PERIOD; SECTARIAN DEVELOPMENT

Gibb, H. A. R., "The Structure of Religious Thought in Islam," Muslim World 38 (1948), pp. 17-28, 113-123, 185-197, 280-291.
Hodgson, Marshall G. S., "How did the early Shi'a become Sectarian?," JAOS 75 (1955), pp. 1-13.
Ivanow, W., "Early Shi'ite Movements," Journal of the Bombay Branch of the Royal Asiatic Society 17 (1941), 1-23.
Kohlberg, Etan, "From Imamiyya to Ithna-'Ashariyya," BSOAS 39 (1976), pp. 521-534.
Kohlberg, Etan, "Shî'î Hadîth," in Cambridge History of Arabic Literature, vol. 1, pp. 299-307.
Lewis, Bernard, "'Ali al-Rida," EI (new ed.).
Madelung, Wilferd, "Imama," EI (new ed.).
Omar, Farouk, "Some Aspects of Abbasid-Husaynid Relations during the Early Abbasid Period," Arabica 22 (1975), pp. 170-179.
A. A. Sachedina, Islamic Messianism: the idea of the mahdi in Twelver Shi'ism (Albany, 1981).
Watt, W. Montgomery, "The Reappraisal of Abbasid Shi'ism," in George Makdisi (ed.), Arabic and Islamic Studies in Honor of H. A. R. Gibb
Watt, W. Montgomery, "The Rafidites: A Preliminary Study," Oriens 16 (1963), pp. 110-121.

THE FATIMIDS & ISMA'ILISM

READING LIST

General Works on the Fatimids

Marius Canard, "Fatimids", Encyclopaedia of Islam (2nd ed.)
Stanley Lane-Poole, A History of Egypt in the Middle Ages (London: Methuen, 1901)
De Lacey E. O'Leary, A Short History of the Fatimid Khalifate (London: Kegan Paul, 1923)
M. J. de Goeje, Mémoire sur les Carmathes du Bahrain dt les Fatimides (Leiden, 1886).
Abbas Hamdani, The Fatimids (Karachi, 1962).
Heinrich F. Wüstenfeld, Geschichte der Fatimiden-chalifen (Göttingen, 1881).

Isma'ilism, Fatimid Doctrine

Bernard Lewis, The Origins of Isma'īlism (Cambridge: W. Heffer, 1940)
Wilferd Madelung, "Imâma", Encyclopaedia of Islam (2nd ed.)
Wilferd Madelung, "Das Imamat in der frühen ismailitischen Lehre," Der Islam 37 (1961), pp. 43-135.
Tilman Nagel, Frühe ismailitische und fatimidische Lehre im Lichte der Risâlat Iftitâh al-Da'wa (Bonn: Orientalisches Seminar der Universität, 1972)
S. M. Stern, "Isma'ilis and Qarmatians," L'Elaboration de l'Islam (Paris, 1961)
Heinz Halm, "Die Söhne Zikrawayhs und das erste fatimidische Kalifat," Die Welt des Orients 10 (1977), pp.
J. Salt, "The military exploits of the Qarmatians (al-Qarâmitah)," Abr-Nahrain 17 (1976-77), pp.
Farhat Dachraoui, "Les commencements de la prédication ismailienne en Ifrîqîya," Studia Islamica 20 (1964), pp. 89-102.
Heinz Halm, "Die Sîrat Ibn Hausab. Die ismailitische da'wa in Yemen und die Fatimiden," Die Welt des Orients 12 (1981), pp. 107-135.
S. M. Stern, "Isma'ili Propaganda and Fatimid Rule in Sind," Islamic Culture (1949), pp. 1-10.
W. Ivanow [Vladimir Alekseevich Ivanov], "The Organization of the Fatimid Propaganda," Journal of the Bombay Branch of the Royal Asiatic Society 15 (1939), pp. 1-35.
Abbas Hamdani, "Evolution of the Organizational Structure of the Fatimi Da'wah: the Yemeni and Persian Contribution," Arabian Studies 3 (1976), pp. 85-114.
Marshall Hodgson, "Al-Darazi and Hamza in the Origin of the Druze Religion," JAOS 82 (1962), pp. 6-20.
N. M. Abu-Izzeddin, The Druzes. A new study of their history, faith, and society (Leiden, 1984).

Fatimids: Miscellaneous Topics

W. Ivanow, Ismaili Tradition concerning the Rise of the Fatimids [Islamic Research Association Series, no. 10] (Oxford, 1942) [tr. of Sîrat Ja'far]
Heinz Halm, "Der Mann auf dem Esel. Der Aufstand des Abû Yazîd gegen die Fatimiden nach einem

Fatimids and Isma'ilism-Reading List

Augenzeugbericht," Die Welt des Orients 15 (1984), pp. 144-204.
Wilferd Madelung, "Fatimiden und Bahrainqarmaten," Der Islam 34 (1959), pp. 34-88.
Thierry Bianquis, "La prise du pouvoir par les Fatimides en Egypt (357-363/968-974)," Annales Islamologiques 11 (1972), pp. 48-108.
Yaacov Lev, "The Fatimid Conquest of Egypt--Military, Political, and Social Aspects," Israel Oriental Studies 9 (1979), pp. 315-328.
Marius Canard, "L'impérialisme des Fâtimides et leur propagande," Annales de l'Institut d'Etudes Orientales de la Faculté des Lettres d'Alger VI (1942-47), pp. 156-193 [repr. in Canard, Miscellanea Orientalia, ch. II]
Marius Canard, "La procession du Nouvel An chez les Fâtimides," Annales de l'Institut d'Edutes Orientales de la Faculté des Lettres d'Alger X (1952), pp. 364-398 [repr. in Canard, Miscellanea Orientalia, ch. IV]
Marius Canard, "Un vizir chrétien à l'époque fâtimite, l'Armenien Bahrâm," Annales de l'Institut d'Etudes Orientales de la Faculté des Lettres d'Alger XII (1954), pp. 84-113 [repr. in Canard, Miscellanea Orientalia, ch. VI]
Josef van Ess, Chiliastische Erwartunge und die Versuchung der Göttlichkeit: der Kalif al-Hâkim (Heidelberg: Carl Winter, 1977) [Abhandlungen der Heidelberger Akademie der Wissenschaften, Philosophische-historische Klasse, Jahrgang 1977, no. 2]
S. A. Assaad, The Reign of al-Hakim bi-Amr Allah, 386/996-411-1021. A Political Study (Beirut, 1974).
P. J. Vatikiotis, "Al-Hâkim bi'Amrillah: the god-king idea realised," Islamic Culture 29 (1955), pp. 1-8.
Marius Canard, "Badr al-Djamâlî," Encylopaedia of Islam (2nd ed.)
Yaacov Lev, "The Fatimid vizier Ya'qub ibn Killis and the Beginning of Fatimid Administration in Egypt," Der Islam 58 (1981), pp. 237-249.
A. A. A. Fyzee, "Qâdî an-Nu^c^mân the Fatimid Jurist and Author," Journal of the Royal Asiatic Society (1934), pp. 1-32.
R. Gottheil, "A distinguished family of Fatimide cadis (al-Nu'mân) in the tenth century," JAOS 27 (1906), pp. 217-296.
Adel Allouche, "The Establishment of Four Chief Judgeships in Fatimid Egypt," JAOS 105 (1985), pp. 317-320.
Yaacov Lev, "The Fatimids and the ahdâth of Damascus, 386/996-411-1021," Die Welt des Orients 13 (1982), pp. 97-106.
Boaz Shoshan, "Fatimid Grain Policy and the post of the muhtasib," IJMES 13 (1981), pp. 181-189.
Thierry Bianquis, "Un crise frumentaire dans l'Egypte Fatimide," JESHO 23 (1980), pp. 67-101.
Yaacov Lev, "The Fatimid Army, A.H. 358-427/968-1036 C.E.--Military and Social Aspects," Asian and African Studies 14 (1980), pp. 169-181.
B. J. Beshir, "Fatimid military organization," Der Islam 55 (1978), pp. 37-56.
S. M. Stern, "The Epistle of the Fatimid Caliph al-Amir (al-Hidâya al-Amiriyya), its Date and its Purpose," JRAS 1950
S. M. Stern, "The Succession of the Fatimid Imam al-Amir," Oriens 4 (1951), pp. 193-255.
S. M. Stern, Fatimid Decrees (London: Faber & Faber, 1964)

SELJUKS, ATABEGS, CRUSADES

READING LIST

Seljuks

Claude Cahen, Pre-Ottoman Turkey

W. Barthold, Turkestan down to the Mongol Invasion (London, 1928)

Claude Cahen, "Mouvements populaires et autonomisme urbain dans l'Asie musulmane du moyen-age," Arabica 5-6 (1958-59)

Claude Cahen, "The Historiography of the Seljuqid Period," in B. Lewis and P. M. Holt (eds.), Historians of the Middle East (London, 1962), pp. 59-78.

George Makdisi, "Hanbalite Islam", in Merlin Swartz (ed.), Studies in Islam

Jean Aubin, "La ruine de Siraf et les routes du golfe persique," Cahiers de civilisation mediévale 2 (1959)

Ann K. S. Lambton, "Quis Custodiet Custodies?", Studia Islamica 5-6 (1956)

Ann K. S. Lambton, "Justice in the Medieval Persian Theory of Kingship," Studia Islamica 17 (1962)

Crusades

Hans Eberhard Mayer, The Crusades

K. M. Setton & H. Baldwin (eds.), A History of the Crusades (5 vv., Philadelphia & Madison,)

William B. Stevenson, The Crusaders in the East (Cambridge, 1907)

Joshua Prawer, Histoire du Royaume Latin de Jérusalem (Paris, 1969)

Claude Cahen, La Syrie du Nord à l'époque des Croisades, et la principalité franque d'Antioche (Paris, 1940)

Atabegs, Zengids, Ayyubids

EI, "Atabak"

Nikita Elisséeff, Nur al-Din (Damascus, 1967)

H. A. R. Gibb, "The Armies of Saladin," in his Studies on the Civilization of Islam (Boston, 1962)

H. A. R. Gibb, The Life of Saladin (Oxford, 1973)

Andrew Ehrenkreutz, Saladin (N.Y., 1972)

Andrew Ehrenkreutz, "The Place of Saladin in the naval history of the Mediterranean Sea in the middle ages," JAOS 75 (1955), pp 100-116

Andrew Ehrenkreutz, "The crisis of the dinar in the Egypt of Saladin," JAOS 76 (1956), pp. 178-184

Malcolm C. Lyons & D. E. P. Jackson, Saladin (Cambridge, 1982)

Hassanein Rabie, The Financial System of Egypt, A.H. 564-741/A.D. 1169-1341 (Oxford, 1972)

Claude Cahen, Makhzûmiyyât (Leiden,)

A. N. Poliak, "The Ayyubid Feudalism," JRAS (1939), pp. 428-432

S. D. Goitein, A Mediterranean Society (4 vv., Berkeley & Los Angeles, 1967-)

M. H. M. Ahmad, "Some notes on Arabic historiography during the Zengid and Ayyubid Periods," in B. Lewis and P. M. Holt (eds.) Historians of the Middle East (London, 1962)

GEORGETOWN UNIVERSITY
Department of History

Middle East History I: Classical Islam — Professor Ruedy
1-44-411-01 — Fall 1986

Undergraduate Syllabus

Course Requirements:

1. Examinations.--There will be two mid-term examinations and a final. The examinations are primarily essay in form, but will include a small number of one paragraph identification questions.

   One half of the final examination deals with the last third of the course, while the other half is a question requiring you to take a broader look at the whole experience of classical Islam.

Mid-term #1	First or second week in October
Mid-term #2	First or second week in November
Final	Monday, December 22, 4:00-6:00 p.m.

2. Book critiques.--Each student is asked to read two books on aspects of the classical Islamic experience of special interest to him or her. These books are normally selected from the attached list of collateral readings, but any scholarly study in the field which interests you and of which the instructor approves may be substituted.

   Written critiques of 400-600 words for each book should follow the attached outline and be submitted by the following deadlines:

Critique #1	October 15
Critique #2	November 12

Study Aids

Encyclopedia of Islam
Index Islamicus
Cambridge History of Islam
Cambridge Medieval History

Required Reading

Lewis, Bernard	The Arabs in History
Gibb, H.A.R.	Mohammedanism
Schacht, J. and Bosworth, C.E.	The Legacy of Islam

Collateral Reading: Library

Abbot, Nabia	Two Queens of Baghdad
Ahmad, Aziz	A History of Islamic Sicily
Arberry, A.J.	The Legacy of Persia
________	Revelation and Reason in Islam
________	Sufism
Ashtor, E.	A Social and Economic History of the Near East in the Middle Ages
Ayoub, Mahmoud	Redemptive Suffering in Islam
Bell, Richard	The Origins of Islam in its Christian Environment
Blachère, Régis	Introduction au Coran
Barthold, Wilhelm	Turkestan down to the Mongol Invasion
Bulliet, Richard	The Camel and the Wheel
Cahen, Claude	Pre-Ottoman Turkey
Chejne, Anwar	Muslim Spain
Corbin, Henri	Histoire de la Philosophie Islamique, Vol I
Daniel, Norman	Islam and the West: The Making of an Image
Dashti, Ali	In Search of Umar Khayyam
deBoer, T.	The History of Philosophy in Islam
Ehrenkreutz, Andrew S.	Saladin
Frye, Richard	The Golden Age of Persia
Gabrieli, P.	Arab Historians of the Crusades
Gardet, Louis	La Cité musulmane
Gaudefroy de Mombynes	Muslim Institutions
Gibb, H.A.R.	Arabic Literature
Grousset, René	The Empire of the Steppes
von Grunebaum, G.E.	Islam: Essays in the Nature and Growth of a Cultural Tradition
Guillaume, Alfred	The Tradition of Islam: An Introduction to the Study of Hadith Literature
Iqbal, Azfal	The Life and Thought of Muhammad Jalal ud Din Rumi
Elgood, Cyril	A Medical History of Persia and the Eastern Caliphate
Julien, Charles-André	History of North Africa
Katsh, Abraham L.	Judaism in Islam
Lammens, H.	La Mecque à la veille de l'Hégire
Lapidus, Ira	Muslim Cities in the Later Middle Ages
Lassner, Jacob	The Shaping of Abassid Rule
Latourneau, Roger	Fez in the Age of the Marinids
Levi-Provencal, E.	La civilisation arabe en Espagne
Lewis, Archibald	Naval Power and Trade in the Mediterranean
Mez, Adam	The Renaissance of Islam
Mieli, Aldo	La science arabe et son rôle dans l'évolution scientifique mondiale
Peters, R.E.	Aristotle and the Arabs: The Aristotelean Tradition in Islam
Pipes, Daniel	Slave Soldiers of Islam
Planhol, Xavier de	Les fondements géographiques de l'histoire de l'Islam
Rodinson, Maxime	Islam and Capitalism
Schact, Joseph	An Introduction to Islamic Law
Shaban, M.A.	The Abassid Revolution
Spuler, Barthold	Die Mongolen in Iran
________	Iran in Früh-Islamischer Zeit

Watt, W.M.	The Faith and Practice of Al Ghazali
___________	Bell's Introduction to the Quran
___________	Islam and the Integration of Society
Wellhausen, Julius	The Arab Kingdom and its Fall
Wiet, Gaston	Baghdad: Metropolis of the Abassid Caliphate

Collateral Reading: Paperback (Most of these books are also in the librarY)

Andrae, Tor	Mohammed: The Man and His Faith
Arberry, A.J.	Aspects of Islamic Civilization: The Moslem World Depicted
Baynes, N.H. & Moss, H.	Byzantium: An Introduction to East Roman Civilization
Fernea, Elizabeth	Guests of the Sheikh
Hodgson, Marshall	Venture of Islam, Vol. I and/or II
Levy, Rueben	The Social Structure of Islam
Smith, W.R.	Kinship and Marriage in Early Arabia
Rahman, Fazlur	Islam
Rosenthal, E.K.J.	Political Thought in Medieval Islam
Talbot Rice, David	Islamic Art
Watt, W.M.	Muhammad: Prophet and Statesman
Said, Edward	Orientalism
von Grunebaum, G.E.	Medieval Islam
Moscati, Sabatino	Ancient Semitic Civilization

Middle East History I: Classical Islam

Projected Lecture Topics - Fall 1986

Please note that following is an approximate list of lecture topics. Occasionally the order may change, and certain elements may be added or deleted.

I. Introduction. "Civilization." Civilization in the Middle East. Perceptions of Islam.

II. Human and physical geography of the Middle East. Some ways they have influenced historical processes.

III. Religious and political development in the Middle East before Islam.

IV. Arabia and the context of the Islamic revelation. Muhammad and the revelations at Mecca.

V. The Community at Medina. The Fundamentals of Islam.

VI. The Fundamentals of Islam.

VII. The expansion of the Arabs: some historical interpretations. Abû Bakr, the Ridda Wars and the first conquests.

VIII. The conquest of Syria, Iraq and Egypt. Evolution of the Orthodox Caliphate (the Râshidûn). The statute of dhimma.

IX. cUthmân, cAli, and the First Civil War. Religious schism and the end of the Orthodox Caliphate.

MID-TERM EXAMINATION

X. The Umayyad Empire: consolidation and the Second Civil War. The historical roots of Shîcism.

XI. The Umayyad Empire: apogée and decline. Institutional developments; problems of societal integration.

XII. The cAbbâsid Revolution: origins; interpretations; results.

XIII. The cAbbâsid Empire: institutional successes and shortcomings.

XIV. Cultural life: Poetry and humanism in the medieval Arabo-Islamic tradition.

XV. Cultural life: The religious sciences. Law, hadith, theology.

XVI. Cultural life: The religious sciences. Law, hadith, theology.

MID-TERN EXAMINATION

XVII. The decline of the caliphate, the militarization of the state and the process of political decentralization. Central Asia, Iran and the Central Islamic lands.

XVIII. Political Decentralization: the Maghrib and Egypt. Ismâ^{c}îlism and the Fâtimids.

XIX. Social and economic bases of the medieval Islamic synthesis I.

XX. Social and economic bases of the medieval Islamic synthesis II.

XXI. The profane sciences: Translation and philosophy.

XXII. The profane sciences: mathematics, chemistry, medicine.

XXIII. The conversion and expansion of the Turks: social, economic and political implications.

XXIV. The crisis of the 11th century. Internal and external pressures on the medieval Islamic synthesis. The Ayyûbids, the Mamlûks and the Crusaders.

XXV. Disasters of the 13th century: the Castillians and the Mongols; Interpretations of the Medievel Islamic experience.

Outline of Undergraduate Book Critique
Classical Islam

General Format:

Critique should consist of between 400 and 600 words, typed double spaced. The five main elements of its content are as follows:

1. Who is the author? That is, who is the author professionally and what is her or his relationship to the field of Middle East history? Generally, this part of the critique can be covered in three or five short sentences.

2. What kind of book is this and what does it cover? Kind of book refers to genre: historical monograph, literary analysis, historical survey, essay, memoires, translation with commentary, etc. Coverage is what the book is about. Two or three sentences in this paragraph.

3. Main thesis or conclusion. This is the heart of your critique and should be three or four paragraphs in length. Here, tell what principle idea or ideas the author develops, and/or what his main conclusions are. NOTE: A thesis is never "about" anything; a thesis _is_.

4. Organization and presentation. A discussion in two or three paragraphs of salient aspects of the mechanics of the book. Here you could discuss style, organization, method or argument, documentation, or other aspects of the structure of this work.

5. Your own evaluation, in about a paragraph, of the value or utility of this work.

GEORGETOWN UNIVERSITY
Department of History

Middle East History I: Classical Islam — Professor John Ruedy
History 144-411-01 — Fall 1986

Graduate Reading List

Study Aids

Index Islamicus
Encyclopedia of Islam (EI1 or EI2)
Cambridge History of Islam (CHI)
Cambridge History of Iran
Cambridge Medieval History (CMH)

Texts

Gibb, H.A.R., Mohammedanism
Gibb, H.A.R., Studies in the Civilization of Islam
Goldziher, Ignaz, Introduction to Islamic Theology and Law
Lewis, Bernard, The Arabs in History
Swartz, Merlin L., Studies on Islam
Schacht, Joseph & Bosworth, C.E., The Legacy of Islam

Interpretive and Analytical Readings

I. Pre-Islamic Arabia
*Shahid, Irfan, "Pre-Islamic Arabia," CHI
Levi della Vida, Giorgio, "Pre-Islamic Arabia," The Arab Heritage, ed. Nabih A. Faris (Princeton, 1944)
Henninger, Joseph, "Pre-Islamic Bedouin Religion," in Swartz, Merlin L., Studies on Islam, 3-22
Kister, M.J., Studies in Jâhiliyya and Early Islam
Salibi, Kamal, A History of Arabia, pp. 1-74
Donner, Fred McGraw, "The State and Society in Pre-Islamic Arabic," in ibid., The Early Islamic Conquest, pp. 11-49

II. Muhammad
*Rodinson, Maxime, "A Critical Survey of Modern Studies on Mohammad," in Swartz, ibid., 23-85
*Fueck, Jl, "The Orginiality of the Arabian Prophet," ibid., 86-98
Andrae, Tor, Mohammed, His Life and Doctrine
Blachère, Régis, Le Problème de Mahomet
Buhl, Frantz, "Muhammad," EI1, vol. II, 641-657
Watt, W. Montgomery, Muhammad: Prophet and Statesman

III. The Qur'an

*Watt, W. Montgomery, Bell's Introduction to the Qur'an
Blachèrre, Régis, Introduction au Coran
Buhl, Frantz, "Kor an," EI1
Nöldeke, Theodore, Geschichte des Qorans

IV. Overviews of the Expansion of Islam and its Significance

*Gibb, H.A.R., "An Interpretation of Islamic History," Studies in the Civilization of Islam, 3-33
*Becker, Carl, "The Expansion of the Saracens," CMH, 1st ed.
Hodgson, Marshall G.S., The Venture of Islam, I, Book I, Chs. II and III
Gabrieli, Francseco, Muhammad and the Conquests of Islam
Donner, Fred, "Introduction" and "Conclusion" in ibid.

V. The Umayyads and the cAbbâsid Revolution

*Cahen, Claude, "Points de vue sur la Révolution abbasside," Revue historique, 230 (1963)
*Lewis, Bernard, "Abbasids," EI2, I
Wellhausen, Julius, The Arab Kindgom and its Fall
Gibb, H.A.R., "The Evolution of Government in Early Islam," in Studies in the Civilization of Islam, 34-46
Hodgson, Marshall G.S., The Venture of Islam, I, Book II, Ch. I, "The Islamic Opposition"
Sha'ban, The Abbasid Revolution
Kennedy, Hugh, The Early Abbasid Caliphate: The Political History, Ch. 2

VI. The Religious Sciences

*Goldziher, Ignaz, Introduction to Islamic Theology and Law
*Fueck, J. "The Role of Traditionalism to Islamic Law," in Swartz, ibid., 99-111
Schacht, Joseph, Introduction to Islamic Law
Guillaume, Alfred, The Tradition of Islam: An Introduction to the Study of Hadith Literature
Gardet, Louis, Introduction à la théologie musulmane

VII. High Civilization of Medieval Islam

*Von Grunebaum, G.E., Medieval Islam, Chs. I, VI, and VII
*Goldziher, Ignaz, "The Attitude of Orthodox Islam Toward the 'Ancient Sciences'", in Swartz, Ch. VIII
Hodgson, Venture of Islam, I, "Absolutism in Flower, 750-813," "Speculation: Falsafah and Kalam"
Von Grunebaum, G.E., Classical Islam: A History, 600-1258
Sourdel, D. and J., La Civilisation de l'Islam Classique
Mez, Adam, The Renaissance of Islam

VIII. Social and Economic Interpretation

*Amin, Samir, The Arab Nation, foreword, Ch. I
Cahen, Claude, "Economy, Society, Institutions" in CHI, II, 511-538
Goitein, S.D., "The Rise of the Medieval Muslim Bourgeoisie," "The Rise of the Bourgeoisie in Early Islamic Times," and "The Mentality of the Middle Classes in Medieval Islam," in ibid., Studies in Islamic History and Institutions
Rodinson, Maxime, Islam and Capitalism
Lombard, Maurice, The Golden Age of Islam

Gran, Peter, "Political Economy as a Paradigm for the Study of Islamic History," in International Journal of Middle East Studies, XI (1980), 511-526

Duri, Abdal Aziz, Muqaddima fîl tarîkh al iqtisâdi al[c]arabi; tr. Arabische Wirtschafts geschichte

IX. The Study of Islamic History

*Said, Edward, Orientalism

Cahen, Claude, "L'Histoire économique et sociale de l'Orient musulman medieval," Studia Islamica, III (1955), 93-115

Tibawi, A.L., "English-Speaking Orientalists: A Critique of their Approach to Islam and to Arab Nationalism," Muslim World, LIII (1963), 185-204, 98-313

Hourani, Albert, "History," in Leonard Binder, The Study of the Middle East

Abdel-Malek, A., "Orientalism in Crisis," Diogenes, XLIV (1963) 103-140

Owen, Roger, "Studying Islamic History," Journal of Interdisciplinary History, IV (1973), 287-298

Sabagh, Georges, "Sociology" in Leonard Binder, The Study of the Middle East

*Required reading for all graduate students.

ISLAMIC CIVILIZATION: THE IMPERIAL AGE

Course Outline and Reading Assignments

H466B

I. The Muslim World, 1250-1500
   A. The Mongols
      1. The Mongol invasions (Feb. 3, 5, 7)
      2. The Mongol states
         i. The Ilkhans (Feb. 10, 12)
         ii. The Jagatai Khanate (Feb. 14) — Kritzeck, pp. 247-61, 267-73, 281-84
         iii. The Golden Horde (Feb. 19, 21)
   B. Mamluk Egypt (Fe. 24) — Kritzeck, pp. 285-88
   C. The Slave Sultanate of Delhi (Feb. 26) — Kritzeck, pp. 337-43
   D. The Rise of the Ottoman Turks (Feb. 28, March 3)
   E. Spain and the Maghrib (March 5, 7)
   F. Iran and the Sheep States (March 10)
   G. The Expansion of Islam, 1250-1500 (March 12)
   H. Post-Caliphal Culture and Institutions-Law, History, Science, Art (March 14, 17)
   I. Sharia-Mindedness and Tariqa Sufism (March 19, 21) Kritzeck, pp. 262-266, 274-80
   J. The Medieval Muslim Intellectual Achievement-Ibn Khaldun, Jami, Ibn Battuta, etc. (March 31, April 2)

MIDTERM EXAMINATION on April 4, covering material presented in lecture and Hoggson, Vol. II, pp. 369-574

II. The Muslim World, 1500-1800
   A. Moghul India (April 7, 9, 11) — Kritzeck, pp. 344-51
   B. Birth of Modern Iran-Safavida, Afsharids, Zends (April 14, 16, 18)
   C. Islam in Central Asia (April 21, 23)
   D. The Maghrib (April 25, 28)
   E. Islam and Black Africa (April 30)
   F. The Ottoman Empire — Kritzeck, pp. 352-77
      1. Ottoman territorial expansion and conquests (May 2, 5, 7)
      2. Ottoman administration (May 9, 12)
      3. The Empire and its non-Turkish subjects-millets and the devshirre (May 14, 16)
      4. Foreign Policy and education (May 19)
      5. Ottoman culture (May 21, 23)

FINAL EXAMINATION on May 28 at 2:15 p.m. The final examination is comprehensive but will stress the material presented in II, above, and the readings from Hodgson, Vol. III, pp. 3-161.

ISLAMIC CIVILIZATION: THE IMPERIAL AGE

Course Syllabus

H466B

This course is a continuation of H466A. The Arab Ascendancy and deals with the history of the Muslim world from the thirteenth to the nineteenth century. It is the most obscure period in Islamic history and probably also the most difficult to grasp, since by this time the Muslim world has become immense. From Vienna to Timbuktu, from Granada to Kashgar, Bengal and the Malaysian Archipelago, its sheer territorial extent and diversity pose unique problems of understanding. The map quiz (letter A below) will hopefully offset some of the initial geographical difficulties and should not be underestimated as an aid to understanding of the course.

Given the vastness of the area, it would not be practical to try to retain any clear picture of the succession of rulers. We will accordingly concentrate on trends and institutional changes within Islam, ignoring as much of the chronological framework as possible. Both 466A and 466B are"civ" courses. Students should therefore understand that course content often focuses on culture rather than political or dynastic history per se.

Texts

Students are asked to purchase the following textual materials---
Marshall G.S. Hodgson, The Venture of Islam, Vols. II and III
James Kritseck (ed.), Anthology of Islamic Literature

Course Requirements

A. A map quiz scheduled for February 21.
B. A midterm examination scheduled for April 4.
C. Two short quizzes over the assigned reading in the Hogarson text.
D. A comprehensive final examination scheduled for Wednesday, May 28, at 2:15 p.m.
E. Class discussion of the Kritzeck readings. This element of the student's grade is less important than the first four.

Students are expected to demonstrate use of correct, academic English in all their written work. Examinations may not be made up unless the instructor has been notified in advance of the absence and then only for reasons of serious nature. Makeup examinations will not be of the same type as those administered in class. There are no extra-credit assignments in this course.

Dr. Crabbs
Office: Humanities 825E
Phone: (714) 773-3567 or
773-3474

Instructor: Carl Petry
Place: Harris 313
Time: MWF 11
Office: Harris 103B
Phone: 492-7448
Office Hours: WF 1:00 and by appt.

History C70-2, Fall Quarter, 1986
The Islamic Middle East, 1258-1789; The Age of Empires

Required Texts (all paperbacks) (available at SBX)

N. Itzkowitz, Ottoman Empire and Islamic Tradition (Chicago)
I. M. Lapidus, Muslim Cities in the Later Middle Ages (Cambridge)
F. J. Rosenthal, ed., Ibn Khaldun, The Muqaddima (Princeton)
W. H. McNeill, The Islamic World (Chicago)
B. Lewis, Istanbul and the Civilization of the Ottoman Empire (Oklahoma)
Set of data sheets to be purchased from dept.

Required and Recommended works on Reserve

B. Lewis, Islam, 2 vols

J. J. Saunders, The History of the Mongol Conquests
L. Stavrianos, The Balkans Since 1453
M. G. S. Hodgson, The Venture of Islam, 3 vols.
H. Inalcik, The Ottoman Empire: The Classical Age, 1300-1600
P. M. Holt, Egypt and the Fertile Crescent, 1516-1922
B. Lewis, ed., The Cambridge History of Islam, Vol I (CHI) for detailed outlines
A. J. Arberry, Shiraz

Course Description:

Although this survey is the second in a three-term sequence, it does not presume familiarity with events covered during the first quarter. We shall begin with an analysis of the Mongol invasions in the Middle East. Topics to be discussed will include: the related phenomena of alien governments, economic depression and communal realignment; emergence of the military empires: Mamluks, Ottomans and Safavids; the multi-ethnic Islamic empire as an alternative to the European national monarchy during the Renaissance period; and the issue of cultural and economic decline to 1789.

To provide the student with an opportunity for exploring more widely in the field, a reading list of publications in western languages will be distributed.

Course Requirements

There will be an in-class mid-term and a choice between a take-home final and a substantial research paper or analytical essay. Students electing the essay option should decide on how they wish to approach their topic in consultation with the instructor. Final examinations or essays are due on or before Thursday, December 11 at 11:00 A.M. Extensions beyond this date will be granted only for compelling reasons (instructor's discretion).

Schedule of Lectures

1. Introductory Remarks
McNeill 249-253; Lapidus 1-8, rec. Hodgson II 369-385, Saunders 1-55, CHI 160-165.

2. Impact of the Mongol Invasions
Lewis I 77-80, McNeill 253-273; rec. Saunders 55-70, 91-118.

3. Legacy of the Ilkhanids
Lewis I 81-96, II 170-172, McNeill 274-208; rec. Hodgson II 386-437, Saunders 119-139, 175-191, CHI 165-174.

4. Establishment of the Mamluk Empire
Lapidus, 9-43; Lewis I, 97-99; rec. CHI 201-214.

5. Egyptian and Syrian Society during the Mamluk Period
Lapidus, 44-78; Lewis II, 35-39, 43-44, 135-136, 228-235; rec. CHI 214-230, Holt 1-19.

6. The Silver Age of Arabic Islam: Scholasticism in Mamluk Cairo
Lapidus, 79-115; Rosenthal 333-459, Lewis II 3-18.

7. Medieval Sociology: the Work of Ibn Khaldun
Lapidus, 116-191; Rosenthal vii-332.

8. Art and Architecture during the Mamluk Period
rec. Hodgson II 501-531.

9. Pre-Ottoman Anatolia
rec. CHI 251-262 (for background, 231-251).

10. Origins of the Ottoman State
Itzkowitz 3-16, Stavrianos 20-32, Lewis I 135-140; rec. Hodgson III 1-15, CHI 263-277.

11. From Beylik to Empire: Murad I and Bayazid Yilderim
Itzkowitz 16-20, Stavrianos 33-49, Lewis I 226-227, II 45-49; rec. Hodgson II 532-574, Holt 23-32.

12. The Timurid Invasions
Lewis I 100-109; rec. CHI 277-280.

13. Recovery of the Ottomans and Mamluks

Itzkowitz 20-24, Stavrianos 50-55, rec. Holt 33-45.

14. The Dar-al Harb in Eclipse
Itzkowitz 24-34, Lewis, Istanbul 3-64, McNeill 312-336, Stavrianos 55-72; rec. Hodgson III 99-133.

15. The Sunni World State
Itzkowitz 34-37, Stavrianos 72-80, Lewis, Istanbul 65-95, McNeill 344-352; rec. Holt 46-57.

16. The Middle East in the World Economy of the Fifteenth Century
Lewis II 137-140, 251-256; rec. CHI 333-342.

MID-TERM EXAMINATION

17. Ottoman Society and Institutions
Itzkowitz 37-61, Lewis, Istanbul 145-176, Stavrianos 81-95.

18. Constantinople during the Reign of Sulayman Qanuni
Lewis, Istanbul, 96-144.

19. Iranian Society during the Fifteenth Century
Arberry 30-60; rec. CHI 169-174, 394-397.

20. Shi'ism and Charisma: Establishment of the Safavid State
McNeill 337-344; rec. Hodgson III 16-58, CHI 397-413.

21. The Great Sophy
McNeill 373-391; rec. CHI 413-423.

22. Isfahan in the Age of Shah Abbas
Arberry 3-29, 61-171.

23. The Dar al-Harb Ascendant: The Challenge of Renaissance Europe
Itzkowitz 62-72, Stavrianos 96-115; rec. CHI 350-356.

24. The Ottoman Empire in Decline
Itzkowitz 72-85, Stavrianos 117-136 (rec. 154-197); rec. CHI 342-350, 354-356, Holt 61-70.

25. Traditional Theories of Reform and Rejuvenation
Itzkowtiz 87-109; rec. Hodgson III 134-162.

26. Fragmentation of the Safavid State
rec. CHI 423-440.

27. Provincial Autonomy: Syria, Egypt and the Maghrib during the Seventeenth and Eighteenth Centuries
rec. CHI 374-378, Holt 71-148.

28. The Economic Eclipse of the Early Modern Period
    Stavrianos 137-153.

29. The Middle East on the Eve of the Napoleonic Adventure
    rec. Holt 149-163.

INTRODUCTION TO ISLAMIC CIVILIZATION II
Social Sciences 221
Section 1
Winter 1987

John E. Woods
212 Pick Hall
w: 702-8343, 702-8297
h: 955-1225

Kate Lang
410 Kelly Hall
w: 702-8298
h: 493-0932

I. Texts

A. Books recommend for purchase (available at CTS)

M. G. S. Hodgson. **The Venture of Islam**, vol. 2
Ibn Khaldun. **The Muqaddimah**. Ed. N. J. Dawood

B. Bound supplementary readings may be purchased at Kinko's

II. Requirements and Grades.

A quality grade in this course may be earned by selecting either the structured or independent study option outlined below. Please indicate in writing which you have chosen by the end of 3rd Week.

A. <u>Option 1</u> - **Structured Study** (2 examinations, 1 paper)

1. **Examinations** (based on Hodgson, Ibn Khaldun, supplementary readings, lectures, discussions)

   a. take-home mid-term (based on Hodgson, Book 3; Ibn Khaldun; readings; lectures, discussions), distributed Friday of 5th Week; due the following Monday (25%).

   b. take-home final (based on Hodgson, Books 3 and 4; Ibn Khaldun; readings; lectures; discussions) distributed Friday of 10th Week; due the last day of Exam Week (25%).

2. **Essay.** A paper of 10-15 pages in length on any topic of your choice relating to Islamic civilization during the Middle Periods. Due Friday of 10th Week (50%).

B. <u>Option 2</u> - **Independent Study** (3 papers)

1. **Essay.** You are required to prepare a report on the readings you have done for the course. You may read intensively in a single area or range extensively across a variety of topics. In addition to assessing the significance, major thesis, or point of view of each author, you should also indicate the depth to which you have studied each

work (skimmed, read thoroughly, rejected, etc.). Complete publication information should also be included for each item. Your results may be submitted in the form of an integrated essay or an annotated list. The books or articles do not necessarily have to be chosen from the attached reading list, but relevancy to the course material should certainly be one of your criteria of selection. A written outline of your progress is due at the end of 5th Week and the final annotated list is due by the last day of 10th Week.

2. **Course Evaluation.** In addition, you are required to write a paper as brief or as lengthy as you wish about your own personal attitudes, views, and values, and the ways they have changed (or not changed) as a result of this course. I would sincerely appreciate any specific criticisms, both positive and negative, you have to make about the course, the instructor, and the way the course has been carried out, along with your recommendations for improvement. This evaluation will in no case have any influence on your final mark, but if you are concerned that it might do so, place the paper in a sealed envelope marked "Please do not open until the final grades have been turned in," and I assure you I will honor your request. Due the last day of Exam Week.

3. **Self-Evaluation.** Finally, you are required to turn in a statement of your own evaluation of your work along with the grade that you think is appropriate. The statement should include the following:

   a. the goals you set for yourself in the course,

   b. the specific criteria by which you are judging your work,

   c. a description of the ways in which you have achieved or failed to achieve your goals, and

   d. the grade you think appropriately rates your performance.

   If I find that my own estimate of your work is quite at variance with yours, I will have a personal talk with you and we will try to arrive at some mutually satisfactory grade which I can in good conscience sign and hand in. My perception of your commitment to the aims of independent study and your academic citizenship will be the deciding factor in determining your final mark. Due the last day of Exam Week.

Islamic Civilization II

C. **Common Requirements.**

1. **Disscussion/Study Groups.** You will be divided into groups for assignment to discussions sessions held during regular class times. Remember that these groups may also be used outside class in any way and as often as you find helpful; for example, you may meet to discuss the readings, to propose class activities, and to plan class presentations, or you may not meet at all. Kate and I will attend the meeting of any group by invitation extended two days in advance. I would like to be informed of the status of each group by the end of 3rd Week.

2. **Conference.** You are required to set up a 15-minute appointment with me at some mutually convenient time during the quarter to discuss your study plans and progress. A sign-up sheet will be posted outside my office.

III. Resource People in Islamic Civilization at the University of Chicago

R. Austen - Islam in Africa
B. Bezirgan - Arabic bibliography and women's studies
R. Bianchi - political science
J. Carswell - Islamic art
R. Chambers - Turkish history
B. Craig - Islamic bibliography
R. Dankoff - Turkish literature
F. Donner - Arab history
N. Golb - medieval Jewish history and civilization
H. Inalcik - Turkish history
W. Kaegi - Byzantine history
H. Moayyad - Persian literature
F. Mustafa - Arabic literature
M. Naim - Urdu and Persian literature
R. Nelson - Islamic art
J. Perry - Persian literature and Iranian history
F. Rahman - Islamic philosophy, theology, and law
J. Stetkevych - Arabic literature
J. Woods - Iranian and Central Asian history
M. Zonis - contemporary Middle Eastern issues

Islamic Civilization II

IV. Class Schedule (* - indicates combined sessions)

Problems of the Middle Periods

Week 1, Jan. 5-9
M: Introduction to the Course
W: *Islamic Civilization in the Middle Periods
F: *"The Night Journey," slide lecture
Readings: Hodgson, pp. 3-11, 371-385; Ibn Khaldun, pp. 5-69; "The Night Journey"

Politics and Government in the Middle Periods

Week 2, Jan. 12-16
M: *"Unity," film and discussion
W: *The Arab World, lecture
F: *The Irano-Turkish World and Beyond, lecture
Readings: Hodgson, pp. 12-61, 255-292, 386-436, 532-574

Week 3, Jan. 19-23
M: *Evolution of the Caliphate, lecture
W: Nizam al-Mulk's **Book of Government**, class discussion
F: Discussion Sections
Readings: Ibn Khaldun, pp. 123-183, 188-261; "Rules and Regulations of the 'Abbasid Court," "On the Contract of the Caliphate," "Execution of the Minister Hasanak"

NOTE: Grading option selections and discussion group reports due.

Islamic Society in the Middle Periods

Week 4, Jan. 26-30
M: *Pastoral Nomadism
W: Ibn Khaldun, pp. 91-122, class discussion
F: Discussion Sections
Readings: Hodgson, pp. 62-105, 391-410; "Dede Korkut," "The Reign of Osman Ghazi"

Week 5, Feb. 2-6
M: *"Man and Nature," film and discussion
W: *Settled Society, lecture
F: Discussion Sections
Readings: Hodgson, pp. 105-151, 329-368, Ibn Khaldun, pp. 263-332; "Ma'aruf the Cobbler," "The Maqamat," "The Assassins"

NOTE: Mid-term exams distributed; reading progress reports due.

Islamic Civilization II

Philosophy and Theology

Week 6, Feb. 9-13
- M: *Islamic Philosophy, guest lecture, Fazlur Rahman
- W: *"Knowledge of the World," film and discusssion
- F: Discussion Sections

Readings: Hodgson, pp. 170-200, 315-325, 467-500; Ibn Khaldun, pp. 333-358, 371-411; "Life of a Philosopher, The After-Life," **Two Treatises, The Bezels of Wisdom**

Religion and Mysticism

Week 7, Feb. 16-20
- M: *"The Inner Life," film and discussion
- W: Ghazali's **Deliverance from Error**, class discussion
- F: Discussion Sections

Readings: Hodgson, pp. 201-254, 455-467; Ibn Khaldun, pp. 70-89, 358-367; **An Unconventional Pir**

The Mirror of Literature

Week 8, Feb. 23-27
- M: *"A King's Book of Kings," film and discussion
- W: *Philosophy and Literature, lecture
- F: Discussion Sections

Readings: Hodgson, pp. 152-169, 293-325; Ibn Khaldun, pp. 411-459; **The Epic of the Kings, Nine Quatrains, The Ethics of the Aristocracy**

The Visual Arts

Week 9, Mar. 2-6
- M: *"Patterns of Beauty", film and discussion
- W: *The Variety of Islamic Art, guest lecture, John Carswell
- F: *Tour of the Islamic Gallery, The Art Institute, 11:30 AM-2 PM

Readings: Hodgson, pp. 325-328, 501-531

Week 10, Mar. 9-13 - Class Presentations and Reading Period

***

NOTE: All essays, final exams, and evaluations should be deposited at the Center for Middle Eastern Studies, Kelly 411.

INTRODUCTION TO ISLAMIC CIVILIZATION III

Soc. Sci. 222
Spring 1987

M. W. F. 11:30 a.m. - 12:30 p.m.
Pick 016

Richard Chambers
Kelly 408
702-8295

Kate Lang
Kelly 410
702-8298
493-0932

Course Requirements:

1) Midterm examination - in class - Friday, May 1.
2) Essay - based on readings in contemporary literature for classes May 27 - June 1 - due in class on Wednesday, May 27.
3) Final examination - Friday, June 12, 10:30 a.m. - 12:30 p.m..

Readings:

The following readings are on reserve in Regenstein Library. Those marked with an asterisk (*) are also available in paperback editions at the CTS Co-op bookstore (5757 University Ave.).

Abrahamian, E., Iran Between Two Revolutions.
Bezirgan, B., and E. Fernea, Middle East Muslim Women Speak.
Cottrell, A.J. et. al., The Persian Gulf States: A General Survey.
*Hodgson, M.G.S., The Venture of Islam, vol. 3.
*Hourani, A.H., Arabic Thought in the Liberal Age.
*Itzkowitz, N., Ottoman Empire and Islamic Tradition.
*Iz, Fahir (ed.), An Anthology of Modern Turkish Short Stories.
*Johnson-Davis, Denys (ed.), Modern Arabic Short Stories.
Landen, R., The Emergence of the Modern Middle East
*Lewis, B., The Emergence of Modern Turkey.
*McNeill, W.H., and M. Waldman, The Islamic World.
Perry, J.R., Karim Khan Zand: A History of Iran. 1747-1779.
Quandt, W.B., Saudi Arabia in the 1980's.
*Rahman, F., Islam.
*Soc. Sci. 222, Syllabus of Selected Readings.
*Southgate, Minoo (ed.), Modern Persian Short Stories.
Walton, "Economic Development and Revolutionary Upheavals in Iran," in Cambridge Journal of Economics, vol. 4 (1980), pp. 271-292.

Class Topics; Assigned and Suggested Readings:
(Assigned readings are marked with an asterisk "*".)

M., March 30 (1) Lecture: Post Caliphate Government.

W., April 1 (2) Discussion: Ibn Khaldun's view of History: A Review
*Ibn Khaldun selection in the syllabus.

F., April 3 (3) Slide Lecture: The Golden Age of the Gunpowder Empires
*Hodgson, 3-133.
McNeill and Waldman, 344-391.

M., April 6 (4) Lecture: The Post-Classical Ottoman Empire to 1789 A.D..
*Hodgson, 134-144.
*Lewis, Part 1: Chapters 2 and 3.

W., April 8 (5) Iran from the Safavis to the Qajars.
*Hodgson, 144-158.
Perry, 1-47, 205-271, 297-301.

F., April 10 (6) Lecture: Timuri India and the Islamic Periphery.
*Hodgson, 144-158.

M., April 13 (7) Lecture: The Material and Cultural Changes Of the Modern West.
*Hodgson, 165-222.
Landen, 3-33.

W., April 15 (8) Discussion: Universalism and Localism in The Middle East.
*Hodgson 223-248.
*Hourani 1-33.

F., April 17 (9) Lecture: Revivalism - the Wahhabis of Arabia And Shah Wali Allah of India.
*Hodgson, 158-161.
*Rahman, Chapter 12.

M., April 20 (10) Lecture: Reform in the Ottoman Empire (and Egypt).
*Lewis, Part 1: Chapters 4 and 6.
Landen, 33-75.

W., April 22 (11) Lecture: Qajar Iran - Reforms and Concessions
*Hodgson, 303-316.
Landen, 76-81, 127-143, 174-177.

F., April 24	(12)	Lecture: British India - Iqbal and Modernism. *Hodgson, 333-356. McNeill and Waldman, 396-406. *Rahman, Chapter 13.
M., April 27	(13)	Lecture: New Ottomans and Young Turks. *Hodgson, 249-259. *Lewis, Part 1: Chapters 5 and 7. Landen, 94-106, 119-125. *Ziya Gokalp (in syllabus).
W., April 29	(14)	Discussion: Jamal al-Din al-Afghani and Muhammad `Abduh. *Hourani, 103-160. *McNeill and Waldman, 423-431. Landen, 106-110. *Muhammad `Abduh (in syllabus).
F., May 1	(15)	Midterm Examination.
M., May 4	(16)	Lecture: Legal Reform. *Anderson (in syllabus). *Rahman (in syllabus).
W., May 6	(17)	Lecture: Arab Nationalism. *Hodgson, 272-302. *Hourani, Chapter 11. Landen, 125-126, 227-230, 265-272.
F., May 8	(18)	Film/Lecture: Nationalism and Secularism In the Turkish Republic. *Hodgson, 259-271. *Lewis, Part 1: Chapters 8 and 9.
M., May 11	(19)	Lecture: The Islamic World in the 20th Century: A Political Overview. *Hodgson, 357-384. Landen, 294-366.
W., May 13	(20)	Discussion: Economic Development and Social Change. *Hodgson, 384-441. Landen, 294-366.
F., May 15	(21)	Film/Lecture: Women and Family Life. *Loyah (in syllabus). *Idris (in syllabus). *Kamal (in syllabus). Bezirgan and Fernea, I - XXXVI, 193-200.

M., May 18	(22)	Lecture: Iran: The Constitutional Revolution Of 1905-1911 and the "Islamic" Revolution Of 1978-1979. *Abrahamian, Chapters 1, 2, and 11.
W., May 20	(23)	Discussion: Education, Journalism, And Communications. *Lewis, 419-436, (Review Part 1: Chapters 5 and 6). *Hourani, Chapter 10.
F., May 22	(24)	Lecture: Oil, Economics, and Politics. *McLachlan, "Oil in the Persian Gulf Area," (in Cottrell). *Walton, "Economic Development and Revolutionary Upheavals in Iran," (in *Cambridge Journal of Economics*).
M., May 25	(25)	Memorial Day Holiday.
W., May 27 ESSAY DUE	(26)	Lecture/Discussion: Contemporary Persian Literature. See attached assignment for readings.
F., May 29	(27)	Lecture/Discussion: Contemporary Arabic Literature. See attached assignment for readings.
M., June 1	(28)	Lecture/Discussion: Contemporary Turkish Literature. See attached assignment for readings.
W., June 3	(29)	Slide Lecture: Western Views of the Middle East. 10:30 a.m. Breasted Hall, Oriental Institute
F., June 5	(30)	Reading Period - No Class.
F., June 12	(31)	Final Examination. 10:30 a.m. - 12:30 p.m..

Essay Assignment

Introduction to Islamic Civilization III

Spring 1987

The written assignment for this quarter of Islamic Civilization is due in class, Wednesday, May 27. It is to be in the form of an essay (ca. 5-6 double spaced, typed pages) based on the short stories assigned for the Contemporary Literature sessions on May 27, May 29, and June 1.

Contemporary authors in the Islamic World, as elsewhere, frequently use fiction as a vehicle for social commentary and criticism. Your essay should focus on what you perceive as some of the issues raised by the authors of the short stories you have read. What are the authors of these stories saying about their own societies? What do they criticize? What do they praise? Are they optimistic or pessimistic? Do they suggest the causes and possible solutions for problems which they identify? Do the authors address, either directly or indirectly, the roles of Islam, religion, or religious representatives in contemporary society? If so, what do they seem to be saying? Do Arab, Persian, and Turkish authors express common concerns about their respective societies? Are there certain concerns associated with one or two of these societies, but not all three?

Develop your perceptions systematically, with references to specific authors, stories, characters, or other elements in the stories which illustrate the points you make. This essay should be written in the context of this course (Islamic Civilization) and should reflect an understanding of the issues and developments we have been discussing.

Read:	Johnson-Davies:	"Farhat's Republic" "Sundown" "The Man and the Farm" "Miracles for Sale" "A Space Ship of Tenderness to the Moon" "Zaabalawi" "Summer Journey"
	Southgate:	"Seeking Absolution" "The Game is Up" "Joyous Celebration"
	Iz:	"My Nephew"

"The Secret Shrine"
"The Peach Orchard"
"The Girl Who Heard Voices"
"Wasting Government Time"
"The Voice"
"The Valley of Violets"
"The Marriage of Shepherd Ali"
"Sebati Bey's Expedition to Istanbul"
"Civilization's Spare Part"
"Yaran Dede's Stories"
"The River"

E. L. Daniel
Sakamaki B-205
8:00-9:00 MWF
x-6759

HISTORY 355: THE MODERN MIDDLE EAST

Spring, 1986

Course Description: This course is intended to be a survey of the history of the Middle East from the post-Mongol era to the present day, with the major emphasis on the period since the First World War. The topics to be studied in depth include imperialism and nationalism in the Middle East; problems of modernization and development; the Arab-Israeli-Conflict; and the Iranian revolution.

Course Requirements: Attendance at lectures; completion of assigned readings; participation in discussions; a map quiz; a midterm examination; and a final examination. Grades will be determined on the basis of the final examination (30%); the midterm exam (30%); the map quiz (20%); classroom activities (20%).

Required Textbooks:

Don Peretz, *The Middle East Today* (fourth edition)
Kanafani, *Men in the Sun* (any edition)
Al-e Ahmad, *Gharbzadegi* (any edition)

TENTATIVE SCHEDULE OF LECTURES AND READINGS

		Lecture Topic	*Suggested Readings*
Jan.	27:	Introduction	
	29:	The Middle East: Geography	1-9
	31:	Peoples of the Middle East	9-22
Feb.	3:	Islam and the Middle East	23-49
	5:	Safavids and Mamluks	
	7:	The Ottoman Empire	50-52
	10:	Ottoman Institutions	53-61
	12:	Ottoman Decline and Reforms	61-76
	14:	Middle East and the West	77-84
	17:	HOLIDAY	
	19:	The "Eastern Question"	85-95
	21:	Congress of Berlin to World War I	95-103
	24:	Mustafa Kemal Ataturk	103-5;169-178
	26:	The Turkish Republic	160-169
	28:	Modern Turkey	184-200
Mar.	3:	Turkey and NATO	
	5:	Arab Nationalism	135-159
	7:	World War I and the Arabs	105-112

	10:	Jordan	337-357
	12:	Syria and Iraq	396-415;428-445
	14:	MIDTERM EXAMINATION	
	17:	The Arabian Peninsula	462-495
	19:	Lebanon	358-384
	21:	Egypt	202-211
March 24-28:		SPRING RECESS	
	31:	Egypt and the British	211-226
Apr.	2:	The Egyptian Revolution	227-270
	4:	Modern Syria and Iraq	415-427;445-461
	7:	The Zionist Movement	272-281
	9:	The Palestine Mandate	281-298
	11:	Independent Israel	299-336
	14:	Arab-Israeli Conflict to 1956	
	16:	The Six Day and October Wars	
	18:	The Palestinians	*Men in the Sun*
	21:	Camp David/Lebanese Crisis	385-395
	23:	Afghanistan	
	25:	Pahlavi Iran	496-518
	28:	Iran Since World War II	518-522
	30:	Iran and Modernization	*Gharbzadegi*
May	2:	The Iranian Revolution	522-527
	5:	The Islamic Republic	
	7:	REVIEW	

May 16: FINAL EXAMINATION (9:45 A.M.)

UNIVERSITY OF WISCONSIN

RIVER FALLS

HISTORY 145 - HISTORY OF THE MODERN MIDDLE EAST

Prof. Stephen Feinstein

Objectives of the Course: Probably the most important area of the world today is the Middle East. In the aftermath of the Viet Nam War and with the perpetuation of the Arab-Israeli problem and the advent of the "oil crisis," the events and history of the Middle East loom with greater importance. In short, while the Middle East has always played a great role in the history of the world, its presence now is being felt even more because for the first time, it directly affects us as Americans. To understand fully the present events, it would seem logical to look back and try to relate and understand some of the historical events of Middle Eastern history to the present world situation.

The term "Modern Middle East" has a double meaning. In overall terms it denotes that history of the Middle East since the rise of the Islamic religion, or it may refer to the recent history of the region in the twentieth century which has become well known because of its political pressures and instability. The term "Middle East" is often attached only to the Arab world and Israel. In actuality, as this course will hopefully show, the dimensions of the Middle East are far greater, including the histories of the Ottoman Turks, Egypt, Modern Turkey, Iran and the foreign influences which have been a consistent part of Middle Eastern history. The obvious subject matter of Palestine, Arabs, and Israelis, and the oil crisis will also be covered.

In short, then, the purpose of the course is to familiarize the student with the history of a part of the world which is usually neglected in high school and sometimes even in the university curriculum.

*** Note on names and spellings: One of the reasons for the apparent difficulty many people have in understanding the Middle East centers on the issue of names and unfamiliar terms. In reading the assigned material for the course, the student should prepare a list of such new names as he or she is confronted with them, spell them out, and define them to one's own satisfaction. It is only by comprehending these names that one can fully understand the material.

Readings:

I. From the textbook library:

Glenn E. Perry — The Middle East (consult reading schedule)

R.M. Savoury (ed.) — Introduction to Islamic Civilization

Readings (cont.)

II. To be purchased from bookstore (paperback) or available in the the reserve room of the library.

Richard Critchfield Shahhat: An Egyptian (Syracuse)

III. Book to be selected from Library by student for second book report.

See page 4 of this syllabus for details on both reports

Examinations: There will be two examinations of substantial depth, a mid-term and a final. There will also be several quizzes based on the readings in Savoury, which taken together, are equivalent to a midterm examination.

Progress in the Course: Grading is done on a ten-point division system, which means that grades are as follows: 100-90--A; 89-80--B; 79-70--C; 69-60--D; Below 60--F. Students may always judge their position in the class on this basis. If you are uncertain of your class standing, please consult with me during office hours.

Office hours: Students are encouraged to meet with the instructor if they have any questions or difficulties about the class or the assignments.

Office: 355C F.A.

Times: As indicated in class or by appointment

Feel free to drop in, especially if you are having problems, or if you cannot fulfill an assignment. Phone Ext. 3376

Map Assignment: Since the Middle East is generally unfamiliar to Americans geographically, it is useful to acquaint yourself with the geography of the area. You are urged to study the list of names of places enclosed, and to fill out the enclosed map. A short map test will be given during the second week of classes.

Modern Middle East -- Lecture Topics

1. Geography and Ethnography of the Middle East
   Perry, Chapter 1 and Savoury, Chapter 1

2. Islam and its Legacy, including Caliphates
   Perry, Chs. 2 & 3, and Savoury, Chs. 2,3,4,5.

3. Crusades and European Penetration
   Perry, Ch. 4, pp. 95-104, and Savoury, Chs. 6,10,11,12.

4. Ottoman Empire I
   Perry, Ch. 4, pp. 104-119, and Savoury, Chs. 7 & 8.

5. Ottoman Empire II
   Perry, Ch. 4, pp. 119-133.

6. Art and Architecture of the Moslem World
   Class lecture (slides). Read Savoury, Ch. 9.

7. Imperialism and the Birth of Modern Nationalism in the Middle East
   Perry, Ch. 5, pp. 133-144.

8. British Imperialism and the Suez Canal
   Perry, Ch. 5, pp. 144-166.

9. Ottoman Empire - Reform and Revolution
   Perry, Ch. 5

10. World War I and Peace Settlements - Perry, Ch. 6

11. Kemal and Modern Turkey - Perry, Ch. 7, pp. 190-194;205-208.
    Ch. 8, pp. 237-238;278-280.
    Ch.10, pp. 310-311.

12. Mandate System and its successors
    Perry, Ch. 7, pp. 197-201
    Ch. 8, pp. 225-227; 239-242

13. Rise of Modern Egypt I - Perry, Ch. 7, pp. 194-196; 212-218
    Ch. 8, pp.219-224

14. Creation of Israel and TransJordan - Perry, Ch. 7, pp. 201-204
    Ch. 8, pp. 229-235; 245-249

15. Arab-Israeli and Palestinian Conflict - Perry, Ch. 9, pp. 266-275
    Ch.10, pp. 282-290

16. Rise of Modern Egypt II - Perry, Ch. 8, pp. 242-245
    Ch. 9, pp. 249-266

17. Modern Iran - Perry, Ch. 7, pp. 196-197; 208-210
    Ch. 8, pp. 227-228; 235-237; 297-312

18. Oil, Saudi Arabia and OPEC - Perry, Ch. 7, pp. 210-212; 238-239; 275-281
    Ch.10, pp. 290-297.

Book 1. Richard Critchfield - <u>Shahhat: An Egyptian</u>

In a paper of about 5-7 pages, examine the main sociological and religious issues raised. Write the report in a book report format, with the full range of criticisms or analysis which you think are useful. Things which you <u>might</u> bring into your report are as follows:

1. How may the way of life in the Arab world be compared to other parts of the Arab world and non-Arab (Western) world?
2. Analyze the status of women and men.
3. Examine the relationship of religion, work, social & political relationships to the lives of these people and compare it to your own experience.
4. Compare the status of the family in the Arab world with the status of the family in industrial-urban societies. Which is better off?

PAPER DUE: ______________________________

Book 2. Pick a historical account (not a novel) from the works which are to be found in the library regarding the Middle East and write a 3-5 page analytical book report which reflects your knowledge of the Middle East and your specific interest in this topic. Since this is the second assignment, there is a presumption that you know a bit more by the time you do this report.

Suggested areas of interest:

1. Histories of states in particular periods--try to pick recent books rather than dated editions. If, however, you wind up with an older edition, make certain to analyze its faults.

2. Biographies of people associated with Middle Eastern history--Mohammed, Sulieman the Magnificent, Mohammed Ali, Attaturk, Golda Meir, Chaim Weizmann, Theodore Herzl, Gamal Abdul Nasser and the like.

3. Memoirs of people who travelled in the Middle East. In evaluating these, be careful as many erroneous facts often creep into the texts which, as a reviewer, you must be able to pick out!

4. Books about Middle East art and architecture and sociology and religion are acceptable.

PAPER DUE: ______________________________

MAP ASSIGNMENT: Locate the following items on a map of the Middle East:

COUNTRIES

Sudan
Turkey
Iraq
Iran
Jordan
Lebanon
Syria
Israel
Yemen Arab Republic
People's Democratic Republic of Yemen
Kuwait
Bahrain
Cyprus
Qatar
Saudi Arabia
Oman
Dubai
Abu Dhabi
United Arab Emirates

RIVERS AND SEAS

Bosporus
Dardanelles
Sea of Marmora
Aegean Sea
Tigris
Euphrates
Nile
Lake Van
Red Sea
Gulf of Aqaba
Gulf of Aden
Persian Gulf
Gulf of Oman
Caspian Sea
Suez Canal
Strait of Hormuz
Straits of Bab El Mandab
Shatt-al-Arab
Strait of Tiran
Arabian Sea
Litaini River

CITIES

Contantinople - Istanbul
Ankara
Izmir
Mosul
Mecca
Cairo
Alexandria
Jerusalem
Haifa
Tel Aviv
Tyre
Beirut
Baghdad
Damascus
Amman
Aleppo
Medina
Aswan
Teheran
Riyadh
Elath
Erzurum
Kars
Batum
Basra
Muscat
Dhahran
Abadan
Acre
Nicosia

PLACES

Sinai
Mesopotamia
Nafud Desert
Negev
Kurdistan
Gallipoli Peninsula
Sharm-El-Sheik
Salonika
Armenia
Anatolia
Chios
Dodecanese Islands
"West Bank"

MOUNTAINS

Zagros
Taurus
Elburz
Caucasus
Hejaz
Pontic
Anti-Lebanon
Red Sea Mountains

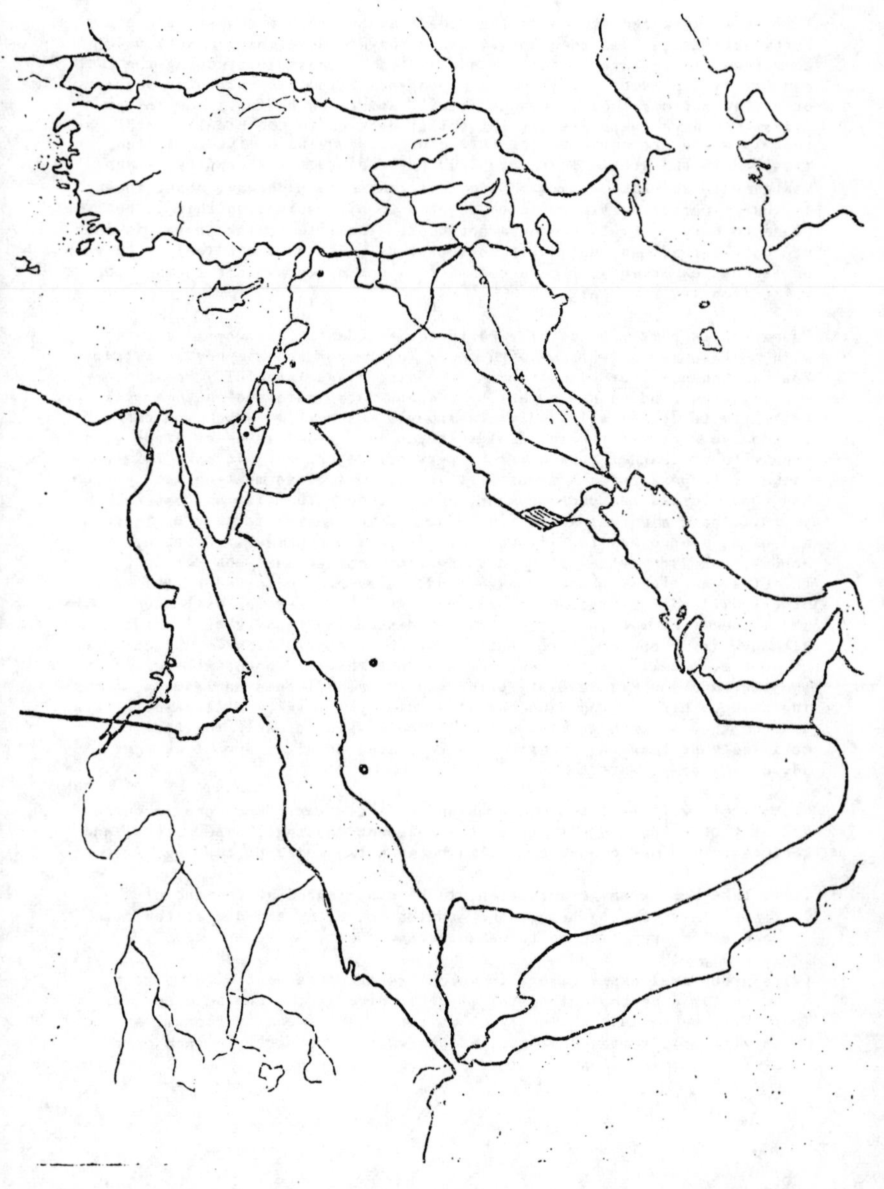

History 473 **THE CONTEMPORARY MIDDLE EAST** Dr. Goldschmidt

Schedule of Classes and Reading Assignments (spring 1986)

This is an advanced course on the modern history of Southwest Asia and Northeast Africa, designed for students who are developing a serious commitment to the use of their minds and an interest in studying the 20th century Middle East. It is not a propaganda forum, an encounter session, or a play period, though we hope it will sometimes be fun. Most of your classmates have taken History 181 ("Introduction to the Middle East"), but that is not a prerequisite for this course. Some have lived, studied, or traveled in the area. There are 2100 pages of required reading, a map assignment, and three exams. Once this course is underway, about three fifths of our class time will be devoted to discussion, so this is not the place to bury yourself behind a notebook. The time to take notes is when you do the readings, not during discussions. If you don't feel up to such an intense experience, please consider switching to another course. Now, while drop-add is free!

Education is partly a social experience. Students learn by interacting with one another as well as with their instructor and his/her assistants. You can enhance <u>your</u> education by attending class faithfully and by completing each reading assignment by the due date indicated on this syllabus. We'll try to create a friendly classroom atmosphere in which you can get to know your classmates and feel that you may either agree or argue with them without fear of antagonism or personal rejection. To make this possible, I'll pass out a student list at our next class meeting, ask you to add your address and phone number, and reproduce the list so that each of you will have a copy. We'll try to help this process further by learning and using your names (or, if you say so, your nicknames). Starting on Monday, the 20th, you will be divided into smaller sections for most of the class meetings. Lecture dates and titles are indicated by (L); all others will be for small group discussions. Each section will have a name and a specified meeting place, but the discussion leaders will rotate. Although in my opening lecture I'll introduce Anat and Chris Manson (plus, of course, myself), let me say for now that they are both well-versed in the contemporary Middle East, being experienced discussion leaders, minoring in both history and Middle East studies. I think you'll enjoy getting to know them as much as I have. We'll be working closely together to maximize your learning experience. Feel free to offer any of us your advice--or complaints.

History 473 will have two midterms and a final exam. Each one is worth 25% of your grade and will cover the relevant readings, discussions, and lectures. You may choose each time between two modes of testing:

(1) **a take-home essay examination**, to be distributed at the end of the last class meeting before the examination date, and due at the time and place specified on the examination sheet,

(2) **a group oral examination**, in which 3-4 students meet with me at a mutually acceptable time and place to discuss the course material.

There will be no in-class essay or multiple choice examinations. Anat and Chris will hold review sessions, if you want them, early in each exam period. I'll grade all oral and written exams, although Chris and Anat may take part if they wish. The remaining 25% of your grade will be based on class participation.

My office is in 614 Liberal Arts Tower (phone 863-0086, or leave message at 865-1367). Don't hesitate to stick your head in my door whenever it's open or leave me a note on the message board if it isn't. My official office hours will be Mondays 10 to 11:55 AM and Thursdays 2 to 3:45 PM. I'm willing to meet with you at other times and places, provided I don't thereby endanger my health, break the law, miss my other classes, fail to get my writing done, or blow off my other appointments. You can usually call me at home (237-3517) between 7 and 9 AM or at 7 PM, right after the evening news. My wife can take messages, and our phone has a message recorder if we're all out when you call. Casual discussions about the contemporary Middle East are more welcome than drawn-out arguments about grades and course requirements.

There is no official textbook; students taking this course should buy as many of the following books as possible:

James A. Bill and Carl Leiden, Politics in the Middle East (2nd ed.; Little Brown, 1984) "B & L"

Jimmy Carter, The Blood of Abraham: Insights into the Middle East (pb Houghton Mifflin Co., 1985) "C"

David Gilmour, Lebanon: the Fractured Country (St. Martin's Press, 1984)

Fred J. Khouri, The Arab-Israeli Dilemma (Syracuse U. Press, 1985) "K"

Edward Mortimer, Faith and Power: the Politics of Islam (Random House, 1982) "M"

Barry Rubin, Paved with Good Intentions: the American Experience and Iran (Penguin Books, 1981) "R"

For maps, tables of rulers, and general reference, some students will find use for:

Jere L. Bacharach, A Middle East Studies Handbook (University of Washington Press, 1984)

Here, at last, is your syllabus:

13 Jan. INTRODUCTION TO THE STUDY OF THE CONTEMPORARY MIDDLE EAST (L)

15 EARLY ISLAMIC HISTORY AND INSTITUTIONS (L)
M, 15-55 (two movies will be shown at 7:15 PM in 165 Willard)

17 ISLAMIC ECLIPSE AND WESTERN IMPERIALISM (L)
M, 56-117

20 THE WESTERNIZATION OF TURKEY
M, 121-158

22 WAHHABI ISLAM AND OIL IN SAUDI ARABIA
M, 159-185

24	NATIONALISM AND RESURGENT ISLAM IN THE ARAB WORLD (L) M, 230-295
27	REVOLUTIONARY IRAN M, 296-376
29	THE USSR AND THE MIDDLE EAST M, 377-407
31	DEVELOPMENT AND MODERNIZATION (L) **map assignment due** B & L, 1-37
3 Feb.	RELIGION AND POLITICS IN THE MIDDLE EAST B & L, 38-73
5	SOCIAL STRUCTURES IN THE MIDDLE EAST B & L, 74-131
7	TRADITIONAL LEADERSHIP B & L, 132-176
10	MODERNIZING LEADERSHIP B & L, 177-234
12	THE POLITICS OF COERCION B & L, 235-285
14	THE POLITICS OF PERSUASION (L) B & L, 286-323
17-19	**FIRST EXAMINATION** (covering all material to date)
21	INTRODUCTION TO THE ARAB-ISRAELI CONFLICT (L) B & L, 324-371
24	BRITISH POLICY AND THE PALESTINE CONFLICT K, 1-42
26	THE UNITED NATIONS AND THE BIRTH OF ISRAEL K, 43-101
28	TWO INTRACTABLE ISSUES: JERUSALEM AND REFUGEES (L) K, 102-181
3-8 Mar.	**Spring Break**
10	THE SUEZ WAR, 1956 K, 182-241
12	THE JUNE 1967 WAR K, 242-292
14	EARLY ARAB-ISRAEL PEACE EFFORTS K, 293-355
17	THE ARAB-ISRAELI CONFLICT, 1968-1976 K, 356-389
19	CARTER'S AND REAGAN'S PEACE EFFORTS (L) K, 390-467
21	BACKGROUND ON LEBANON (L) G, 1-51

- over -

24 NATIONALIST MOVEMENTS IN LEBANON
G, 53-105

26 THE LEBANESE CIVIL WAR, 1975-1982
G, 107-157

28 ISRAELI INTERVENTION AND ITS AFTERMATH
G, 158-199

31 SUMMARY AND CONCLUSION (L)
K, 468-523

2-4 Apr **SECOND EXAMINATION** (covering all material since first exam)

7 Apr. THE UNITED STATES AND IRAN (L)
R, 3-53

9 FROM MOSSADEGH TO THE WHITE REVOLUTION
R, 54-123

11 IMPERIAL IRAN
R, 124-189

14 THE COLLAPSE OF THE SHAH
R, 190-251

16 THE IRANIAN REVOLUTION
R, 252-299

18 THE AMERICAN HOSTAGE CRISIS
R, 300-364

21 IMPLICATIONS OF IRAN'S REVOLUTION FOR THE GULF STATES
B & L, 372-412

23 CARTER AND THE ISRAELIS (L)
C, 1-60

25 CARTER LOOKS AT SYRIA AND LEBANON
C, 61-106

28 CARTER LOOKS AT JORDAN AND THE PALESTINIANS
C, 107-151

30 CARTER LOOKS AT EGYPT AND SAUDI ARABIA
C, 153-192

2 May THE FUTURE OF THE MIDDLE EAST (L)
C, 195-208; B & L, 413-445

FINAL EXAMINATION (covering material since the second exam) will be held during the Final Examination period.

M.I.T.
HISTORY FACULTY

SYLLABUS

21.481: THE MIDDLE EAST IN THE TWENTIETH CENTURY

Prof. Philip S. Khoury
14N-314
X3-2601
Office Hours: MW, 2:30-3:30
(or by appointment)

Spring 1986
HUM-D
MW, 9-10:30
5-233

This subject surveys the major political, socioeconomic, and cultural changes in the post-World War I Middle East through the lenses of religion, state, and nationalism. We shall first investigate interwar independence struggles against Europe and then the emergence of American and Soviet influence, radical nationalist, socialist, and Islamic movements, and the growth of modern states and societies after 1945. We shall conclude with an examination of several contemporary problems in historical perspective: Arab-Israeli conflict, Lebanese civil war, oil and regional security, Islamic revivalism and the Iranian revolution.

PART I: BACKDROP TO THE CONTEMPORARY MIDDLE EAST

Feb. 5 The Middle East in the 20th Century: An Overview
Feb. 10 Religion and State/Islam and Politics
Feb. 12 The Rise of Modern Nationalism
Feb. 17 HOLIDAY
Feb. 19 The Great Partition: World War I and the Peace Settlement

Readings: Lois A. Aroian and Richard P. Mitchell, The Modern Middle East and North Africa, 1-28, 67-160
Edward Mortimer, Faith and Power: The Politics of Islam, 31-117

Feb. 24 DISCUSSION SECTION: Social Change and the Rise of Nationalism

Readings: Middle East Sourcebook, Part I

PART II: NATIONALISM AND IMPERIALISM: THE INTERWAR YEARS

Feb. 26 Ataturk and the Creation of Modern Turkey
March 3 The Mandate System: British and French Imperialism Compared

March 5 The Struggle for Palestine - I
March 10 The Struggle for Palestine - II
March 12 Egypt: The Failure of Liberalism

BOOK REVIEW DUE

Readings: Aroian and Mitchell, 160-262
William P. Quandt, et. al., The Politics of Palestinian Nationalism, 7-42
Don Peretz, The Government and Politics of Israel, 1-50
Rosemary Sayigh, Palestinians: From Peasants to Revolutionaries, 10-63
Bernard Lewis, The Emergence of Modern Turkey, 236-319
Derek Hopwood, Egypt: Politics and Society, 1945-1984, 1-33

March 17 DISCUSSION SECTION: The Struggle for Palestine

Readings: Middle East Sourcebook, Part II
Arthur Hertzberg, The Zionist Idea, 201-226, 249-269, 353-366, 557-570

PART III: RADICALISM AND REGIONALISM: POST-1945

March 19 General Trends in Post-World War II Politics and Society

March 24-28 SPRING VACATION

March 31 Egypt's Uncertain Revolution under Nasser and Sadat
April 2 Syria and the Ba^cth Party
April 7 Saudi Arabia: A House Built on Sand?

Readings: Aroian and Mitchell, 313-421
Hopwood, 33 to end
Mortimer, 159-185

April 9 DISCUSSION SECTION: Radicalism and Regionalism

Readings: Middle East Sourcebook, Part III
Denys Johnson-Davies, trans., Modern Arabic Short Stories, 1-18 (Idris), 83-94 (Salih), 135-145 (Mahfouz)

ESSAY I DUE

Part IV: **THE IRANIAN REVOLUTION: A CASE STUDY**

April 14 Iran under the Shahs
April 16 Structural Causes of the Iranian Revolution
April 21 HOLIDAY
April 23 The Iran-Iraq War

Readings: Nikki Keddie, Roots of Revolution: An Interpretive History of Modern Iran, 1-23, 79-276

April 28 DISCUSSION SECTION: Interpreting the Revolution

Readings: Middle East Sourcebook, Part IV

PART V: CONTEMPORARY PROBLEMS IN HISTORICAL PERSPECTIVE

April 30 The Turkish Experiment in Democracy
May 5 Israel: Challenges to Zionism and Democracy
May 7 Lebanon: Between a Rock and a Hard Place
May 12 The Middle East: Prospects and Perspectives

Readings: Aroian and Mitchell, 267-278, 292-312
Peretz, 51-118, 141-256
David Gilmour, Lebanon: The Fractured Country
Sayigh, 64 to end

SUGGESTED: Amos Oz, In the Land of Israel

May 14 DISCUSSION SECTION: Suffer the Future

Readings: Middle East Sourcebook, Part V

ESSAY II DUE

COURSE MECHANICS (read carefully!!)

1. Subject breaks down into five parts, each consisting of a number of formal lectures followed by a required discussion section.

2. READINGS:
a) books and articles which complement my lectures and serve as background for discussion sections and your essays. The Course text is L.A. Aroian and R.P. Mitchell, The Modern Middle East and North Africa

b) primary materials (in translation) which will form the basis of our discussion sections. Included are travellers' accounts, memoirs, treaties and other international agreeements, tracts on politics and religion, economic plans, literary works, interviews, and speeches. Most of these primary materials are collected in a bound volume (Middle East Sourcebook) which I have assembled and which you must purchase. The Sourcebook may only be purchased in the History Faculty Office, 14N-408. @$7.00

All readings on the Syllabus are required (unless otherwise indicated). They can be located in the Reserve Book Room (14N-132) of the Humanities Library. You may also purchase the following books which can be found in the textbook section of the MIT COOP.

L.A. Aroian and R.P. Mitchell, The Modern Middle East and North Africa (MacMillan)
Edward Mortimer, Faith and Power: The Politics of Islam (Vintage)
Derek Hopwood, Egypt: Politics and Society, 1945-1984 (Allen & Unwin)
Nikki R. Keddie, Roots of Revolution: An Interpretive History of Iran (Yale)
Don Peretz, The Government and Politics of Israel (Westview)
Denys Johnson-Davies, ed., Modern Arabic Short Stories
Rosemary Sayigh, Palestinians: From Peasants to Revolutionaries (Zed)
Amos Oz, In the Land of Israel
David Gilmour, Lebanon: Fractured Country (St. Martin's)

3. COURSE REQUIREMENTS

This is a HUM-D subject. You are asked to write one 6-7 page Book Review and two 9-10 page essays. I shall provide you with a list of books for review on a wide variety of Middle Eastern topics. Your two essays will address questions raised in my lectures, the required readings, and in discussion sections. You will have a choice of questions on which to write. I shall circulate these questions well in advance and I shall help you formulate (if necessary) your topic and provide you with additional bibliographic references. Book reviews and essays must be typewritten and doublespaced. Make certain to produce at least one extra copy of your essays for your own files.

DATES TO KEEP IN MIND: MARCH 12 (Book Review)
APRIL 9 (ESSAY I)
MAY 14 (ESSAY II)

n.b. I DO NOT ACCEPT INCOMPLETES!!!
n.b. THERE WILL BE NO QUIZZES, MIDTERM OR FINAL EXAMINATION!!!

History 336
MiddleEast - Modern

Peter von Sivers

SYLLABUS

(1) Course Description

This course description offers you a survey of Middle Eastern history from 1500 to the Present. For our purposes the Middle East shall be defined as the area now comprised by Egypt, Israel, Lebanon, Syria, Turkey, Iraq, the Arabian peninsula, Iran and Afghanistan. The survey nature of the course demands a concentration on long-range developments and overall trends rather than a detailed examination of developments in specific Middle Eastern countries. Therefore we shall focus in the early part of the course on the economic stagnation which became a more and more pronounced feature during the period from c. 1500 to c. 1800 and which was a result of European economic expansion in the Atlantic and Indian Oceans. This expansion made a by-passing of the traditional Middle Eastern trade routes possible. Once the Middle East was economically weakened, it became the victim of European political and, in the 19th century, colonial interference. Both English and French colonial interferences were met with fierce resistance, but it was only after World War I and the rise of nationalist movements that the Middle East was able to turn the tide of colonialism. Nationalism reached its climax in the middle of the 20th century. During the 1950's the last remnants of formal political control by the colonial powers disappeared, as demonstrated by Egypt's takeover of the Suez canal from the English in 1954-56. However, in one instance national aspirations remained unfulfilled. The Palestinian Arabs were not only unable to achieve self-rule but also lost their lands to the Israeli state in two wars (1948-1967).

While political self-rule became a fact by the middle of the 20th century for most Middle Eastern people, economic dependence on the West continues unabated. Most Middle Eastern governments have opted for industrialization in imitation of the West in order to overcome what is called "underdevelopment". The exploitation of large oil deposits has made many Middle Eastern countries able to finance their industrialization efforts. But the economic aspirations of the people have risen faster that the ability of the governments to provide for permanent, well-paying industrial jobs and so the Middle East has been beset with monumental social tensions. The most glaring case, of course, is that of Iran but similar tensions have become visible also in Egypt, Syria, Turkey, Saudi Arabia and Iraq. These tensions have become so overwhelming that they have caused a backlash among a sizeable portion of Middle Easterners against efforst to imitate Western industrialization -- a backlash which has expressed itself in anti-Westernisms and an attempt to revive religious fundamentalism. How successful this backlash will be remains to be seen, but since there is no quick way out of the all-pervasive social tensions pitting a decayed traditional way of life against an alien modernity adopted by a razor-thin minority of people Middle Eastern history is likely to remain volatile for some time to come.

(2) Course Requirements

(a) The class generally shall meet four times a week (M, Tu, W, Th). However, a few times we shall have to add Friday sessions in order to cover the course materials thoroughly. Fridays without classes are reserved for reading and preparation. I expect everyone to attend classes regularly, since in my lectures I shall analyze rather than repeat the content of the assigned readings. I also expect each of you to set aside enought time each weekend to prepare the readings assigned for the following week. It is absolutely mandatory that you read ahead of the lectures so as to be able to absorb the often complicated materials and be properly prepared for the exams.

(b) The basic texts for this class are P.M. Holt et al., eds., The Cambridge History of Islam; Peter Mansfield, The Arabs; Bernard Lewis, The Emergence of Modern Turkey; Fred Halliday, Iran: Dictatorship and Development; and Fred Khouri, The Arab-Israeli Dilema. All books are available in the bookstores on and near the campus.

(c) I shall distribute lecture outlines before each class meeting. These outlines are designed to help you orient yourself in the materials. Each outline contains a summary of the lecture and further readings which will be helpful aids for the preparation of your exams and for the general understanding of the materials discussed in class.

(d) There will be three tests in this class. The first test is a 15 minute exam dealing with the book of Mansfield and is scheduled for Monday, April 7. The second and third tests are 50 minutes each and are scheduled for Monday, April 28, and Monday, May 19, respectively. They will cover both assigned readings and lecture materials. All three tests will consist of essay questions of varying lengths (short questions asking for identification and statement of significance in one paragraph and/or long essay questions asking for the detailed development of a historical theme covering time periods of up to 25 years). You will have a choice of questions. I have not scheduled a final exam. The first test is worth 20%, the second and third are worth 40% each of the final grade.

(e) If you are prevented from taking one of the exams, please let me know in advance, so that we can make different arrangements. If you miss an exam unexcused I shall be forced to fail you on the exam.

(f) This class shall require a serious intellectual effort from you. Academic progress and working for a living do not mix easily, so if you have divided loyalties please seriously examine your place in this class. Likewise, if your mind is not geared towards the achievement of academic excellences and if you do not care abut reading books or immersing yourself in historical problems, perhaps you should look for another course. On the other hand, if you are fascinated by a foreign culture and civilization, such as that of the Middle East, and seriously want to learn about it, I shall give you the strongest encouragement and support possible. I want you to vigorously participate in our class discussions and I am also available, outside the class context, for private discussions in my office. You can come to me with any academic or personal concern. Don't hesitate to contact me directly or by phone (581-8312 or 363-4143). My office is in 301 Carlson Hall and my hours are M 1-2 or by appointment.

(3) Lecture Schedule

Week 1 - The Ottoman Empire, Safavid Iran and the West: Struggle for Predominance, 1500-1700 (Ottoman expansion into Balkans, Egypt and ndian Ocean, Iranian-Ottoman struggles, Ottoman economy and society)

Reading assignments: Holt, III 3 and III 5; Mansfield, I 1-3

Week 2 - Middle Eastern Decentralization, 1700-1800 (provincial autonomy in the Ottoman empire, Iran from the Safavids to the Qajars, the Wahhabi-Ibn Sa ud movement in Arabia)

Reading assignments: Holt, III 3, 4 and 6; Mansfield I 5; Lewis, I-III

Week 3 - Middle Eastern Re-Centralization, 1800-1850 (Tanzimat reforms in the Ottoman empire, Muhammad Ali in Egypt)

Reading assignments: Mansfield I 6, Lewis IV

Week 4 - European Colonial Interference, 1850-1900 (constitutional reforms and Abdul Hamid in the Ottoman empire, Egypt under Isma[c] il and the British, the Mahdi of Sudan, Jewish immigration into Palestine)

Reading assignments: Mansfield I 7, Lewis V and VI, Khouri I

Week 5 - The Climax of European Control Over the Middle East, 1900-1920 (Young Turks in the Ottoman empire, king Faysal and Arab nationalism, the constitutional revolution in Iran)

Reading assignment: Mansfield, I 8; Lewis VII; Halliday 1

Week 6 - and 7 - The Ascendancy of Middle Eastern Nationalism, 1920-50 (development in Turkey and Iran, the Wafd party in Egypt, the British mandate over Palestine, the French in Syria and Lebanon, oil in Iraq and Arabia, the emergence of Israel)

Reading assignments, week 6: Mansfield, I 9 and 10; Lewis VIII, X and XI; Khouri, II and III

Reading assignments, week 7: Mansfield, I 10 and 11; Lewis, IX and XII-XIV; Khouri, IV; Halliday, 2 and 3

Week 8 - and 9 - The Middle East Politically Independent, 1950-70 (Nasser's leadership of the Middle East, the Ba[c]th party in Syria and Iraq, Arab-Israeli wars in 1956 and 1967, uneasy democracy in Turkey, hectic economic development in Iran)

Reading assignments, week 8: Mansfield, I 12; Khouri, V and VI; Halliday, 4 and 5

Reading assignments, week 9: Mansfield, 13-14; Khouri, VII and VIII; Halliday, 6-7

Page 2

Week 10 - Rapid Economic Development and Social Crises, 1970-80 (Sadat and the October 1973 war against Israel, Palestinian nationalism; development schemes in Syria, Iraq, Sudan, Egypt; civil war in Lebanon, extremism in Turkey, the fall of the Shah of Iran, Marxist regimes in Yemen and Afghanistan)

Reading assignments: Mansfield, II 17-25 and III, 30-31; Khouri, IX and X; Halliday, 8-10.

Anthropology 119
PEOPLES OF THE MIDDLE EAST
Spring, 1987 Tufts University
M,Th 2:30-3:45, Braker 2

Professor: Janet Bauer
Office: 129 Eaton, x2509
Office Hours: M,Th 4-5; Tuesdays 1:30-3:30 by appointment only

Course Description

This course surveys cultures, religious practices, social institutions, political economies, and social change in contemporary Middle Eastern and North African societies. Particular attention is given to the relationship of these societies to the west.

Course Goals

1. To learn the geography of the Middle East and North Africa.
2. To understand the historical relationships between the Middle East and the West.
3. To understand the similarities and differences among cultures of the Middle East from both an emic and an etic perspective and be able to relate this knowledge to contemporary events in the region.
4. To understand the impact of economic and historical change on culture and society in the Middle East.
5. To demonstrate this knowledge in both oral and written form.

Course Requirements

1. Ongoing journal of media coverage of the Middle East, preferably limited to one society or culture for which you will also provide the background paper in class. This will be submitted in April with some analysis based on what you have learned in this course.
2. Background paper (@ 6-8 pages) on one culture of the Middle East to be presented in class orally (will be related to media reporting)
3. Midterm and Final exams.
4. Occasional class exercises (one page)
5. Completion of all class assignments and attendance at assigned campus lectures or events.

Course Organization

Course will be held as a lecture/discussion class. You are responsible for material presented in class, guest lectures and assigned readings.

Required Reading--main selections

Eickelman, The Middle East: An Anthropological Perspective
Asad and Owens,ed., The Middle East
Crapanzano, Tuhami. Portrait of a Moroccan
Nawal el-Saadawi, Two Women in One
Fernea and Bezirgan, eds., Middle Eastern Muslim Women Speak
Behnke, The Herders of Cyrenaica...the Bedouin of Eastern Libya
Selections from Said, Covering Islam; El-Asmar, Through the Hebrew Looking Glass; Lewis, Semites and Anti-Semites
Tessler, "Ethnic Change and Nonassimilating Minority Status: Jews in Tunisia and Morocco and Arabs in Israel"

Course Outline
Peoples of the Middle East

I. Introduction to the Anthropological Study of the Middle East
1/15

Exercise #1--Survey media or journal sources for information on Middle Eastern/North African societies; choose a particular culture--not your own--for your future concentration in the class and write one page on your impressions of that culture (for 1/29). Also begin locating "natives" of that culture among students on campus.

1/22 Unity and Diversity--evening lecture on Jerusalem
8:00 AV room of Wessell Library
Dr. Heilman, "Jerusalem: Attachments and Cultural Memory"
meet at 7:30 in Braker 2 first

What are the simlarities in societies of Middle East and North Africa. Do we explain similaritites by shared culture or by similar ecology?

assigned reading: Eickelman, Chapter 1, "Anthropology and the Middle East"

**Specific reading and writing assignments will be distributed in advance of each major section below.

II. Cultural History and Oral Traditions
1/26 First Impressions (Historical and Personal)

How do Westerners and Middle Easterners view self and each other?
What are the sources of bias in these perceptions?
What is the relation of culture and cultural bias to behavior?

Assigned Readings: Eickelman, Chapters 2 and 3; begin Crapanzano
Exercise #2 for 1/29--Bring folk tales or proverbs or stories from the culture you have elected to focus on.

1/29 continued
2/2

III. Variations in Gender and Ethnic Identity, Social Structures, Religio-Cultural Traditions (Music, Food, Dress, Ritual, Healing).
2/5 Sex Roles and Society
2/9
2/12
2/19 Culture Life--Manners and Dress
2/20 Kinship, family and community
2/23

Assigned Reading: Eickelman, Chapters 6,7,8 ;Additional Assignments--
El-Saadawi; Fernea and Bezirgan

Film fest--Fernea's view of the Middle East
Communal ritual dinner--Exercise #3: students will report on meals/foods/local agriculture in their society--we'll have meal
2/26 Popular Religion and World View
3/2
3/5
Films on sufism, popular Islam
Exercise #4--Reports on the religious traditions and world view of the group you are focusing on
Assigned reading: Eickelman, chapter 9; selections from Fernea

3/9 Ethnicity and Music--guest lecturer, Rabbi Summit on Yemmeni Jews
3/12
Assigned reading: Tessler; readings from El-Asmar and Bernard Lewis
3/23 Midterm

IV. Political Economies of Middle Eastern Societies
3/26 Historical systems of production and political systems; kinship, tribe and politics
3/30
4/2
Exercise #5--know the political economy of your group
film: Grass
Assigned reading: Eickelman, Chapters 4 and 5
Begin Behnke

V. Economic Development, "Westernization", and Social Change
4/6
4/9
4/13
Assigned Readings: Eickelman, Chapters 10 and 11; Behnke, continued
selections from Asad and Owens

4/16 Responses to Change--Religious Revivalism, nationalism, revolution--Focus on Iran
4/23

What are the political economic explanations for revival and protest and what are the cultural explanations for the form this takes?

Assigned Readings: selections from Fernea and Asad and Owen

V. Another look at western and eastern misperceptions: media and literature
4/27
Oral Reports on Media Coverage--Written Assignment due
Paper on chosen Culture due; must have checked out impressions with student from that culture--include comments and reactions

Assigned reading: selections from Said, Covering Islam
Final Exam

Anthro 404
Spring 1986
Tuesday 10:00-12:30
McMillan 101

Dr. Lois Beck
Office: 121 McMillan
Hours: by appointment and to be posted

ETHNICITY, RELIGION, AND CHANGE IN THE MUSLIM WORLD

This course offers a study of contemporary social systems in the Muslim world, with emphasis placed on types of ethnic and religious groups and movements in this vast region and on issues of modernization and change in Muslim society. The course is identical with Asian 435 and International Development 404.

Books for purchase

Dale Eickelman	The Middle East: An Anthropological Approach
Michael Gilsenan	Recognizing Islam: Religion and Society in the Modern Arab World
Edward Mortimer	Faith and Power: The Politics of Islam
Nikki Keddie	Roots of Revolution: An Interpretive History of Modern Iran
Roy Mottahedeh	The Mantle of the Prophet: Religion and Politics in Iran
Rosemary Sayigh	Palestinians: From Peasants to Revolutionaries

Schedule of readings and assignments

Jan. 14 Introduction to the course

Jan. 21 Dale Eickelman, The Middle East

Jan. 28 Dale Eickelman, The Middle East

Feb. 4 Michael Gilsenan, Recognizing Islam

Feb. 11 John Esposito, "Islamic Revivalism," American Institute for Islamic Affairs, Occasional Paper No. 3, 1985 (copies on reserve in Anthropology Office)
Edward Mortimer, Faith and Power, pp. 1-117.

Feb. 18 Edward Mortimer, Faith and Power, pp. 121-407.
Three-page paper on the anthropological study of Islam and Islamic society

Feb. 25 Nikki Keddie, Roots of Revolution

Mar. 4 Nikki Keddie, Roots of Revolution

Spring vacation

Anthro 404

Mar. 18 Roy Mottahedeh, The Mantle of the Prophet

Mar. 25 Roy Mottahedeh, The Mantle of the Prophet
Three-page paper on the relationship of religion and politics in modern Iran

Apr. 1 Rosemary Sayigh, Palestinians

Apr. 8 Individualized readings on ethnicity in Muslim society
Student reports and discussion

Apr. 15 Individualized readings on ethnicity
Student reports and discussion

Apr. 22 Individualized readings on ethnicity
Student reports and discussion

Fifteen-page paper on a topic developed by the student and teacher, relating to ethnicity, religion, and change in the Muslim world

Course requirements

This course is a seminar, and student participation in each week's discussions is essential. This requires regular attendance and thorough reading of the assignments. Each student will write three papers and present one report.

ashington University, St. Louis
nthropology 302BQ
all 1986
, Th 9:30-11:00

Dr. Lois Beck
Office: 121 McMillan
Hours: T, Th 11:15-12:00
and by appointment

PEOPLES AND CULTURES OF THE MIDDLE EAST

ooks for purchase

aniel Bates and Amal Rassam	Peoples and Cultures of the Middle East
onald Cole	Nomads of the Nomads: The Al Murrah Bedouin of the Empty Quarter
mos Elon	The Israelis: Founders and Sons
lizabeth Fernea	Guests of the Sheik: Ethnography of Iraqi Village
dward Mortimer	Faith and Power: The Politics of Islam
osemary Sayigh	Palestinians: From Peasants to Revolutionaries
oy Mottahedeh	Mantle of the Prophet: Religion and Politics in Iran

ecommended:

ay Cleveland	Middle East and South Asia 1986
dward Said et al.	Profile of the Palestinian People

chedule of readings and assignments

ug. 28	Introduction
ept. 2, 4	Elizabeth Fernea, Guests of the Sheik (first half)
ept. 9, 11	Elizabeth Fernea, Guests of the Sheik (last half) Sept. 9: film, Naim and Jabar (rural Afghanistan) (we meet in Olin 252)
ept.16, 18	Donald Cole, Nomads of the Nomads (first half)
ept. 23, 25	Donald Cole, Nomads of the Nomads (last half)

Sept. 30, Oct. 2	Daniel Bates and Amal Rassam, Peoples and Cultures of the Middle East (first half)
Oct. 7, 9	Daniel Bates and Amal Rassam, Peoples and Cultures of the Middle East (last half)
Oct. 7	Films, A Veiled Revolution (Islam and veiling in Egypt) and The Painted Truck (Afghanistan) (we meet in Olin 252)
Oct. 14, 16	Paper due: eight-page anthropological analysis of Middle Eastern societies and cultures and the process of change, based on the readings to date Edward Mortimer, Faith and Power: The Politics of Islam (first half)
Oct. 21, 23	Edward Mortimer, Faith and Power: The Politics of Islam (last half)
Oct. 23	Films, Unity and The Inner Life (Islam) (we meet in Olin 252)
Oct. 28, 30	Mottahadeh, Mantle of the Prophet
Oct. 28	Film, Saints and Spirits (Islam in Morocco) (we meet in Olin 252)
Nov. 4, 6	Amos Elon, The Israelis: Founders and Sons (first half)
Nov. 11, 13	Amos Elon, The Israelis: Founders and Sons (last half)
Nov. 18, 20	Rosemary Sayigh, Palestinians (first half)
Nov. 20	Film, Women Under Siege (Palestinians in south Lebanon) (we meet in Olin 252)
Nov. 25	Rosemary Sayigh, Palestinians (last half)
Dec 2, 4	No new reading
Dec. 8	Paper due: two-part essay totalling eight pages on 1) Islam and politics and 2) the issue of Israel and the Palestinians

The course will feature lectures, discussions of our readings, discussions of current events in the Middle East, several guest speakers, slides and films.

Columbia University
Graduate School of Architecture, Planning, and Preservation

A 4351y Architecture of Islam Spring 1986
Instructor: Zeynep Celik

Introduction:

This course is an introduction to Islamic architecture in the Middle East, North Africa, and Spain. It is not a comprehensive survey, but an analysis of selected programs from the seventh to the twentieth century. The approach is contextual. The individual monuments and building types are studied in terms of their relation to the surrounding urban fabrics, to economic, political, and socio-cultrual factors, and with reference to the pre-Islamic heritage.

The required bibliography is on reserve in the library. It is a good idea to buy Oleg Grabar's THE FORMATION OF ISLAMIC ART- an essential text for early periods.

Schedule:

Lecture 1: Introduction
(Jan. 24)

E. Said, ORIENTALISM, 1977. Introduction.
O. Grabar, THE FORMATION OF ISLAMIC ART, 1973. Ch. 1.
I. Lapidus, "Traditional Muslim Cities" in FROM MADINA TO METROPOLIS (C. Brown, ed.), 1973.
A. H. Hourani, "The Islamic City in the Light of Recent Research" in THE ISLAMIC CITY (A.H. Hourani and S.M. Stern, eds.), 1970

Lecture 2: The Mediterranean Setting, Arabia, and the Birth of Islam
(Jan. 31)

H. A. R. Gibb, "Structures of Religious Thought in Islam" in STUDIES IN THE CIVILIZATION OF ISLAM (S. Shaw and R. Polk eds.), 1962.
M. Godfroy-Demombynes, MUSLIM INSTITUIONS, 1950, Ch. 11 and 12.
O. Grabar, THE FORMATION, Ch. 2.

Lecture 3: The Early Mosque
(Feb. 7)

O. Grabar, "The Architecture of the Middle Eastern City" In MIDDLE EASTERN CITIES (I, Lapidus, ed.) 1969.
O. Grabar, THE FORMATION, Ch. 5.
O. Grabar, "The Umasyyad Dome of the Rock in Jerusalem" in ARS ORIENTALIS, 1959.
J. Hoag, ISLAMIC ARCHITECTURE, 1977. Ch. 1 and 2

Lecture 4: Umayyad Palaces and Abbasid Cities
(Feb. 14)

R.W. Hamilton, KHIRBAT AL MAFJAR, 1959.
O. Grabar et al., CITY IN THE DESERT, 1978. Ch. 1.
O. Grabar, THE FORMATION, Ch. 6.
S.A. El-Ali, "The Foundation of Baghdad" in THE ISLAMIC CITY.
J.M. Rogers, "Samarra" in THE ISLAMIC CITY.

Lecture 5: North Africa and Cordoba, Spain
(Feb. 21)

D. Hill, ISLAMIC ARCHITECTURE IN NORTH AFRICA, 1976. "The Maghrib", pp. 40-72, 91-132.
P. Sebag, THE GREAT MOSQUE OF KAIROUAN, 1965.
E. Sorda, MOORISH SPAIN, 1963.
Hoag, Ch. 4 and 5.

Lecture 6: Islam in Persia
(Feb. 28)

A.U. Pope, PERSIAN ARCHITECTURE, 1965. Ch. III and IV.
Hoag, Ch. X and XI

Lecture 7: Cairo
(March 7)

J. Abu-Lughod, CAIRO, 1971. Ch. 2,3, and 4.
Hoag, Ch. VIII and IX.

Lecture 8: Granada and Alhambra
(March 21)

O. Grabar, THE ALHAMBRA, 1978.

Lecture 9: Isfahan
(March 28)

N. Ardalan and L. Bakhtiar, THE SENSE OF UNITY, 1973.
Hoag, Ch. XVIII.
Pope, Ch. VIII.

Lecture 10: Istanbul
(April 11)

B. Lewis, ISTANBUL AND THE CIVILIZATION OF THE OTTOMAN EMPIRE, 1963. Ch. 5.
D. Kuban, "Sinan", in MACMILLAN ENCYCLOPEDIA OF ARCHITECTURE, 1982. S. Kostof, A HISTORY OF ARCHITECTURE, 1985. Ch. 19.
Z. Celik, THE REMAKING OF ISTANBUL, 1986. Ch. 1.

Lecture 12: The Ottoman Provinces
(April 18)

A. Raymond, THE GREAT ARAB CITIES IN THE 16TH-18TH CENTURIES, 1984.
I. Andric, THE BRIDGE ON THE DRINA, 1959.

Lecture 13: The 19th and 20th centuries
(April 25)

Abu Lughod, Ch.
Celik, Ch. 6.
R. Holod, ed., ARCHITECTURE AND COMMUNITY, 1983.

Requirements:

Midterm: A research paper, 12-15 pages long and on a subject approved by the instructor is due March 28. A draft outline should be submitted no later than February 28.

Final: An Exam on the material covered by the lectures and the readings.

SYLLABUS

PAGE 230, Sect. 4480 Fall 1986
Cross-Cultural Perspectives:
Change and Continuity in
Modern North Africa
Thompson 126, MWF 1230-1320

Dr. Don Holsinger
Office: 3536 5th fl. Library
Off. Tel.: 323-3035
Off. Hrs.: MWF 0830-0915
1030-1115 and
other times by appointment

Course Description

This course enables students to broaden cultural horizons and to understand human behavior by studying a society different from their own. The course is organized around five general goals:

1. To observe and experience the daily lives of individuals in a cultural setting far removed from contemporary American life.

2. To understand similarities and differences in social, political, economic, and cultural organization across space and time.

3. To develop an historical perspective, an awareness of the forces of change and continuity over varying time spans.

4. To gain a geographical orientation, an ability to situate oneself in relation to the physical world.

5. To cultivate analytical skills through reading, listening, observing, writing, and speaking.

The geographical scope of this section ranges from the Middle East through North Africa, Algeria, and a northern Saharan oasis community called the Mizab (or Mzab). The time frame encompasses the period since the rise of Islam with special emphasis on the past two centuries during which unprecedented social transformations have taken place. The choice of time frame and geographical scope is explained by the instructor's experience living in this area for several years and research carried out on northern Saharan societies during modern times.

Course Procedures and Requirements

This course is organized into lectures, class discussions, and workshops, and is supplemented by slide and film presentations. Regular class attendance is essential to successful completion of the course since class sessions often transcend assigned readings and will include workshop sessions analyzing documentary materials. Active class participation is encouraged and you are invited to raise questions at any time.

There will be three exams, including the final, consisting of identification and essay questions. Bring blue examination booklets (available in the University Bookstore) and write in ink for the exams. The GMU Honor Code is is effect. Please be familiar with your responsibilities in upholding it.

Please take seriously all due dates in this course. Late work will not be accepted unless late submission has been approved by me in advance. Please be prepared to provide me with written documentation of illness or other urgent factors that make late submission of work unavoidable. If an exam is missed because of an emergency, I must be contacted immediately.

The main writing requirement consists of a course journal which will contain class summaries as well as a variety of written assignments. (See attached journal instruction sheet for details.) The journal will be checked periodically and will be submitted on December 8 for final evaluation. Final course evaluation will be based on the following scale: course journal and general class contributions-1/3; the first two exams combined-1/3; the final exam-1/3.

My expectations are that you will attend class regularly, arrive on time, take an active part in class discussions, and complete course assignments as requested. If, because of special circumstances, you are unable to fulfill any one of these expectations, please see me as soon as possible.

Required Texts (available for purchase at the University Bookstore in SUB II)

ANTHROPOLOGY 86/87 (Annual Editions, 1986)
Elizabeth Fernea, A STREET IN MARRAKECH (Doubleday, 1976)
Arthur Goldschmidt, A CONCISE HISTORY OF THE MIDDLE EAST (Westview, 1983)
John P. Entelis, COMPARATIVE POLITICS OF NORTH AFRICA (Syracuse University Press, 1980)

Works on Reserve in Fenwick Library

E. A. Alport, "The Mzab," from Louise E. Sweet (ed.), PEOPLES AND CULTURES OF THE MIDDLE EAST (Vol. 2)
Pierre Bourdieu, "The Mozabites," from THE ALGERIANS
Clifford Geertz, "Thick Description: Toward an Interpretive Theory of Culture," from THE INTERPRETATION OF CULTURES
D. C. Holsinger, "Muslim Responses to French Imperialism: An Algerian Saharan Case Study," INTERNATIONAL JOURNAL OF AFRICAN HISTORICAL STUDIES (1986)

TENTATIVE CLASS SCHEDULE

I. Introduction: Dimensions of the Middle East and North Africa

Readings: Fernea, all
Goldschmidt, Chapter 1
ANTHROPOLOGY, #10, #34, #16, #18, #31, #26
Bourdieu (on Reserve)
Alport (on Reserve)

Sept. 3-5	Introduction; Myths and Stereotypes
8-12	Physical, Political and Human Geography
15-19	Urban life: From Marrakech to Mizab; HAND IN JOURNALS (19th)
22-24	Exploring a Saharan Community
Sept. 26	EXAM NO. 1

II. Islam in Middle East History and Society; Challenge of the West

Readings: Goldschmidt, Chapters 2-21

S. 29-Oct 3	Introducing Islam - Religion, Culture, Civilization
Oct. 6-10	Foundations and Development of Islam
15-17	The Middle East and Europe
20-24	Challenge and Response in the Modern Era; HAND IN JOURNALS (24th)
27-29	Conflict over Palestine
Oct. 31	EXAM NO. 2

III. Change and Continuity in Modern North Africa

Readings: Entelis, all
Holsinger (on Reserve)
Geertz (on Reserve)
ANTHROPOLOGY, #21, #39, #35, #36, #29, #32, #41

Nov. 3-7	Historical Perspectives on North Africa
10-14	Algerian Case Study - The Imperial Challenge
17-21	Nationalist Awakening - Colonial Defense
24-26	The French-Algerian War and Aftermath
Dec. 1-5	Challenges of Independence - Strategies of Development
Dec. 5	HAND IN JOURNALS
Dec. 8-12	Interpreting Culture and History

December 19 FINAL EXAMINATION 10:30 - 1:15

WRITING TO LEARN - KEEPING A COURSE JOURNAL

Writing, someone has said, enables us to see what we know. It is the physical record of a mysterious interaction between conscious and subconscious thought. Often used as a means of evaluating knowledge, writing is, in its own right, an effective learning tool. It helps to identify what we do not yet understand, thereby pointing the way toward future growth.

An essential requirement in this course is the keeping of a course journal. The journal is designed to be a relatively painless way to do a substantial amount of writing. It is a record of the main concepts of the course along with your elaborations (comments, questions, responses . .) on them. Experience has shown that journals facilitate the comprehension of new ideas and that they help make students better listeners and writers.

The journal should be kept in an 8½ by 11 inch notebook (no thick spines please) separate from your lecture notes. It is important to date each entry and to write legibly, but don't worry excessively over minor details of spelling and grammar. The essential task is to record clearly, directly, and accurately the ideas brought out in class and your responses to them. Occasionally I shall check to see that the journals meet expectations and will make comments for improvement. At the end of the course they will be evaluated on the basis of length, regularity, authenticity, comprehensiveness, and depth of insight. (Note: If there are journal entries that you would prefer that I not read, just fold the page over that particular entry.)

The journal will contain three main types of entries:

1) After each class period summarize the main points of the class lecture or discussion and write down your immediate reactions (in the form of comments, questions, illustrations . .) Write in <u>complete sentences and paragraphs</u>, as this focuses your attention on the all-important relationships among main ideas. Record your responses. What makes sense based on your experience? What appears vague or puzzling or imbalanced? These class summaries constitute the core of the journal and must be done regularly. (Whatever you do, don't fall behind! Much better to write even a very brief summary than to put it off and fall behind.)

2) At times I shall make writing assignments to be completed in the journal. Some are designed to focus your thinking in preparation for upcoming discussions. Some may require greater reflection and organization of ideas. (Feel free to revise and rewrite in your journal). Toward the end of the course there will be a more substantial assignment involving cross-cultural analysis. Some of these assignments may be done in class, so have your journal on hand.

3) Use the journal to comment on and summarize items outside the classroom that relate somehow to the subject matter of the course (Islam, the Middle East, North Africa, etc.). Read the newspaper on a daily basis. Watch for items in magazines, TV, radio, movies, ads, conversations . . that deal with the Middle East. When you encounter something of interest, summarize it briefly in your journal and explain its significance. Howdid you react to it intellectually and emotionally?

At the end of the course you should have an interesting and valuable record of your progress in the course and a useful study aid for the final exam. Regular thinking and writing are keys to learning. Set aside a few minutes after each class session. Begin today!

UNIVERSITY OF WISCONSIN-MADISON
Department of History
Semester I, 1986-87

COURSE NO.	COURSE TITLE	INSTRUCTOR
137	The Traditional Middle East: Society, Politics, and Culture	Prof. Humphreys

COURSE DESCRIPTION

In this course we survey the development of society, culture, and political institutions in the Middle East and North Africa from the emergence of Islam down to early modern times (ca. 600-1500 A.D.). In order to locate Islamic culture and society in time and space, we will survey, in a very general manner, the sequence of states and rulers in the area during this long period. However, the course will focus on four topics: (1) basic patterns of political organization and ideology produced within traditional Islamic society; (2) religious orientations -- in particular law and mysticism -- within Islam; (3) the ideals of human conduct produced within Islamic culture; (4) the character of everyday life, in city, village, and nomadic tribes, and the varying relations between town and countryside.

There is no one textbook for the course. As far as possible, readings will be drawn from original texts in translation, and their significance will be developed through class discussions and written exercises. Where appropriate, films and slides will be used.

The course is open to all undergraduates. It is intended to stand as a useful presentation of the material in its own right; however, it is also an appropriate introduction to further coursework in this field.

LECTURES

Lectures meet Tuesday and Thursday, 9:30 - 10:45. Students taking the course for 4 credits will attend a discussion section with the instructor, Wednesday, 1:20 - 2:10. THE LECTURES DO NOT REPEAT THE READINGS: YOU ARE RESPONSIBLE FOR ALL MATERIALS ASSIGNED AND DISCUSSED IN THE COURSE.

WRITTEN ASSIGNMENTS AND EXAMINATIONS

One map exercise.

Three essays (3-5 pp. each), each one based on your choice out of several assigned topics or problems. These are not research papers, but essays relating to the regular assigned readings.

Final Examination (as in Timetable).

GRADING SYSTEM

Map: 10% Essays: 20% each Final Exam: 30%

REQUIRED READINGS (Assignments will average about 75 pp./week)

The Koran, trans. N.J. Dawood (Penguin Classics)
F.M. Denny, An Introduction to Islam (Macmillan)
Richard Critchfield, Shahhat, an Egyptian (Avon)
History 137: Selected Readings (at Kinko's, 626 University Ave.)

SCHEDULE OF READINGS AND CLASS SESSIONS

1. (Tues., Sept. 2) Introduction

2. (Thurs., Sept. 4) Geography and Ethnography of the Central Islamic Lands: an overview

3. (Tues., Sept. 9) The societies of the Middle East on the eve of Islam (6th cen. A.D.)

4. (Thurs., Sept. 11) Nomadism in ancient Arabia: Social values and cultural expression

READINGS, Sessions 3-4:

Denny, Pt. I (pp. 1-61)
Musil, "Manners and Customs of the Rwala Bedouin" (Selected Readings)
Lyall, "Ancient Arabian Poetry" (Selected Readings)

5. (Tues., Sept. 16) The Koran: form and structure

6. (Thurs., Sept. 18) The Koran: teachings and themes

READINGS, Sessions 5-6:

The Koran (Dawood transl.), 15-38, 214-220, 246-264, 386-407.
Denny, Ch. 8 (pp. 153-173)

7. (Tues., Sept. 23) Muhammad's career

8. (Thurs., Sept. 25) Muhammad's teaching

READINGS, Sessions 7-8:

Denny, Chs. 5-6 (pp. 65-124)
Ibn Ishaq, "Life of Muhammad" (Selected Readings)
Tibrizi, Mishkat al-Masabih (Selected Readings)

SCHEDULE OF READINGS AND CLASS SESSIONS, continued.

9. (Tues., Sept. 30) The Arab conquests and the creation of an Islamic empire

READINGS, Session 9:

Denny, Ch. 7 (pp.125-149)

10. (Thurs., Oct. 2) The Primitive Caliphate and its downfall, 632-692

READINGS, Session 10:

Tabari and Ibn Ishaq, "The Election of Abu Bakr" (Selected Readings)

11. (Tues., Oct. 7) The High Caliphate, 692-945

READINGS, Session 11:

Tabari, "Accession Sermon of al-Saffah (749)" (Selected Readings)
Tabari, "Denunciation of Mu^{c}awiya (897) (Selected Readings)

12. (Thurs., Oct. 9) The Sunni ideology of the Caliphate

READINGS, Session 12:

Wali al-Din al-Tibrizi, "Offices of Commander and of Qadi" (Selected Readings)
Mawardi, "Contract of the Caliphate" (Selected Readings)

13. (Tues., Oct. 14) The Shi'a and its political concepts

READINGS, Session 13:

Qadi Nu'man, "Book of Faith" (Selected Readings)
Shaykh al-Mufid, "Speeches of Ali" (Selected Readings)

14. (Thurs., Oct. 16) Military government, 945-1500: amirs, sultans, and padshahs.

15. (Tues., Oct. 21) Military government: ethos and ideology

READINGS, Sessions 14-15:

Bayhaqi, "Gibbeting of the Minister Hasanak" (Selected Readings)

SCHEDULE OF READINGS AND CLASS SESSIONS, continued.

16. (Thurs. Oct. 23) Religion as a code of conduct: the shari'a

17. (Tues., Oct. 28) The shari'a in practice: justice and education in medieval Islam

READINGS, Sessions 16-17:

Denny, Chs. 9, 11 (pp. 174-189, 216-238)
Malik ibn Anas, "al-Muwatta" (Selected Readings)
Shaybani, "Islamic Law of Nations" (Selected Readings)
Reread: Tibrizi, Mishkat al-Masabih

18. (Thurs., Oct. 30) Sufism: mystical interpretations of Islam

READINGS, Session 18:

Denny, Pt. IV (pp. 241-292)

19. (Tues., Nov. 4) Shari'a, sufism, and rational speculation -- the synthesis of al-Ghazali

READINGS, Session 19:

Ghazali, "Deliverance from Error" (Selected Readings)

20. (Thurs., Nov. 6) Human ideals in Islamic culture (I): Arabic Humanism.

READINGS, Session 20:

Jahiz, selected writings (Selected Readings)

21. (Tues., Nov. 11) Human ideals in Islamic culture (II): Persian epic

READINGS, Session 21:

Firdawsi, Shah-nameh (Selected Readings)

22. (Thurs., Nov. 13) Human ideals in Islamic culture (III): Persian didactic satire

READINGS, Session 22:

Sa'di Gulistan (Selected Readings)

SCHEDULE OF READINGS AND CLASS SESSIONS, continued.

23. (Tues., Nov. 18) — Human ideals in Islamic culture (IV): Turkish inscriptions and tales

READINGS, Session 23:

"The Turks" (*Selected Readings*)

Thurs., Nov. 20 — NO CLASS (Instructor out of town)

24. (Tues., Nov. 25) — Social Life and Personal Conduct: Actualities

READINGS, Session 24:

Denny, chs. 14-15 (pp. 295-348)

Thurs., Nov. 27 — THANKSGIVING DAY

25. (Tues., Dec. 2) — Topography of the Middle Eastern city.

26. (Thurs., Dec. 4) — Politics, economy, and the social order in Middle Eastern cities.

READINGS, Sessions 25-26:

English, *City and Village in Iran* (*Selected Readings*)

27. (Tues., Dec. 9) — The Egyptian Peasant

READINGS, Session 27:

Critchfield, *Shahhat: An Egyptian* (all)

28. (Thurs., Dec. 11) — Recapitulation and Review

MASSACHUSETTS INSTITUTE OF TECHNOLOGY

THE "ISLAMIC" CITY: HISTORY, CULTURE, AND FORM

4.683J
(same 21.482J)

Fall 1986
T, Th: 12:30-2:00
Bldg. 3, Rm. 133.

Instructors: Philip S. Khoury (History Faculty)
Yasser Tabbaa (Architecture Department)

SYLLABUS

This course introduces Islamic civilization, past and present, through a study of the city in the Muslim world. It illustrates how the lenses of social and architectural history, anthropology and planning reveal different phenomena in the city, and different aspects of urban culture and form. It poses the question: How far can the socioeconomic, political, architectural and spatial features of such cities as Fez, Cairo, Istanbul, and Isfahan be explained in terms of Islam?

INTRODUCTION

Sept. 9: The City: Visual Images and Intellectual Contours
(Khoury and Tabbaa)
Sept. 11: What is Islam?
(Tabbaa)

Readings: Joseph Schacht (ed.), The Legacy of Islam, 2nd ed. pp. 9-143
Michael Gilsenan, Recognizing Islam: Religion and Society in the Modern Arab World, pp. 142-191
J.J. Saunders, A History of Medieval Islam (recommended)

PART I: THE ISLAMIC CITY

Sept. 16: Is There an Islamic City?
(Khoury)
Sept. 18: The Evolution of Muslim Urban Society
(Khoury)
Sept. 23: The Islamic City: Physical Environment
(Tabbaa)
Sept. 25: Film and Discussion: "Mecca: The Forbidden City"

Sept. 30: DISCUSSION

Readings: S.M. Stern, "The Constitution of the Islamic City, A.H. Hourani and S. M. Stern, eds., The Islamic City pp. 25-50.

Eugen Wirth, "The Middle Eastern City: Islamic City? Oriental City? Arabian City? The specific characteristics of the cities of North Africa and Southwest Asia from the point of Geography." (xerox copy on reserve at Rotch Library circulation desk)

Ira M. Lapidus, Muslim Cities in the Later Middle Ages (entire)

J.M. Wagstaff, "The Origin and Evolution of Towns, 4000 BC to AD 1900," in G.H. Blake and R. I. Lawless, eds., The Changing Middle Eastern City (1980) pp. 11-33.

Ibn Khaldun, The Muqaddimah, Trans. F. Rosenthal; edited and abridged by N. J. Dawood, pp. 263-295. (xerox at Rotch)

Al-Muqaddasi selection on "capitals and provinces" in Bernard Lewis, ed., Islam from the Prophet Muhammad the Capture of Constantinople, vol. II, pp. 69-81. (xerox at Rotch)

Max Weber, The City (1958), (recommended)

Michael E. Bonine, "From Uruk to Casablanca. Perspectives on the Urban Experience of the Middle East." Journal of Urban History 3 (Feb. 1977), 141-180 (recommended for those interested in historiography)

PART II: MEDIEVAL MUSLIM CITIES: SOCIETY AND ARCHITECTURE

Oct. 2: The Urban Heritage of Early Islam (Tabbaa)

Oct. 7: Medieval Muslim Cities (Tabbaa)

Oct. 9: Medieval European Cities (David H. Friedman, Dept. of Architecture, MIT)

Readings: J. Schacht, ed., The Legacy of Islam, pp. 244-273.

Oleg Grabar, "The Architecture of the Middle Eastern City from Past to Present: The Case of the Mosque," in Ira M. Lapidus, ed., Middle Eastern Cities, pp. 26-46.

J. M. Rogers, "Samarra: A Study in Medieval Town Planning," in Hourani and Stern, The Islamic City, pp. 119-156.

Michael E. Bonine, "The Morphogenesis of Iranian Cities," Annals of the Association of American Geographers, 69 (June 1979), pp. 208-224 (xerox in Rotch)

Paul English, "The Traditional City of Herat, Afghanistan," in L. Carl Brown, ed., From Madina to Metropolis, pp. 73-94.

F. Benevolo, The History of the City (1980), pp. 259-287. (recommended)

PART III: CITIES IN THE LATER ISLAMIC EMPIRES

Oct. 14: HOLIDAY
Oct. 16: The Method of the Urban Historian
(Khoury)

MIDTERM EXAMINATION DUE

Oct. 21: Ottoman Cairo: Social Classes and Popular Movements
(Khoury)
Oct. 23: Imperial Urban Planning Under the Ottomans
(Tabbaa)
Oct. 28: Imperial Urban Planning Under the Safavids and Mughals
(Tabbaa)
Oct. 30: DISCUSSION

TERM PAPER ABSTRACT DUE

Readings: Janet Abu-Lughod, Cairo: 1001 Years of the City Victorious, pp. 27-79
André Raymond, "The Residential Quarters of Cairo during the Ottoman Period." (xerox at Rotch)
André Raymond, The Great Arab Cities of the Sixteenth to the Eighteenth Century (1984), entire
Albert Hourani, "The Ottoman Background to the Modern Middle East," in Hourani, The Emergence of the Modern Middle East, pp. 1-18.
Excerpts from Narratives of Travels, by Evliya Effendi [Celebi], vol. I, part 2, pp. 103-128, 136-146. (xerox at Rotch).
Excerpts from Travels in Persia, by Sir John Chardin (London, 1927), pp. 6-11, 248-279 (xerox at Rotch).
Heinz Gaube, Iranian Cities (1978), pp. 65-96

PART IV: THE CASE OF THE DUAL CITY: CAIRO BETWEEN OLD AND NEW

Nov. 4: Cairo in the Age of European Expansion: the 19th Century
(Khoury)
Nov. 6: Cairo in the Age of Independence: the 20th Century
(Khoury)
Nov. 11: HOLIDAY
Nov. 13: Contemporary Cairene Planning
(Mona Serageldin, Aga Khan Program)

Readings: Janet Abu-Lughod, "Varieties of Urban Experience: Contrast, Coexistence, Coalescence in Cairo," in Ira M. Lapidus, ed., Middle Eastern Cities, pp. 159-187.
Gabriel Baer, Studies in the Social History of Modern Egypt, pp. 133-148.
Naguib Mahfouz, Miramar (entire novel)
Edward Lane, Manners and Customs of the Modern Egyptians (1978) (recommended)
Janet Abu-Lughod, "Perspective and Prospectus," in L.C. Brown, ed., From Madina to Metropolis, pp. 95-113.
Philip S. Khoury, Urban Notables and Arab Nationalism. Politics of Damascus, 1860-1920, (1983), 1-74. (recommended)

PART V: CONTEMPORARY CITIES

Nov. 18: Traditional Form and Colonial Image (Tabbaa)
Nov. 20: NO CLASS
Nov. 25: NO CLASS
Nov. 27 THANKSGIVING
Dec. 2: The Town of Sanaa (Ronald Lewcock, Dept. of Architecture, MIT)

Readings: V.F. Costello, Urbanization in the Middle East (entire)
William J. R. Curtis, "Type and Variation: Berber Collective Dwellings of the Northwestern Sahara," Muqarnas, 1 (1982), pp. 181-209.
Philip S. Khoury, "Syrian Urban Politics in Transition: The Quarters of Damascus during the French Mandate." International Journal of Middle East Studies 16 (November 1984), pp. 507-540. (xerox at Rotch)
Clifford Geertz, Islam Observed: Religious Development in Morocco and Indonesia (1968), pp. 1-55.

PART VI: GRADUATE STUDENT PRESENTATIONS

Dec. 4: STUDENT PRESENTATIONS
Dec. 9: STUDENT PRESENTATIONS

PART VII: CONCLUSION AND SUMMATION

Dec. 11: The "Islamic" City Reconsidered (Khoury and Tabbaa)

COURSE MECHANICS
(read carefully!!)

1. Subject meets on Tuesdays and Thursdays at 12:30-2:00, in 3-133. It breaks down into several parts, each consisting of formal lectures normally followed by a required Discussion Section on a selection of themes.

2. All Syllabus readings are designed to complement our lectures and as background for Discussion Sections. Copies of all required readings are on reserve at the Circulation Desk of the Rotch Architecture Library. We have also ordered some of the required and suggested readings for purchase at the MIT Coop. These are:

   Required (if financially possible)

   I.M. Lapidus, Muslim Cities in the Later Middle Ages (paperback)
   N. Mahfouz, Miramar (paper)
   J.J. Saunders, A History of Medieval Islam (paper)
   M. Gilsenan, Recognizing Islam (paper)
   V. Costello, Urbanization in the Middle East (paper)
   C. Geertz, Islam Observed (paper)
   J. Schacht, The Legacy of Islam (paper)

   Suggested

   J. Serjeant, ed., The Islamic City (paper)
   Max Weber, The City (paper)
   J. Abu-Lughod, Rabat (paper)
   P. Khoury, Urban Notables and Arab Nationalism (cloth)
   H. Gaube, Iranian Cities (cloth)
   J. Abu-Lughod, Cairo: 1001 Years of the City Victorious (cloth)
   A. Raymond, The Great Arab Cities of the Sixteenth to the Eighteenth Centuries (cloth)
   L. Carl Brown, ed., From Madina to Metropolis (paper)

3. Rotch Library has an excellent visual collection (slides, etc.) on all aspects of urban life in the Muslim world, past and present, and we recommend that students make full use of this collection.

4. OTHER REQUIREMENTS

a) Take-home midterm: students will write a 1800-2000 word (6-7 typewritten, doublespaced) essay on a question concerning the assigned reading. There will be a choice of questions on which to write and students will have a week to complete the essay. Students will be given a week to write their essays. Due October 16.

b) Each student will undertake a research project during the semester on some aspect of urban life (urban politics, socioeconomic organization, cultural change, architecture and architectural history, planning, etc.) in the Muslim world. We shall assist you in formulating your topic and, when possible, with bibliographic materials. The final result of your project will be a research paper of 25 typewritten (doublespaced) pages. Naturally, we shall evaluate the research and writing of undergraduates with greater compassion than that of graduate students!! All students will be required to submit a 500-word ABSTRACT (including a list of bibliographic sources) of their proposed term paper by October 30. Graduate students will also be asked to give an informal presentation (30 minutes) to the class on their research. These presentations will be made in December.

5. DATES TO KEEP IN MIND

October 16: Take-home midterm examination due
October 30: Research Project title and 500-word project abstract due.
(we consider the abstract to be of great importance!!)

December 12: Research papers due.

THERE IS NO FINAL EXAMINATON!!

** ** **

PEOPLES AND CULTURES OF THE MIDDLE EAST

MWF 1:25-2:20 -- LC 22
Office Hours: MWF 10:00-11:00
and by appointment

Dr. Walter P. Zenner
Fall, 1986

The "Middle East" is a large "cultural continent" which spans Southwestern Asia and North Africa, from Afghanistan to Morocco's Atlantic Coast. In this course, we will provide a general survey of the cultures of this area, concentrating on what is sometimes called the "Central Middle East" (Iran, Turkey, Asian Arabs, Israel, and Egypt). We will also give special attention to peoples most involved in the Arab-Israeli struggle and the Lebanese civil war. Since courses in other departments of this university deal with the history and politics of the conflict, we will devote our attention to providing a background to the actors in those tragic dramas, including Middle Eastern and European Jews. Palestinian Arabs, and the various ethnic groups of Egypt, Lebanon, and Syria. Ethnicity and religion will be among the areas of Middle Eastern cultures which we will examine in this endeavor. While some of this material will be integrated into our general survey, we will also devote several weeks to a more specific discussion.

Course requirements: Each student is expected to attend class regularly and participate in class discussion. There will be 4 short answer examinations. The examinations will be short-answer in character (see below). The quizzes will cover assigned readings and lectures up to the date of the quizzes. Examinations may be preceded by review sessions. Each quiz is weighed by points, depending on the time allotted and lateness in the term.

Required Texts: D. Bates and A. Rassam: Peoples & Cultures of the Middle East.
S. Deshen and W. Zenner: Jewish Societies in the Middle East.
Gilsenan: Recognizing Islam.
Shokeid/Deshen: Distant Relations.

Readings on Reserve:
L. Sweet: Peoples and Cultures of the Middle East, Vols. I and II.
Nakhleh/Zureik: Sociology of the Palestinians.
H. Batatu: Social Roots of Syria's Ruling Military Group. Middle East Journal (1981).
S. Deshen: Israeli Judaism. International Journal of Middle Eastern Studies (1978).
P. Gubser: The Zu'ama of Zahleh. Middle East Journal (1973).

Suggestions for study:

In a course such as this, the student is expected to learn about a new area of the world, one about which he/she knows very little. Many new and unfamiliar words and names must be learned. In addition, the student is expected to learn to test broad generalizations, some specific to the Middle East, and some which may be generalized to other areas of the world. For instance, the concept of ethnicity is central to this course, yet ethnicity in the Middle East is different from ethnicity in the United States. A crucial ethnic marker in the Middle East is membership in a religious sect. This does not mean that all disputes are necessarily religious, only that the religious affiliations of actors is noted by others. In this bewildering jungle of detail, each student should try to find out what is important, as opposed to trivial. For instance, try to find out some basic principle on which you can differentiate Sunni Muslims from Shi'i Muslims. If you read the article on the zu'ama of Zahleh, or Moroccan Jews in Israel, try to relate that article to Bates/Rassam's chapter on politics. That article contains a number of terms; try to figure out which two or three are the most important; the same is true of the characters in the story which that article tells you. Some of this will be aided by handouts, but lectures may contain some additional information. You cannot rely on the handout to substitute for reading and lectures.

There is a certain logic to this course, which is founded on its two basic goals: one is to survey the Middle East as an example of a non-Western "developing" area. The second is to provide some understanding of the Lebanese civil war and the Arab-Israeli dispute, in terms of the background of the major actors. Sometimes these two goals do not mesh.

Examinations will be short-answer in character, but here are examples of different varieties of such questions:

Define the following in the space provided:
za'im, bint 'amm; kuttab; etc....

The country which borders Israel on the north is:
a) Yeman b) Lebanon c) Jordan d) Egypt e) Turkey

In comparing Christian and Muslim sects, we find that
- a) Muslims stress issues concerned with political legitimacy while Christians stress issues related to the nature of God;
- b) Muslims stress the nature of God and Christians stress legitimacy;
- c) both stress legitimacy more than theology:
- d) Christians stress law and Muslims stress theology;
- e) none of the above.

Further hints for study:

Remember the politics of the Middle East have polarized scholar and lay citizen alike. Everyone has a stand. In some ways, no article or book even one which appears bland and factual, is considered objective. Especially when reading about the Arab-Israeli conflict, try to find the author's political standpoint, including that of Professor Zenner. Try to understand other standpoints, no matter how objectionable to your own. Questions and comments by students obviously will represent viewpoints different from that of the professor. They are welcome to raise such questions, if they are relevant to the topic under discussion. Students are welcome to pass questions in writing or to raise their hands.

Try to do the reading in order according to the assignments and use the class handouts, but not as a substitute for reading or attendance.

While we will try to cover most topics in both lectures and readings, some will be covered only in one and not the other. Some topics will be touched on lightly in lectures, but if they are assigned, you are responsible for knowing the material.

Try to plan your reading. Some weeks have lighter reading than others (either due to content or number of pages). Some reading is on reserve in the Library and some is not.

Study in groups whenever possible.

DO NOT BE AFRAID TO ASK QUESTIONS ABOUT SOMETHING WHICH YOU DO NOT UNDERSTAND, either in class or during the Professor's office hours.

Good Luck

Tentative Schedule of Assignments

Week of	Topic and Reading Assignment
Sept. 3	Introduction to anthropological study of Middle East. Readings: Bates and Rassam, pp. ix-xiv; Gilsenan, 9-26.
Sept. 8	Definitions of area; review of geography and history. Readings: Bates and Rassam, 1-27; Deshen/Zenner, 1-30.
Sept. 15	Subsistence Base and Ecological Adaptations Rural Society: Pastoralism and Nomads Readings: Bates/Rassam, 107-128; Sweet, I:346-362 (Asad)--(on reserve).
Sept. 22	Rural Society: Cultivators, Craftsmen and Others. Readings: Bates/Rassam, 107-128; Sweet, II:143-160 (Rosenfeld) (on reserve).
Sept. 26	Quiz (25 minutes).
Sept. 29	Religion and Ethnicity Islam: Major Tenets and Institutions (Parallels with Judaism & Christianity) Readings: Bates/Rassam, 29-58; Gilsenan, pp. 27-54.
Oct. 6 & Oct. 15	Sectarianism and Survey of Religious Sects. Readings: Bates/Rassam, 59-106; Gilsenan, 55-94.
Oct. 20	The "Protected" Ethno-Religious Sects: Example of the Jews. Readings: Deshen/Zenner, review 1-30 again; read 85-118; 211-233; 285-298.
Oct. 24	Quiz (45 minutes)
Oct. 27	Secrecy & Sects Readings: Gilsenan, 116-141; Batatu, Social Roots of Syria's Ruling Elite (on reserve).
Nov. 3	Middle Eastern and European Jews in Israel. Readings: Deshen/Zenner, 137-148; Shokeid/Deshen, 13-28; 96-118; 139-151 Deshen, Israeli Judaism (on reserve).
Nov. 10	Palestinians and Israelis in the State of Israel and the rest of the "Land". Readings: Nakhleh/Zureik, 64-80; 84-108; Shokeid/Deshen, 53-76; 121-136; 154-163.

Week of	Topic and Reading Assignment
Nov. 17	Urbanization and Ethnic Pluralism: Ottoman and Contemporary. Readings: Bates/Rassam, 157-188; Deshen/Zenner, 155-183; Gilsenan, 192-214.
Nov. 21	Quiz (45 minutes)
Nov. 24 & Dec. 1	Understanding Lebanese Pluralism and Conflict. Readings: Gilsenan, 95-115; Sweet II, 257-307 (on reserve); Zureik/Nakhleh, 112-147 (on reserve); Gubser, the Zu'ama of Zahleh (on reserve).
Dec. 8	The Family, Kin and Gender Roles Readings: Deshen/Zenner, 251-284; Bates/Rassam, 189-239; Shokeid/Deshen, 32-48.
Dec. 12	Quiz (25 minutes)

Donna Robinson Divine

SMITH COLLEGE

Government 223b
Spring 1986

MIDDLE EAST POLITICS
Topic for 1986: Identities and Loyalties

Week 1: Introduction

Dale F. Eickelman, The Middle East, pp. 1-63.
John L. Esposito, editor, Voices of Resurgent Islam, pp. 3-63.

Week 2: Ecology

Dale F. Eickelman, The Middle East, pp. 63-175.
Norman Itzkowitz, The Ottoman Empire and Islamic Tradition, pp. 3-37.
A. Reza, S. Islami, and Rostam Mehraban Kavoussi, The Political Economy of Saudi Arabia, pp. 3-35.
Robert W. Stookey, "Yemen: Revolution Versus Tradition," in The Arabian Peninsula, edited by Robert W. Stookey, pp. 79-109.
Alexander Bligh, "The Saudi Religious Elite (Ulama) As Participant in the Political System of the Kingdom," International Journal of Middle East Studies, Volume 17, Number 1 (February, 1985):37-50.

Week 3: People

Dale F. Eickelman, The Middle East, pp. 175-326.
Norman Itzkowitz, The Ottoman Empire and Islamic Tradition, pp. 37-110.

Week 4: Culture

John L. Esposito, ed., Voices of Resurgent Islam, pp. 63-99; 134-175; 191-215; 230-291.
Robert A. Fernea and Elizabeth W. Fernea, "Variation in Religious Observance Among Islamic Women," in Scholars, Saints, and Sufis, edited by Nikki R. Keddie, pp. 385-401.
Clifford Geertz, "The Mysteries of Islam".
Wilfred Cantwell Smith, Islam in Modern History, pp. 11-47.

Government 223b (2)

Weeks 5 and 6: Egypt

P. J. Vatikiotis, The History of Egypt.
Afaf Luth Al-Marsot, A Short History of Egypt.
J. S. Birks, I, Serageldin, C. A. Sinclair and J. A. Socknat, "Who is Migrating Where? An Overview of International Labor Migration in the Arab World," in Migration, Mechanization, and Agricultural Labor-Markets in Egypt, edited by Alan Richards and Philip C. Martin, pp. 103-117.

Week 7: Syria

John F. Devlin, Syria.
Hanna Batatu, "Some Observations on the Social Roots of Syria's Ruling Military Group and the Causes for its Dominance," The Middle East Journal, Volume 35, No. 3 (Summer, 1981):331-344.
Hanna Batatu, "Syria's Muslim Brethren," MERIP Reports, Number 110 (November-December, 1982):12-20.

Week 8: Iraq

Phoebe Marr, The Modern History of Iraq.

Weeks 9 and 10: Iran

Shahrough Akhavi, Religion and Politics in Contemporary Iran.
"Iran Since the Revolution," MERIP Reports, Volume 13, No. 3 (March-April, 1983):3-26.

Weeks 11 and 12: Divided Loyalties, Hyphenated Identities

Itamar Rabinovich, The War for Lebanon.

University of Wisconsin-River Falls

Political Science 349 Middle East Govt. and Politics

Winter Quarter 1983-84
Prof. Stephen Feinstein

Object of the Course:

The object of this course is to examine the major events, personalities and strategies connected with Middle East Politics in the 20th century. Special emphasis will be placed on major contemporary issues which are dominant in current events: The Iranian Revolution, Iraqi-Iranian War, the Civil War and relevant issues regarding Lebanon, the Arab-Israeli Conflict, the Palestinians, the oil issue and American relations with Middle Eastern countries.

The classroom format is viewed as being one mixed between lectures and discussions. Since the class will presumably be manageable in size and the topics so volatile that everyone has some predisposed views toward the subject matter, classroom discussions will be expected. Students must, in order to make the participation meaningful, read the assignments by the scheduled date. Although not a formal requirement, you are advised to keep abreast of current events in the Middle East. In fact, political structures and arrangements in the Mideast change so quickly and so often that one cannot rely upon the most recent readings in the course to keep up to date.

TEXTS: Available from the textbook library, DL

James A. Bill and Carl Leiden. Politics in the Middle East.

Available in the Reserve Room, DL

McLaurin, Mughisuddin & Wagner. Foreign Policy Making in the Middle East.

Quandt, Jabbar and Lesch. The Politics of Palestinian Nationalism (only to be read in parts)

Other Readings: Available for purchase in the bookstore or in the reserve room DL.

Fawaz Turki. The Disinherited: Journal of a Palestinian Exile.

Barry Rubin. Paved with Good Intentions. (note: if you read this book for me in another class, choose another book on Iran from the Library for reading).

Outside Readings: Two books will be selectedfrom the Library by each student for reading and writing a comparative book report. Topics covered should be from the 20th century and should deal with relevant issues. If you are not certain, please ask instructor.

Course requirements:

Reading materials and class discussion
Midterm Examination
Final Examination
Paper on Turki, The Disinherited.
Paper on Rubin, Paved with Good Intentions.
Comparative Report from outside readings.

Reading and Study Schedule

Dec. 2 Introduction to the Politcs of the Middle East

Dec. 5 Political Development, Modernization add Islam. Read Bill and Leiden, Chapter 1 and 2.

Dec. 7 Groups in the Middle East and Patrimonial Leadership. Read Bill and Leiden, Chapters 3 and 4.

Dec. 9 & Dec. 12 Leadership in the 20th century. Several models from Islamic countries. Read Bill and Leiden, Chapter 5.

Dec. 14 Violence and Ideology. Read Bill and Leiden. Chapter 6 and 7.

Dec. 16 Video tape on Gulf States.

WINTER BREAK

Jan. 4 Zionism and the Genesis of the Arab-Israeli Conflict. Read Bill and Leiden, Chapter 8

Jan. 6 Arab-Israeli conflict

Jan. 9 Peace plans and prospects--read handouts.

Jan. 11 The Palestinians--hand in report on Turki, The Disinherited. Read Quandt et al, Chapter 1-3 in Reserve Room.

Jan. 13 Midterm examination

Jan. 16 Video tape on the PFLP.

Jan. 18 The Lebanon conflict and relation to the Arab-Israeli conflict. Handouts.

Jan. 20	Foreign policy objectives in Middle East politics. Read chapters 1 and 2 of McLaurin, Mughisuddin and Wagner. <u>Foreign Policy Making in the Middle East</u>. in the Reserve Room.
Jan. 23	American Foreign Policy in the Middle East.
Jan. 25	The Soviet Union and the Middle East
Jan. 27	The Power of Petroleum. Read Bill and Leiden, Chapter 9.
Jan. 30	Video tape on Saudi Arabia.
Feb. 1	The Politics of the Iranian Revolution. Reza Shah and American Involvement. Rubin, Chapters 1-3
Feb. 3	Mohammed Reza Pahlavi's dreams of Empire, problems of Modernization and oil dependency of the West. Read Rubin, Chapters 4-6.
Feb. 6	The Iranian Revolution. Rubin, Chapters 6-10.
Feb. 8	The Hostage Crisis and the Media, the Current State of the Revolution. Read Rubin, Appendiz A and handouts.
Feb. 10	The Iraq-Iran War and Shiite Islam. Politics of the War.
Feb. 13	Women's Politics in the Middle East
Feb. 15	Film on Women in the Middle East.
Feb. 17	Turkish Politics--Democracy or dictatorship (handouts)
Feb. 20-24	Catch up week--we usually lose at least 3 sessions because of extensive discussions earlier in the course.

UNIVERSITY OF WISCONSIN
Department of History

Semester Autumn Year 1985

COURSE NO.	COURSE TITLE	INSTRUCTOR
435	Politics and the State in the Medieval Islamic World (600-1500)	Humphreys

COURSE DESCRIPTION

An investigation of the development of political life, and the linkages between political action and social structure, in the Islamic world from the time of Muhammad (570-632) down to the rise of the Ottoman Empire (ca. 1500). Among the topics to be explored are the following: (1) the origins of the Islamic state; (2) the attempt to construct a universal empire (the Caliphate) comprehending the whole body of Muslims, and its failure; (3) the age of military dictatorship; (4) the Turkish domination of politics after the eleventh century; (5) the Mongol invasions of the thirteenth century; (6) military oligarchy in Egypt and Syria in the later Middle Ages.

Through these topics we shall examine a number of themes which recur in a variety of historical settings: concepts of political authority, relationships between governments and their subjects, the recruitment of political elites, the connections between military and political power, conflicts of ideologies, the political significance of ethnic change in the region.

LECTURES

Two times per week, Tuesdays and Thursdays, 2:25-3:40. The class meetings will include both lectures and discussions. For the latter to be useful instead of mutually frustrating, the assigned readings must be done on time.

WRITTEN ASSIGNMENTS AND EXAMINATIONS

Mid-term examination (20%)
Final Examination (40%)
A term paper, 10-15 pp. in length, on a topic to be chosen by the student in consultation with the instructor (40%).

GRADING SYSTEM

A-F

REQUIRED READINGS

J.J. Saunders, A History of Medieval Islam (pb., purchase)
W.M. Watt, The Majesty That Was Islam (pb., purchase).
Syllabus of Selected Readings, to be purchased from Kinko's (620 University Ave.).
Assigned pages from several books held on three-hour reserve in Helen C. White.
Average readings per week: 80 pp.

History 435 Autumn 1985 Prof. Humphreys
Politics and the State in the Medieval Islamic World

REQUIRED READINGS

A) Purchase

W.M. Watt, The Majesty That Was Islam (Sidgwick & Jackson, pb.)
J.J. Sanders, A History of Medieval Islam (RKP, pb.)

Selected Readings, History 435 - from Kinko's, 630 University Avenue

B) On Reserve (Helen C. White, 3-hr., unless otherwise noted)

F.M. Donner, The Early Islamic Conquests
R.P. Mottahedeh, Loyalty and Leadership in an Early Islamic Society
C.E. Bosworth, The Ghaznavids
Encyclopaedia of Islam, New edition (Reference Room, Memorial 263)
Cambridge History of Iran, vol. V
I.M. Lapidus, Muslim Cities in the Later Middle Ages

SCHEDULE OF CLASSES AND READINGS

1. (Sept. 3) - Introduction to the Course

I. The Origins of the Islamic State: Muhammad and the Primitive Caliphate (600-680)

General Readings, sessions 2-8:
Watt, 1-12
Saunders, 1-70

2. (Sept. 5) - The Historical Milieu: Rome and Iran

3. (Sept. 10) - The Historical Milieu: Arabia before Islam

Readings, sessions 2-3:
Donner, Early Islamic Conquests, 11-49 (reserve)

4. (Sept. 12) - Muhammad in Mecca

Readings, session 4:
Qur'an, early suras (Syllabus)

5. (Sept. 17) - Muhammad in Medina: a Chronological Sketch

6. (Sept. 19) - Muhammad in Medina: the Structure of the Community

Readings, sessions 5-6:
Donner, Early Islamic Conquests, 50-90 (reserve)
Qur'an, later suras (Syllabus)
Ibn Hisham, Life of Muhammad (Syllabus)
Constitution of Medina (Syllabus)

History 435 Autumn 1985 Prof. Humphreys

Policics and the State in the Medieval Islamic World

7. (Sept. 24) - The Arab Conquests

Readings, session 7:
Donner, Early Islamic Conquests, 251-78 (reserve)
Conquest (Syllabus)

8. (Sept. 26) - The Crisis of the Early Caliphate

Readings, session 8:
The Election of Abu Bakr (Syllabus)
The Murder of Uthman (Syllabus)

II. The High Caliphate (680-945)

9. (Oct. 1) - The Umayyad Caliphate: the Emergence of an Autocracy

Readings, session 9:
Watt, 15-75
Saunders, 70-94
Jahiz, "Arrival of al-Hajjaj" (Syllabus)

10. (Oct. 3) - The Abbasid Revolution

Readings, session 10:
Saunders, 95-105
Sharon, "The Abbasid Da'wa" (Syllabus)
Revolution From the East, Fall of the Umayyads, Heresy & Revolt (Syllabus)

11. (Oct. 8) - The Century of Abbasid Ascendancy, 750-850: New Elites, New Models of Government

Readings, session 11:
Watt, 93-120
Saunders, 106-123
Ethnic Groups (Syllabus)
Mawardi, "Caliphate" (Syllabus)

12. (Oct. 10) - The Creation of the Mamluk System and the Internal Crisis of the Abbasid Caliphate, 833-945.

Readings, session 12:
Watt, 150-181
Jahiz on the Turks (Syllabus)
The Death of al-Mutawakkil; a Spy; Confessions (Syllabus)

III. Challenges to the Abbasid Order

13. (Oct. 15) - The Ismaili Revolt (875-969)

Readings, session 13:
Saunders, 125-140

History 435 Autumn 1985 Prof. Humphreys
Politics and the State in the Medieval Islamic World

Book of Faith (Syllabus)
Revolutionaries in Power (Syllabus)

14. (Oct. 17) - The Fatimid Caliphate in Egypt, 969-1171

Readings, session 14:
History of al-Hakim (Syllabus)
Army of the Fatimid Caliph (Syllabus)

15. (Oct. 22) - MID-TERM EXAM

16. (Oct. 24) - The Era of Military Dictatorship in Iran and the Fertile Crescent, 860-1055.

Readings, session 16:
Watt, 191-219

17. (Oct. 29) - The Buyid Confederation, 945-1055

18. (Oct. 31) - Patterns of Behavior in Buyid Society

Readings, sessions 17-18:
Mottahedeh, Leadership and Loyalty, in toto (Reserve)

IV. The Beginnings of Turkish Paramountcy, 1000-1250: Perso-Islamic Autocracy and Family Confederation

19. (Nov. 5) - The Ghaznavid State

Readings, session 19:
Bosworth, The Ghaznavids, 48-65, 91-114, 126-128 (Reserve)

20. (Nov. 7) - Ideology and Practical Politics in a Perso-Islamic Monarchy

Readings, session 20:
The Gibbeting of the Minister Hasanak (Syllabus)
Nizam al-Mulk, "Book of Government" (Syllabus)

21. (Nov. 12) - The Ghaznavids and their Subjects

Readings, session 21:
Bosworth, The Ghaznavids, 145-202 (Reserve)

22. (Nov. 14) - Peoples of the Eurasian Steppe: the Origins of the Seljukids

Readings, session 22:
Bosworth, The Ghaznavids, 241-268 (Reserve)
The Ancestor of the Seljuks, The Looting of Amul, The Empire of the Turks, Abu Hanifa and the Turks (Syllabus)

History 435 Autumn 1985 Prof. Humphreys

Politics and the State in the Medieval Islamic World

23. (Nov. 19) - The Seljukid Empire: Structure and Evolution, 1040-1194

24. (Nov. 21) - The Seljukids, the Caliphate, and Islam: the Emergence of an Islamic Orthodoxy

Readings, sessions 23-24:
Watt, 235-256
Saunders, 141-153
Encyclopaedia of Islam, "Atabak," "Ikta'" (Mem. Ref. Rm., 263)

Nov. 26-28: NO CLASS

The Mongol Conquest and its Consequences 1218-1350

25. (Dec. 3) - The Mongol Invasion of the Near East, 1219-1260

26. (Dec. 5) - The Il-Khans of Iran

Readings, sessions 25-26:
Saunders, 170-186
Petrushevsky, "The Socio-Economic Condition of Iran under the Il-Khans," Cambridge History of Iran, vol. 5, 483-537 (Reserve)

Chinggiz Khan and his Successors (Syllabus)
Juvaini, "History of the World-Conqueror" (Syllabus)

27. (Dec. 10) - A Military Oligarchy: the Mamluk Empire in Egypt and Syria, 1250-1517

28. (Dec. 12) - The Mamluks and their Subjects

Readings, sessions 27-28:
Lapidus, Muslim Cities in the Later Middle Ages, 44-115 (Reserve)

MIT

HISTORY FACULTY AND POLITICAL SCIENCE DEPARTMENT

21.484J or 17.562J

MODERN EGYPT AND IRAN: ISLAM AND POLITICS IN HISTORICAL PERSPECTIVE

Prof. Philip S. Khoury
14N-314
x2601

Spring 1986
MW, 1-2:30
4-145

SYLLABUS

A comparative historical perspective will be used to examine the process of colonization/decolonization and imperial rivalries, the interplay of human and physical environment, and the role of Islam in shaping the character of state and society in twentieth century Egypt and Iran. Subject explores forces and events that toppled the Egyptian monarchy in 1952-54 and the Shah of Iran in 1978-79, and the radically different changes in economy, society, and culture which Nasser's and Khomeini's revolutions have produced. Subject poses the question: what are the social and ideological bases and aims of Middle Eastern Islamic movements, past and present, and their attitudes to such issues as economic development, women and the family, and international relations?

PART I: INTRODUCTION

Feb. 5 LECTURE: Egypt and Iran: A Framework for Comparison and Analysis

Feb. 10 LECTURE: Theories of Development and Revolution

Harry Eckstein, "On the Etiology of Internal Wars," History and Theory, 4:2 (1965)

Feb. 12 LECTURE: What is Islam?

Edward Mortimer, Faith and Power: The Politics of Islam (New York, 1982) 31-117.

Bernard Lewis, "The Shi^{c}a," New York Review of Books, Aug. 15, 1985, 7-10.

Michael C. Hudson, "Islam and Political Development," in J.L. Esposito, ed., Islam and Development: Religion and Sociopolitical Change (Syracuse, 1980), 1-24

Feb. 17 HOLIDAY

Feb. 19 LECTURE: The Middle East and the West in the 19th Century

Albert Hourani, The Emergence of the Modern Middle East (Berkeley, 1981), 1-18.
Charles Issawi, An Economic History of the Middle East and North Africa (New York, 1982) 1-16.
Charles Issawi, The Economic History of Iran 1800-1914 (Chicago, 1971), 14-19

PART II: EGYPT AND IRAN IN THE LONG 19TH CENTURY, 1800-1914

Feb. 24 DISCUSSION: Egypt and Iran: A Case Study in Comparative Imperialism

Roger Owen, "Egypt and Europe: From French Expedition to British Occupation," in Owen and Bob Sutcliffe, eds., Studies in the Theory of Imperialism (London, 1972), pp. 195-209.
Ronald Robinson, "Non-European Foundations of European Imperialism: sketch for a theory of collaboration," in Owen and Sutcliffe, 117-142.
Nikki R. Keddie, Roots of Revolution, An Interpretive History of Modern Iran, 24-78

PART III: EGYPT AND IRAN: ROOTS OF REVOLUTION AND CRISIS

Feb. 26 LECTURE: Egypt, 1914-1952: Failure of the Liberal Experiment

Anouar Abdel-Malek, Egypt: Military Society (New York, 1967), 3-46

Derek Hopwood, Egypt: Politics and Society, 1945-1984, 20-33

March 3 DISCUSSION: Socio-economic and Cultural Dimensions of Interwar Egypt

Mortimer, Faith and Power, 250-257
Joel Beinin, "Formation of the Egyptian Working Class," Merip Reports, no. 94 (Feb. 1981), 14-23
Afaf Lutfi al-Sayyid-Marsot, "The Revolutionary Gentlewomen in Egypt," in L. Beck and N. Keddie, eds., Women in the Muslim World (Cambridge, Mass., 1978), 261-276
Selections from Ahmad Lutfi al-Sayyid, Taha Husayn, Hasan al-Banna in J.J. Donohue and J.L. Esposito, eds., Islam in Transition (Oxford, 1982), 70-83

March 5 LECTURE: Iran, 1925-1953: The Pahlavis and the Emergence of the Modern State

Keddie, Roots of Revolution, 79-112

March 10 DISCUSSION: The Mossadegh Affair, 1951-53

Keddie, Roots of Revolution, 113-141.
Kermit Roosevelt, Countercoup: The Struggle for the Control of Iran (New York, 1979), 136-210

PART IV: EGYPT UNDER NASSER AND SADAT

March 12 LECTURE: Foundations of Authoritarianism: Nasser's Experiment, 1952-1970

Hopwood, Egypt, 34-104.

March 17 DISCUSSION: Radical Visions: Army Officers, Communists, Muslim Brothers

Raymond W. Baker, Egypt's Uncertain Revolution under Nasser and Sadat (Cambridge, Mass., 1978), 17-43
Maxime Rodinson, "Marxist Views of Nasser's Egypt," in Rodinson, Marxism and the Muslim World, 267-289
Eric Davis, "Ideology, Social Class and Islamic Radicalism in Modern Egypt," in S.A. Arjomand, ed., From Nationalism to Revolutionary Islam, 134-157
Mortimer, Faith and Power, 257-295

March 19 LECTURE: Sadat's Revisionism, 1970-1981

Hopwood, Egypt, 105-121, and Conclusion
Marie-Christine Aulas, "Sadat's Egypt: A Balance Sheet," Merip Reports, no. 107 (July-Aug. 1982), 6-11, 14-15, 18, 30

March 24-28 SPRING VACATION

March 31 DISCUSSION: Cairo: Population and Poverty (Video)

John Waterbury, Egypt: Burdens of the Past/Options for the Future (Bloomington, 1978), 125-198
Alan Richards, "Egypt's Agriculture in Trouble," Merip Reports, no. 84 (Jan. 1980), 3-13

April 2 DISCUSSION: Origins and Nature of Egypt's Islamic Movements

R. Hrair Dekmejian, "Egypt: Cradle of Islamic Fundamentalism," in Dekmejian, Islam and Revolution: Fundamentalism in the Arab World, 79-108, 214-217

Saad Eddin Ibrahim, "Egypt's Islamic Militants," Merip Reports, no. 103 (Feb. 1982), 5-13

PART V: IRAN: CONSOLIDATION OF AUTHORITARIANISM

April 7 LECTURE: The Structural Causes of the Iranian Revolution, 1953-1979: The Shah's Regime

Keddie, Roots of Revolution, 142-182.

April 9 DISCUSSION: Intellectual Trends

Keddie, 183-230

Ervand Abrahamian, "Ali Shari'ati: Ideologue of the Iranian Revolution," Merip Reports, 25-28

Selections from Reza Baraheni, Ayatollah Khomeini, Ali Shari'ati, and in Political and Social Thought in the Contemporary Middle East, ed. Kemal H. Karpat (New York, 1982), 486-491, 496-528

PART VI: THE REVOLUTION

April 14 DISCUSSION: Theories and their Application

Ryszard Kapuscinski, "Revolution" (I - Shah of Shahs and II - The Dead Flame), The New Yorker, 4 and 11 May 1985, 79-96 and 86-101

April 16 LECTURE: Iran - Seven Years After

Eric Rouleau, "Khomeini's Iran," Foreign Affairs (Fall 1980), 1-20

April 21 HOLIDAY

April 23 DISCUSSION: Town and Countryside in the Revolution

Ervand Abrahamian, "The Guerrilla Movement in Iran 1963-1977," Merip Reports, no, 86 (March/April 1980), 3-15
Farhad Kazemi, "Urban Migrants and the Revolution," Iranian Studies 13 (1980), 257-277
Eric Hooglund, "Rural Participation in the Revolution," Merip Reports, no. 87 (May 1980), 3-6
Jim Paul, Eric Hooglund, et al., "Rural Iran and the Revolution," Merip Reports no. 104 (March-April 1982), 22-29

PART VII: COMPARATIVE PERSPECTIVES

April 28 DISCUSSION: Women in Egypt and Iran

Azar Tabari, "The Enigma of the Veiled Iranian Woman," Merip Reports, no. 103 (Feb. 1982), 22-27
Adele K. Ferdows, "Women and the Islamic Revolution," International Journal of Middle East Studies 15 (May 1983), 283-298
Judith Gran, "Impact of the World Market on Egyptian Women," no. 58 (June 1977), 3-7
Mona Hammam,"Egypt´s Working Women," Merip Reports, no. 82 (Nov. 1979), 3-7
Interview: "The Cares of Um Muhammad," no. 82 (Nov. 1979), 8-12, 17.

April 30 DISCUSSION: Islamic Revivalism in Egypt and Iran

Philip S. Khoury, "Islamic Revivalism and the Crisis of the Secular State in the Arab World," in Arab Resources: The Transformation of a Society (London, 1983), 213-236
Nikki R. Keddie, "Islamic Revival in the Middle East: A Comparison of Iran and Egypt," in Samih K. Farsoun, ed., Arab Society: Continuity and Change, (London, 1985)

PART VIII: STUDENT PRESENTATIONS

May 5

May 7

May 12

May 14

COURSE MECHANICS

(Read Carefully)

FORMAT

1. Course will be run in a mixed lecture/seminar format. Lectures are intended to set the background for the discussion sessions that follow. Each student will be required to lead at least once discussion session during the term. This will consist of a summary and analysis of the assigned readings for the specific topic. All students will be expected to have read the assigned readings before each discussion session.

READINGS

1. All readings on Syllabus are required.

2. In addition to the books by Mortimer, Hopwood, and Keddie, students will be required to purchase xeroxes of selected journal articles listed on Syllabus. The MIT History Faculty will provide them at cost. Xeroxes can be purchased from the History Faculty Office, 14N-408 (x4965).

3. Several required and recommended course books are available at the MIT Coop for purchase.

Derek Hopwood, _Egypt: Politics and Society, 1945-1984_ (Allen & Unwin)
Edward Mortimer, _Faith and Power: The Politics of Islam_ (Vintage)
John Waterbury, _The Egypt of Nasser and Sadat_ (Princeton)
Ervand Abrahamian, _Iran Between Two Revolutions_ (Princeton)
Nikki Keddie, _Roots of Revolution: An Interpretive History of Modern Iran_ (Yale)
Fouad Ajami, _The Arab Predicament_ (Cambridge)
John L. Esposito, _Voices of Resurgent Islam_ (Oxford)
Eric Hooglund, _Land and Revolution in Iran_ (Texas)

REQUIREMENTS

1. _Discussion Sessions_ are required for all students

2. _Undergraduates_ and _Graduate students_ are required to write a term paper of 25 typewritten, double-spaced pages (including footnotes and bibliography) on a topic concerned with Egypt or Iran or both. A paper abstract of 250 words (plus appended bibliography) stating paper's main thesis or argument is due on March 19. Each student will make an oral presentation based on his/her research for the paper between May 5 and May 14. Papers are due May 16.

3. Graduate students (only) must also submit a book review of 5-6 typewritten pages on a book relevant to the course topic (instructor's permission required). Guidelines for book reviews and suggested book list will be circulated early in the term. Book review are due on March 5.

GRADES

1. Grade for undergraduates will be based upon contribution to class discussions (30%) and term paper (70%).

2. Grade for graduate students will be based on book review (20%), and term paper (80%) and the paper itself. It is understood that graduate students will participate to the fullest in discussion sessions.

DATES TO REMEMBER

1. MARCH 5: BOOK REVIEW DUE (GRADUATE STUDENTS ONLY)
2. MARCH 19: TERM PAPER ABSTRACTS DUE (ALL STUDENTS)
3. MAY 5-14: ORAL PRESENTATIONS OF TERM PAPERS (ALL STUDENTS)
4. MAY 16: TERM PAPERS DUE (All STUDENTS)

POLITICAL SCIENCE 270G

Comparative Foreign Policies of Middle Eastern States

Don Peretz   Fall 1986

TEXTBOOKS: R.D. McLairin, Don Peretz, Lewis W. Snider, *Middle East Foreign Policy Issues and Processes*; B. Korany, A.E. Hillal Dessouki, *The Foreign Policies of Arab States*; Adeed Dawkha, *Islam in Foreign Policy*; Willard Beling, *Middle East Peace Plans*.

COURSE PLAN AND REQUIREMENTS:

This seminar will compare the foreign policies of major states in the Middle East. They will include Turkey, Iran, Israel, Egypt, Iraq, Syria, Jordan, and Saudi Arabia. The seminar will examine the general policies of each state and its policies on specific issues enumerated below. After a general introduction and discussion of theories in comparative foreign policy studies, the seminar will examine for each country domestic, regional and international factors; the way in which economic, social and political structure influences policy making. The foreign policies of each country toward the United States, the Soviet Union, China, the European common market countries, and toward other Middle Eastern countries will be examined.

Specific issues to be examined will include questions which have come before the United Nations and/or have been central in the area such as: Cyprus, the 1967, 1973 Arab-Israel wars and the 1982 war in Lebanon, Middle East peacemaking and peacekeeping, regional economic cooperation, international petroleum.

The seminar will be divided into small working groups of two or three students each. Each working group will concentrate on the foreign policy of a specific country or problem area mentioned above. Throughout the semester working groups will alternate, so that each group will work on a total of three countries, each country for three or four weeks. Countries and working groups will be selected by lottery.

Instead of examinations or term papers, each student will submit approximately five, four to six-page working papers, that is, two working papers per country on which the student is working. For each of the three countries the student will present a working paper setting out of the general aspects of foreign policymaking, and a working paper on a specific issue from among those enumerated above. Students will present and discuss their working papers in the seminar, and will also discuss other students' papers. Therefore attendance is vital. Grades will be based on the five working papers and on seminar presentation and participation.

Pol. Sci. 270G D. Peretz

BIBLIOGRAPHY:

The following items are suggestive. Students should examine one of the references under general discussion. Ann Schulz's bibliography is an excellent source guide and will be placed on reserve. For specific studies of the policies of countries mentioned above, students should use the following items in the Reference Section of the Library: Keesings Contemporary Archives, Arab Report and Record, the Middle East and North Africa, Middle East Record, Middle East Contemporary Survey, The Middle East: Abstracts & Index, and FMA Arab World File. In the newspaper section of the Library there are English language newspapers from Israel (Jerusalem Post) Egypt (Egyptian Gazette) Iran and other Middle East countries. The following periodicals also have valuable articles, chronologies, and supplementary bibliographic references: the Middle East Journal, International Journal of Middle East Studies, the Journal of Palestine Studies, New Outlook, M.E. and African Economist, M.E. Economic Digest, M.E. International, M.E. News Agency, M.E. Studies, M.E.R.I.P. Reports. In the document section of the library refer to United Nations Records, Congressional Records, and the Foreign Broadcast Information Service (FBIS).

General Discussion of Comparative Foreign Policy

Michael Brecher, The Foreign Policy System of Israel, introductory chapters
Michael Brecher, B. Steinberg and J. Stein, "A Framework for Research on Foreign Policy Behavior," Journal of Conflict Resolution, vol. 13, no. 1, March 1969, pp. 75-101
Leonard Binder. "The Middle East as a Subordinate International System" World Politics, vol. 10, no. 3, April 1958, pp. 408-429
William B. Quandt, Decade of Decisions (an American perspective)
Y.M. Primakov, Anatomy of the Middle East Conflict (a Soviet perspective)

BIBLIOGRAPHY

Ann Schulz, International and Regional Politics in the Middle East and North Africa, a guide to information sources
The Middle East: Abstracts and Index

Turkey

George S. Harris, Troubled Alliance: Turkish-American Problems in Historical Perspective, 1945-1971
Altemur Kilic, Turkey and the World
Ferenc A. Vali, Bridge Across the Bosporus: The Foreign Policy of Turkey
Turkey and the United Nations, Carnegie Endowment for International Peace

Pol. Sci. 270G D. Peretz

Iran

Shahram Chubin & Sepehr Zabih, The Foreign Relations of Iran, A Developing State in a Zone of Great Power Conflict
Rouhollah K. Ramazani, The Foreign Policy of Iran, A Developing Nation in World Affairs, 1500-1941
________, The Persian Gulf, Iran's Role
Richard W. Cottam, Nationalism in Iran
Amin Saikal, The Rise and Fall of the Shah
M.S. Azhary, The Iran-Iraq War
Barry Rubin, Paved with Good Intentions
Gary Sick, All Fall Down
Nikki Keddie, Roots of Revolution
M.S. Azhary, The Iran-Iraq War

Israel

Michael Brecher, Decisions in Israel's Foreign Policy
________, Decisions in Crisis: Israel - 1967 and 1973 ________, The Foreign Policy System of Israel
William R. Brown, The Last Crusade--A Negotiator's Middle East Handbook
Sylvia K. Crosbie, A Tacit Alliance: France and Israel from Suez to the Six Day War
Evan M. Wilson, Decision on Palestine
Avigdor Dagan, Moscow and Jerusalem: Twenty Years of Relations Between Israel and the Soviet Union
Alan Dowty, Decisions In Crisis
Shlomo Aronson, Conflict and Bargaining in the Middle East

Egypt

A.I. Dawisha, Egypt in the Arab World The Elements of Foreign Policy
Richard H. Dekmejian, Egypt Under Nasir
Miles Copeland, The Game of Nations
Mohammed H. Heikal, The Cairo Documents
________, The Road to Ramadan

Iraq

Abid A. al-Marayati, A Diplomatic History of Iraq
Majid H. Khadduri, Independent Iraq, 1932-58, A Study in Iraqi Politics
________, Republican Iraq, A Study in Iraqi Politics Since the Revolution of 1958.
Lorenzo K. Kimball, The Changing Pattern of Political Power in Iraq, 1958-1971
Christine M. Helms, Iraq: Eastern Flank of the Arab World

Syria

Gordon H. Torrey, Syrian Politics and the Military, 1945-1958
Tabitha Petran, Syria
Itamar Rabinovich, Syria Under the Ba'th 1963-66
Patrick Seal, The Struggle for Syria

Po. Sci. 270G D. Peretz

Jordon

Mohammad Ibrahim Faddah, The Middle East in Transition: A Study of Jordan's Foreign Policy
King Hussein, Uneasy Lies the Head. Autobiography.
Vick Vance & Pierre Lauer, Hussein of Jordan: My "War" with Israel
Arthur R. Day, East Bank West Bank--Jordan & Prospects for Peace

Saudi Arabia

Fred Halliday, Arabia Without Sultans
David Holden, Farewell to Arabia
Gerald DeGaury, Faisal, King of Saudi Arabia
Helen Lackner, A House Built on Sand

The Palestinians

Helena Cobban, The Palestian Liberation Organization People, Power and Politics.
John W. Amos, The Palestinian Resistance
John Cooley, Green March, Black September
Galia Golan, The Soviet Union and the Palestine Liberation Organization
William Quandt, Fund Jabber, Ann Lesch, The Politics of Palestinian Nationalism
Brookings Institution, Toward Peace in the Middle East

FIGURE 1

THE RESEARCH DESIGN (1)

INPUTS		
OPERATIONAL ENVIRONMENT		
EXTERNAL	—Global	(G)
	Subordinate	(S)
	Subordinate Other	(SO)
	Dominant Bilateral	(DB)
	Bilateral	(B)
INTERNAL	—Military Capability	(M)
	Economic Capability	(E)
	Political Structure	(PS)
	Interest Groups	(IG)
	Competing Élites	(CE)
COMMUNICATION	—The transmission of data about the operational environment by mass media, internal bureaucratic reports, face-to-face contact, etc.	
PSYCHOLOGICAL ENVIRONMENT		
ATTITUDINAL PRISM	—Ideology, Historical Legacy, Personality Predispositions	
ÉLITE IMAGES	—of the operational environment, including competing élites' advocacy and pressure potential	
PROCESS		
FORMULATION	—of Strategic and Tactical decisions in 4 ISSUE AREAS:	
	Military-Security	(M–S)
	Political-Diplomatic	(P–D)
	Economic-Developmental	(E–D)
	Cultural-Status	(C–S)
IMPLEMENTATION	—of decisions by various structures: Head of State, Head of Government, Foreign Office, etc.	
OUTPUTS	—The substance of acts or decisions	

FIGURE 2

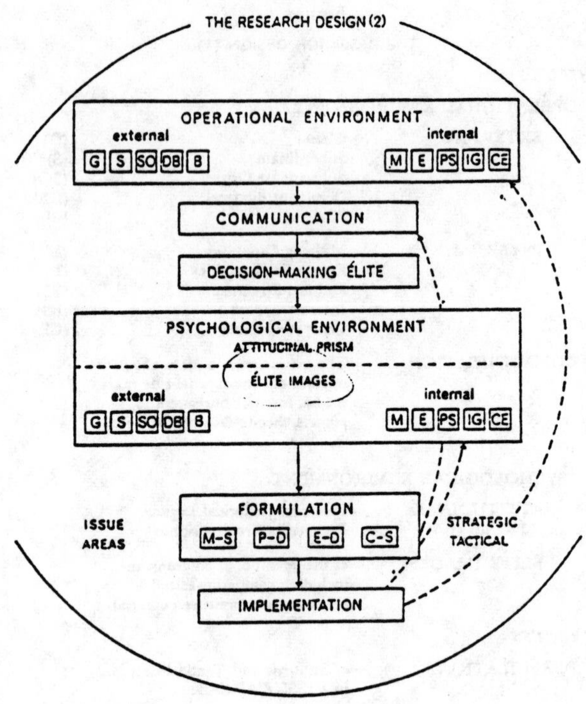
THE RESEARCH DESIGN (2)
OPERATIONAL ENVIRONMENT
external
internal
G S SO DB B
M E PS IG CE
COMMUNICATION
DECISION-MAKING ÉLITE
PSYCHOLOGICAL ENVIRONMENT
ATTITUDINAL PRISM
ÉLITE IMAGES
external
internal
G S SO DB B
M E PS IG CE
FORMULATION
ISSUE AREAS
M-S P-D E-D C-S
STRATEGIC
TACTICAL
IMPLEMENTATION

POLITICAL SCIENCE 129

Professor Peretz Spring 1986

Government and Politics of Israel

Course Syllabus and Bibliography

Political Science 129 meets on Tuesdays and Thursdays from 10:05 to 11:40 a.m. Grades will be based on a mid-term examination, a final examination, a term paper which will be a critical review and comparison of three books, not on the syllabus, about Israel approved by the instructor, and student participation in class discussion. The class will be conducted seminar style with individuals or small groups of students working on selected problems which they will present in class for general discussion. Therefore, attendance is required. Instructor's office hours are Wednesday, 2:30 to 4:30 p.m. room LNG-67. The textbooks in paperback edition available in the Campus Store are: Peretz, Don, *The Government & Politics of Israel*; Arian, Asher, *Politics in Israel*; and Rabinovich, I. and Reinharz, J., *Israel in the Middle East.* Other items listed on this bibliography will be on reserve. Additional bibliography is listed in the text. All students should peruse The *Jerusalem Post* located in the newspaper section on the second floor of the Library at least once a week.

I. Introduction - Political Setting - Overview
   Peretz, Ch. 2, pp. 51-74
   Arian, Ch. 1

II. Political Ideology - Zionism - Its Origins and Relations to the State
   Peretz, Ch. 1, pp. 1-31
   Sachar, Chs. I, II, III, V OR
   Laquer, Walter, *A History of Zionism,* Chs. 1, 2, 3, 4
   Herzl, Theodore, *The Jewish State*
   Arian, Ch. 2

III. Developing Political Institutions - The Pre-State Era: 1900-1948
   Peretz, Ch. 1, pp. 31-50
   Sachar, Chs. IV, VI, VII, XI

IV. Developing Political Institutions - 1948 - present
   Peretz, Ch. 5, pp. 141-170
   Sachar, Chs. XII, XIV, XV, XVIII, XX, XXV
   Arian, Ch. 4
   Rabinovich, Parts I and II

V. Political Parties - Labor and the Left
   Peretz, Ch. 3, pp. 75-104
   Arian, Chs. 5,6
   Laqueur, Ch. 6

VI. Political Paraties - Right, Center, Religious

   Peretz, Ch. 3, pp. 105-118
   Laqueur, Ch. 7
   Arian, Ch. 5,6

VII. Elections and the Electoral System

Peretz, Ch. 4
Don Peretz, "Israel's 1969 Election Issues: The Visible and the Invisible" Middle East Journal, Winter, 1970, Vol. 24, No. 1, pp. 31-46; "The War Election and Israel's Eighth Knesset" MEJ Spring 1974, 28/2, pp. 111-125; "The Earthquake--Israel's Ninth Knesset Elections," MEJ Summer 1977, 31/3, pp. 251-266; "Israel's Tenth Knesset Elections--Ethnic Upsurgence and Decline of Ideology," MEJ Autumn 1981, 34/4, pp. 506-526; Arian, Chs. 7,8,9

VIII. Government Administration and Policy - Internal Issues

Peretz, Ch. 6
Arian, Chs. 3, 10, 11, 12

IX. Oriental Jews - Majority in a Minority Role
Smooha, Sammy, Israel: Pluralism and Conflict, Chs. 5, 6, 7, 8
Oz, Amos, In the Land of Israel, Ch. 2, p. 25

X. The Israel Arab Minority
Smooha, Chs. 5, 6, 7, 8
Fouzi el-Asmar, To Be An Arab in Israel
Lustick, Ian, Arabs in the Jewish State; Israel's Control of a National Minority, Ch. 7
Oz, Amos, Ch. 4, p. 75.

XI. State and Religion
Liebman, Charles S. & Don-Yehiya, Eliezer, Religion and Politics in Israel, or
Abramov, Zalman S, Perpetual Dilemma: Jewish Religion in the Jewish States
Smooha, Passim. See Index References to Religion.

XII. Israel Foreign Policy
Brecher, Michael, The Foreign Policy System of Israel, Part II.
Rabinovich, Foreign Policy Issues in Parts I,II,III, and IV.

XIII. Israel and the Diaspora
Halperin, Samuel, The Political World of American Zionism
Lilienthal, Alfred, The Zionist Connection
Oz, Amos, Ch. 5, p. 85

XIV. The Future of Israel
Smooha, Chs. 9, 10
Oz, Amos - All Chapters

Political Science 243

Professor F. Tachau
1114 BSB by appt.

POLITICAL DEVELOPMENT OF THE MIDDLE EAST

Outline and Assignments

The following books are required reading and may be purchased:

J.A. Bill and C. Leiden, POLITICS IN THE MIDDLE EAST
F. Tachau, ed., POLITICAL ELITES AND POLITICAL DEVELOPMENT IN THE MIDDLE EAST
B. Lewis, THE MIDDLE EAST AND THE WEST

In addition, the following books are on reserve in the library:

D. Lerner, THE PASSING OF TRADITIONAL SOCIETY
G. Baer, POPULATION AND SOCIETY IN THE ARAB EAST
C.S. Coon, CARAVAN

There will be a mid-term examination and a final examination. There will also be a written assignment, details of which will be announced probably during the second week of the term. The mid-term and written assignment will each account for approximately 30% of the final grade; the final exam will account for approximately 35% of the grade; and class participation will account for approximately 5% of the grade.

Class participation is an important part of this course. Students are expected to complete the relevant reading assignment before a particular topic is taken up in class discussion. Scheduling of discussions will be indicated from time to time as the course proceeds. Note: in the following outline, B & L = Bill & Leiden; TBA = to be assigned.

TOPIC	ASSIGNMENT
I. Introduction	
A. Modernization and political development	B & L, Ch. 1 Lerner, Chs. 1,2
B. The Middle East as a culture region	Lewis, Ch. 1
II. Traditional Culture, Society & Politics	
A. Islam	B & L, Ch. 2 Coon, Chs. 6,7,8 Fisher, Ch. 10

III.	Aspects of Change	
	A. Impact of the West and the response of Islam	Lewis, Chs. 2,5
	B. Changes in Function: Leadership and elites	B & L, Ch. 5 Tachau, intro., Chs 2 (pp. 69-84), 5
	C. Changing values and Ideologies	B & L, Ch, 7 Lewis, Ch. 4
	D. Changing Regimes	Tachau, Chs. 1,2 (pp. 84-112), pp. 3,6,7
	E. The Role of Violence and the Military	B & L, Ch. 6
IV.	Current Problems	
	A. The Arab-Israeli Conflict	B & L, Ch. 8
	B. Oil	B & L, Ch. 9
	C. The Iranian Revolution	TBA
	D. Afghanistan	TBA
V.	Conclusions	Tachau, Ch. 8

Spring 1985
Professor N. Choucri
Department of Political Science

17.444

POLITICAL ECONOMY OF THE MIDDLE EAST

Outline and Topics

1. Introduction:

   Evolution of political community, economic regimes, and interaction with the international environment

2. Political Arrangements and Economic Regimes:

   Review of inter-war and post-World War II periods. Efforts toward economic and political coordination

3. Demographic characteristics

   Population profiles in national and regional contexts; ethnic and economic implications

4. Resource Base:

   Review of national and regional endowments; oil price increases and economic effects

5. Petroleum Resources and Politics:

   Asessment of trends since 1973; causes of oil price increases; effects on regional and world markets

6. Economic Transformation:

   Expanding demand and investment programs due to capital flows in the region

7. Migration and Population Change:

   Interdependence of labor markets, effects on national planning, problems of political cohesion

8. Development Planning for the 1980s:

   Review of trends since 1960 and identification of national and regional regimes; options for the 1980s

9. Institutional Development:

   Commercial and development banking, development assistance within and beyond the region

10. Technological change and adaptation

   Problems of technology transfer to the Middle East, criteria for choice, effects of past policies

11. Mapping the Political Economy of the Region:

   Population, resources, technology and policy development

12. Conclusion:

   Development strategies and constraints for the 1980s

17.444

Political Economy of the Middle East

Reading List

All readings on reserve unless noted.

Week 1: Introduction **February 11**

Required

Edith Penrose, Introduction to Peter Mansfield (ed.), The Middle East, Fifth Edition (New York: Oxford University Press, 1980): 2-104.

Charles Issawi, "Middle East Economic Development, 1815-1914: the General and the Specific," in M.A. Cook (ed.) Studies in the Economic History of the Middle East (London: Oxford University Press, 1970): 395-411.

Albert Hourani, "Ottoman Reform and the Politics of Notables," in A. Hourani, The Emergence of the Modern Middle East (Berkeley: University of California Press, 1981): Chapter 3

[Note: This book is also on reserve at the main reserve room.]

Recommended

Halil Inalcik, "Capital Formation in the Ottoman Empire," The Journal of Economic History 29(1) March 1969: 97-140.

Serif Mardin, "Power, Civil Society and Culture in the Ottoman Empire," Comparative Studies in Society and History 11, 1969: 258-81

Peter Gran, Islamic Roots of Capitalism (Austin: University of Texas Press, 1979) Chapter 1: "The Social and Economic History of Egypt 1760-1815: A Study in Merchant Capital and its Transformation," pp. 3-34.

Roger Owen, "Britain and Europe: From French Expedition to British Occupation," in Owens and Sutcliffe (eds.) Studies in the Theory of Imperialism (London: Longman, 1972)

Nikki Keddi, "The Economic History of Iran, 1800-1914, and its Political Impact," in Keddi, Iran: Religion, Politics and Society, Chapter 5 (London: Frank Cass, 1980)

Mohammad Salman Hasan, "The Role of Foreign Trade in the Economic Development of Iraq, 1864-1964: A Study in the Growth of a Dependent Eocnomy," in M.A. Cook: 346-372.

Samir Amin, The Maghreb in the Modern World (London: Penguin, 1970): Part 1.

Week 2: Political Arrangements and Economic Regimes February 25

Required

On Economic Change

Charles Issawi, "Economic Trends in the Middle East and Future Prospects," in U.S. Congress, The Political Economy of the Middle East: 1973-78 (Washington, DC: U.S. Government Printing Office, 1980): 7-24

Fern Racine Gold and Charles K. Ebinger, "Economic Change in the Oil Exporting Countries of the Middle East, The Political Economy of the Middle East: 91-104

On Political Change

Ijaz Gilani, "From Khartoum to Rabat: The Development of Pragmatic Arabism in Inter-Arab Relations: 1967-74," Ph.D. dissertation, MIT 1977: Chaps. 3-6

Samir Amin, The Arab Nation: Nationalism and Class Struggle (London: Zed Press, 1978), especially chapters 3-6

Recommended

Nazli Choucri, The International Politics of Energy Interdependence (Lexington, MA: D.C. Heath 1977), Chapters 2, 4 and 5.

Galal Amin, The Modernization of Poverty: A Study in the Political Economy of Growth in Nine Arab Countries (Leiden: E.J. Brill, 1974)

Samir Amin, The Maghreb in the Modern World: part 2

Malcolm Kerr, "Rich and Poor in the New Arab Order", Journal of Arab Affairs 1(1) October 1981: 1-26.

Ghassame Salamah, "Political Power and the Saudi State," Middle East Research and Information Project (MERIP) 91, October 1980: 5-23. [MERIP reports are on permanent reserve in Dewey.]

Fouad Ajami, The Arab Predicament: Arab Political Thought and Practice Since 1967 (London: Cambridge University Press, 1981.) [n.r.]

William Quandt, Saudi Arabia in the 1980s: Foreign Policy, Security and Oil (Washington, D.C.: Brookings, 1981.) [n.r.]

David Pool, "From Elite to Class: The Transformation of the Iraqi Political Leadership," in Abbas Kalidar (ed) The Integration of Modern Iraq (New York: St. Martin's Press, 1979): 63-87.

Mahmoud Hussein, Class Conflict in Egypt, 1945-1970 (New York: Monthly Review Press, 1977.

Hanna Batatu, The Old Social Classes and the Revelutionary Movements in Iraq (Princeton: Princeton University Press, 1978.) [main reserve room]

Hussein A. Hassouna, The League of Arab States and Regional Disputes (New York: Oceana Publications, 1975.) [n.r.]

Week 3: Demographic Characteristics **March 4**

Required

Nazli Choucri, "Demographic Changes in the Middle East," in The Political Economy of the Middle East: 24-25.

Hanna Batatu, "Some Observations on the Social Roots of Syria's Ruling Military Group and the Causes of its Dominance," The Middle East Journal 25 (Summer 1981).

Janet Abu-Lughod, "The Demographic Transformation of Palestine," in Ibrahim Abu-Lughod (ed), The Transformation of Palestine (Evaston: Northwestern University Press, 1971): 139-64.

Don Peretz, "The Palestinian Issue," in The Political Economy of the Middle East: 531-52.

Walid Kazziha, Palestine in the Arab Dilemma (London: Croom Helm, 1979), "The Lebanese Civil War and the Palestinian Resistance Movement," pp. 37-65.

Recommended

Nicholas Van Dam, The Struggle for Power in Syria: Sectarianism, Regionalism and Tribalism in Politics, 1961-1978 (New York: St. Martins Press, 1978.) [n.r.]

Walid Khalidi, Conflict and Violence in Lebanon (Cambridge, M.A: Harvard Center for International Affairs, 1979.) [n.r.]

Nick Eberstadt and Eric Briendel, Realities Behind Camp David: Demographic Aspects of the Politics of Peace in the Middle East Unpublished paper, 1979.

J.I. Clarke and W.B. Fisher, Populations of the Middle East and North Africa (New York: Africana Publishing Corporation, 1972.) [n.r.]

I. William Zartman (ed). Man, State, and Society in the Contemporary Maghrib (New York: Praeger, 1973.) [n.r.]

Maxime Rodinson, Israel A Colonial Settler State? (New York: Monad Press, 1973.) [n.r.]

Week 4: Resource Base **March 11**

Required

Yusef Sayigh, Economics of the Arab World (New York: St. Martin's Press, 1978): Chapter 14.

Atif Kubursi, "Arab Agricultural Productivity: A New Perspective," in Ibrahim Ibrahim (ed) Arab Resources (Washington, D.C.: Center for Contemporary Arab Studies, Georgetown University, 1983): 71-104.

George T. Abed, "Arab Financial Resources: An Analysis and Critique of Present Deployment Policies," in Arab Resources: 43-70.

Recommended

Robert Mabro, The Egyptian Economy 1952-72 (Oxford: Clarendon Press, 1947). [n.r.]

Robert Mabro and Samir Radwan, The Industrialization of Egypt, 1939-1973 (New York: Oxford University Press, 1976.) [n.r.]

Allan Richards, Egypt's Agricultural Development 1800-1980: Technical and Social Change (Boulder: Westview Press, 1976.) [n.r.]

H. Mahdavy, "The Patterns and Problems of Economic Development in Rentier States: the Case of Iran," in M.A. Cook: 428-467.

Theda Skopol, "Rentier State and Shi'a Islam in the Iranian Revolution," Theory and Society 11(3), 1982: 265-283. [n.r.]

John Wright, Libya: A Modern History (Baltimore: Johns Hopkins University Press, 1982). [n.r.]

Week 5: Petroleum Resources and Politics **March 18**

Required

Albert Danielson, The Evolution of OPEC (New York: Harcourt, Brace and Jovanovich, 1982.)

Nazli Choucri, "OPEC and the World Energy Market," Technology Review 83(1) October 1980: 36-45.

Nazli Choucri, "Power and Politics in World Oil," Technology Review 85(7) October 1982: 1-10.

Nazli Choucri, The International Politics of Energy Interdependence: Chapters 7 and 8.

Recommended

N. Keddi, "Oil, Economic Policy, and Social Change in Iran," in Keddi, Chapter 8: 207-239.

Ruth First, "Libya: Class and State in an Oil Economy," in Petter Nore and Terisa Turner, Oil and Class Struggle (London: Zed Press, 1980): 119-42.

Saad Eddin Ibrahim, The New Arab Social Order: A Study of the Social Impact of Oil Wealth (Boulder: Westview, 1982.) [n.r.]

Tim Niblock (ed) State, Society and Economy in Saudi Arabia (New York: St. Martins Press, 1982.) [n.r.]

OPEC and Future Energy Markets, Proceedings of the OPEC Seminar, Vienna, Austria, 1979 (London: MacMillan, 1980.) [n.r.]

Week 6: Economic Transformation **April 1**

Required

P.J. Vatikiotis, et. al., "Country Studies," Section II in The Political Economy of the Middle East: 105-246.

Philip S. Khoury, "Islamic Revival and the Crisis of the Secular State in the Arab World," in Arab Resources: 213-236.

Elias T. Ghantus, Arab Industrial Integration: A Strategy for Development (London: Croom Helm, 1982.)

Recommended

Malcolm Kerr and Sayid Yassin (eds) Rich and Poor States in the Middle East: Egypt and the New Arab Order (Boulder: Westview, 1982.) [n.r.]

Robert Tignor and Gouda Abdel-Khalek (eds) The Political Economy of Income Distribution in Egypt (London: Holmes and Meier, 1982.) [n.r.]

Mark N. Cooper, The Transformation of Egypt: State and State Captialism in Crisis (Baltimore: Jonns Hopkins University Press, 1982.)

Muhammad Abdel-Fadil, The Political Economy of Nasserism (Cambridge: Cambridge University Press, 1980.) [n.r.]

Edith Penrose "Industrial Policy and Performance in Iraq," in Kalidar: 150-170.

William Hale, The Political and Economic Development of Modern Turkey (New York: St. Martins Press, 1981.)

M.W. Khouja and P.G. Sadler, The Economy of Kuwait: Development and Role of International Finance (

Berch Berberoglu, Turkey in Crisis (London: Zed Press, 1982.) [n.r.]

Feroz Ahmad, "Military Intervention and the Crisis in Turkey" MERIP Reports 93 (January 1981): 5-24.

Daniel Shimshoni, Israeli Democracy: The Middle of the Journey (New York: The Free Press, 1982): Chapter 5, "The Political Economy." [n.r.]

Week 7: Migration and Population Change **April 8**

Required

Nazli Choucri, "The Political Economy of the Middle East: The Dynamics of Labor Migration." Unpublished paper, 1982. [xerox]

Ismail Serageldin, et. al., "Human Resources in the Arab World: The Impact of Migration," in Arab Resources: 17-36.

Janet Abu-Lughod, "Social Implications of Labor Migration in the Arab World," Arab Resources: 237-266.

Nazli Chourci, "Migration in the Middle East: Transformations, Policies, and Processes," Technology and Development Reports 83-9 (July 1983), Volumes I and II.

Recommended

Jon C. Swanson, Emigration and Economic Development: the Case of the Yemen Arab Republic (Boulder: Westview Press, 1979.)

J.S. Birks and C.A. Sinclair, Arab Manpower (1980) [n.r.]

Ian Lustick, Arabs in the Jewish State: Israel's Control of a National Minority (Austin: University of Texas Press, 1980.) [n.r.]

Week 8: Development Planning for the 1980s **April 22**

Required

Yusif Sayigh, "A New Framework for Complementarity Among the Arab Economies," Arab Resources: 147-168.

John Waterbury, "Long-Range Planning and Development in Six Poor Arab States: Syria, Jordan, Sudan, South Yemen, Egypt and North Yemen," The International Journal of Middle East Studies 14, 1982: 35-51. [xerox]

Alan Richards, "Agricultural Mechanization in Egypt: Hopes and Fears," The International Journal of Middle East Studies 13, 1981: 409-25.

Recommended

Naiem A. Sherbiny (ed) Manpower Planning in the Oil Countries (Greenwich, CT: JAI Press, 1981.) [n.r.].

Week 9: Institutional Development **April 29**

Required

Ibrahim M. Oweiss, "The Arab Development Fund and Arab Foreign Aid," in Arab Resources: 115-124.

Clement Henry Moore, Financial Surrogates of Political Order: The Lebanese Banking System: Unpublished paper, 1982.

Ibrahim Shihata, The Other Face of OPEC (London: Longman, 1982.)

John C. Campbell, et. al., "Foreign Relations," The Political Economy of the Middle East, Section IV: 345-422.

Recommended

Alan E. Moore, "The Development of Banking in Bahrain," in May Ziwar-Daftari (ed) Issues in Development: The Arab Gulf States (London, 1980): 76-84.

Samir A. Makdisi, "Arab Economic Cooperation" in Roberto Aliboni (ed) Arab Industrialization and Economic Integration (New York: St. Martins Press, 1979): 90-133. [n.r.]

Robert Mabro, "Oil Revenues and the Cost of Social and Economic Development" in OAPEC, Energy in the Arab World, Proceedings of the First Arab Energy Conference, Abu Dhabi, March 1979, Volume 1 (Kuwait, 1980): 285-322. [n.r.]

Yusif Sayigh, "The Social Costs of Oil Revenues," in Energy in the Arab World (1980): 323-341. [n.r.]

Week 10: Technological Change and Adapation **May 6**

Required

Nazli Choucri, Manpower Issues in Technology Transfer to the Middle East: Report prepared for the Office of Technology Assessment, 1983: Volumes 1-3.

R.D. McLaurin, "Issues in the Transfer of Technology to the Middle East," The Political Economy of the Middle East: 313-344.

Excerpts from Al-Ahram Al-Iqtisadi, "The Description of Egypt in America." Unofficial Translation.

Antoine B. Zahlan, "Constraints on the Acquistion of Technology," in May Ziwar-Diftari (1980): 76-84.

Recommended

Alan Richards, "Agricultural Technology and Rural Social Classes in Egypt, 1920-1939," in Kedourie and Haim (eds) Modern Egypt: Studies in Politics and Society (London: Frank Case, 1980.)

A.B. Zahlan (ed) Technology Transfer and Change in the Arab World (London: Oxford University Press, 1978.) [n.r.]

Joseph Szyliowicz, "The Prospects for Scientific and Technological Development in Saudi Arabia," The International Journal of Middle East Studies 10(1979): 355-72. [n.r.]

Weeks 11 and 12: Mapping the Political Economy **May 13**

Required

Nazli Choucri, "The Arab World in the 1980s: Macro-politics and Economic Change," MIT, 1981.

Malcolm Kerr, "Rich and Poor in the New Arab Order" [see week 2]

Fouad Ajami, "The Arab Road," Foreign Policy 47 Summer 1983: 3-25.

Others to be Assigned.

POLITICS, TECHNOLOGY, AND DEVELOPMENT IN THE MIDDLE EAST

Fall 1986

17.558J Department of Political Science Faculty in charge: N. Choucri
1.255J Department of Civil Engineering Faculty in charge: F. Moavenzadeh
Units: 309

Week 1
September 15

Introduction: Contemporary Conflicts and Competing Ideologies

Focus on systems of conflict, interconnections among conflicts, contemporary state-system.

Choucri

Week 2
September 22

Islam and Politics in Historical and Contemporary Perspectives

Rise of Islam and imperial expansion, Western colonization, shifting state boundaries, resurgent Islam, establishment Islam, Islamic economics.

Choucri, Khoury

Week 3
September 29

Decolonization, Nationalism, and the Cold War

The mandate system, nationalism amidst great power conflicts, changing fortunes of East and West, alliance systems, dealignment, moves toward autonomy. Nationalism and post-war ideologies.

Rotberg, Bloomfield, Khoury

Week 4
October 6

State Building and Contending Institutions of Authority

New states, political processes, the role of the military, regional organizations, political parties, socialization and youth.

Choucri, Khoury, Keniston

[RWP2:course.pc]
[9/11/86]

Week 5
October 20

Inter-State Migration and Interdependence

Demographic pluralism and the forging of national identities, scale and scope of migration, problems of state legimitacy. Cases of Israel, Lebanon, Saudi Arabia, and the Gulf.

Choucri, Weiner, and Khoury

Week 6
October 27

Development in the Urban Context

Urban expansion and mass politics, strains on infrastructure. Cases of Baghdad, Cairo, Rabat, Tehran, Tunis, Yanbu, and Jubail.

Porter, Keniston, and Moavenzadeh

Week 7
November 3

The Middle East as a Source of Capital for International Investment

Growth of capital, nature and composition of capital, impacts on international financial markets, development banks in the Middle East.

Lessard and Choucri

Week 8
November 17

The Middle East as a Context for International Business

Middle East as a market for firms, relation to US foreign policy, strategies of business as it views the region.

Lessard, Westney, and Bloomfield

Week 9
November 24

Role of Technology in Middle East Development

Issues of technological dependence, dependent development in the Middle East, comparisons with other regions.

Moavenzadeh, Trilling, and Simon

Week 10
December 1

Development of Scientific and Technological Institutions

Institutional issues in the development of indigenous scientific and technological capacities, roles of industry, academia, government, and international organizations.

Moavenzadeh, Trilling, and Westney

Week 11
December 8

<u>Development of Regional Institutions</u>

Strategic, financial, scientific, and technological institutions: OPEC, OAPEC, the Gulf Corporation Council, the Arab Development Funds, the Kuwait Fund, the Islamic Fund for Science, Technology and Development.

Choucri

REQUIRED READING

(1) September 15 — Introduction: Contemporary Conflicts and Competing Ideologies

Diana Crane. "Technological Innovation in Developing Countries: A Review of the Literature," Research Policy, 6 (1977): 374-395.

Cheryl Benard and Zalmay Khalilzad. "Secularization, Industrialization, and Khomeini's Islamic Republic," Political Science Quarterly, 94 (2) Summer 1979: 229-241.

Bahgat Korany. "Defending the Faith: The Foreign Policy of Saudi Arabia," The Foreign Policies of Arab States, ed. Bahgat Korany and Ali Dessouki (Boulder, Colo.: Westview Press, 1984).

Technology Transfer to the Middle East (Washington, D.C.: US Congress, Office of Technology Assessment, 1984): Ch. 3.

Hanna Batatu, "Class Analysis and Iraqui Society," Arab Studies Quarterly, 1 (3) Summer 1979: 229-244.

POLITICS, TECHNOLOGY, AND DEVELOPMENT IN THE MIDDLE EAST

Fall 1986

REQUIRED READING

(2) September 22 — Islam and Politics in Historical and Contemporary Perspectives

Wilfred Cantwell Smith. Islam in Modern History (Princeton: Princeton University Press, 1957): Ch. 1.

Hamid Enayat. Modern Islamic Political Thought (Austin: University of Texas Press, 1982): Chs. 1, 2.

Ira M. Lapidus. "Presidential Address: 1984 Meeting of the Middle East Studies Association," MESA Bulletin, 19 (1) July 1985: 1-8.

Michael C. Hudson. "Islam and Political Development," Islam and Development, ed. John L. Esposito (Syracuse, NY: Syracuse University Press, 1980): 1-24.

REQUIRED READING

(3) September 29 — Decolonization, Nationalism, and the Cold War

Sylvia G. Haim, ed. Arab Nationalism (Berkeley: University of California Press, 1976): Introduction.

Charles Issawi. An Economic History of the Middle East and North Africa (New York: Columbia University Press, 1982): Chs. 1, 2, 3, 4, 5.

Albert Hourani. "The Middle East and the Crisis of 1956," A Vision of History (Beirut, Lebanon: Khayats, 1961).

POLITICS, TECHNOLOGY, AND DEVELOPMENT IN THE MIDDLE EAST

Fall 1986

REQUIRED READING

(4) October 6 — State Building and Contending Institutions of Authority

Raymond William Baker. Egypt's Uncertain Revolution under Nasser and Sadat (Cambridge: Harvard University Press, 1978): Ch. 4; 151-165; Ch. 7.

J.C. Hurewitz. Middle East Politics: The Military Dimension (New York: Praeger Press, 1969): Chs. 5, 6, 8, 17.

J.E. Peterson, ed. "Tribes and Politics in Eastern Arabia," The Politics of Middle Eastern Oil (Washington, D.C.: Middle East Institute, 1983): 234-249.

Robert O. Freedman, ed. Israel in the Begin Era (New York: Praeger, 1982): Chs. 2, 3, 4.

William E. Hazen. "Minorities in Revolt: The Kurds of Iran, Iraq, Syria, and Turkey," The Political Role of Minority Groups in the Middle East, ed. R.D. McLaurin (Praeger Publishers, 1979): Ch. 3.

Hanna Batatu. "Some Observations on the Social Roots of Syria's Ruling, Military Group and the Causes for Its Dominance," The Middle East Journal, 35 (3) Summer 1981: 331-344.

REQUIRED READING

(5) October 20 — Inter-State Migration and Interdependence

Myron Weiner. "On International Migration and International Relations," Population and Development Review, 11 (3) September 1985: 441-455.

Nazli Choucri. "A View of Migration and Remittances in the Middle East," Prepared for the Annual Meeting of the Population Association of America, March 1986.

Naiem A. Sherbiny. "Expatriate Labor Flows to the Arab Oil Countries in the 1980s," The Middle East Journal, 38 (4) Autumn 1984: 643-667.

Janet Abu-Lughod. "Social Implications of Labor Migration in the Arab World," Arab Resources: The Transformation of a Society, ed. Ibrahim Ibrahim (Washington, D.C.: Center for Contemporary Arab Studies, 1983): 237-265.

POLITICS, TECHNOLOGY, AND DEVELOPMENT IN THE MIDDLE EAST

Fall 1986

REQUIRED READING

(6) October 27 Development in the Urban Context

Johannes F. Linn. "The Costs of Urbanization in Developing Countries," Economic Development and Cultural Change, 30 (3) April 1982: 625-648.

Michael Pacione, ed. Problems and Planning in Third World Cities (New York: St. Martin's Press, 1981): Ch. 3 (Tunis), Ch. 5 (Tehran).

Samuel H. Preston. "Urban Growth in Developing Countries: A Demographic Reappraisal," Population and Development Review, 5 (2) June 1979: 195-215.

Helen Anne B. Rivlin and Katherine Helmer. The Changing Middle Eastern City (Binghamton, NY: State University of New York, Center for Social Analysis Program in Southwest Asian and North African Studies, 1980): 1-34, 73-95, 149-185.

REQUIRED READING

(7) November 3 The Middle East as a Source of Capital for International Investment

Traute Wohlers-Scharf. Arab and Islamic Banks: New Business Partners for Developing Countries (Paris: Development Center of the Organization for Economic Co-Operation and Development, 1983): Parts II and III.

Mokhtar M. Metwally. "The Role of the Stock Exchange in an Islamic Economy," Journal of Research in Islamic Economics, 2 (1) Summer 1984: 21-30.

Volker Nienhaus. "Profitability of Islamic PLS Banks Competing with Interest Banks: Problems and Prospects," Journal of Research in Islamic Economics, 1 (1) Summer 1983: 37-47.

Donald Lessard, Eugene Floon Jr., and James Paddock, from International Investment and the Multinational firm, unpublished ms., 1986.

POLITICS, TECHNOLOGY, AND DEVELOPMENT IN THE MIDDLE EAST

Fall 1986

REQUIRED READING

(8) November 17 The Middle East as a Context for International Business

Robert A. Kilmarx and Yonah Alexander, eds. Business and the Middle East: Threats and Prospects (New York: Pergamon Press, 1982): Intro., Chs. 7, 8, 9.

Rodney Wilson. "Islamic Business: Theory and Practice, Special Report No. 221" (EIU) The Economist Intelligence Unit, Revised Edition, 1985: Chs. 2, 3, 4, 5.

Technology Transfer to the Middle East (Washington, D.C.: US Congress, Office of Technology Assessment, 1984): Ch. 4.

Theodore H. Moran, "Multinational Corporations and the Developing Countries: An Analytical Overview," in Theodore H. Moran, Multinational Corporations: The Political Economy of Direct Investment (Lexington, Mass.: Lexington Books, 1985), pp. 3-24.

M Michael Porter, "Competition in Global Industries: A Conceptual Framework," in Competition in Global Industries (forthcoming).

REQUIRED READING

(9) November 24 Role of Technology in Middle East Development

Jeffrey James. "Appropriate Technology and Inappropriate Policy Instruments," Development and Change, 11 (1) January 1980: 65-76.

Technology Transfer to the Middle East (Washington, D.C.: US Congress, Office of Technology Assessment, September 1984): Chs. 10, 11.

Joseph S. Szyliowicz. "The Prospects for Scientific and Technological Development in Saudi Arabia," The International Journal of Middle East Studies, 10 (1979): 355-372.

Hussein M. Fahim. Dams, People and Development (New York: Pergamon Press, 1981): Chs. 2, 9.

POLITICS, TECHNOLOGY, AND DEVELOPMENT IN THE MIDDLE EAST

Fall 1986

REQUIRED READING

(10) December 1 Development of Scientific and Technological Institutions

Jack N. Behrman. Industry Ties with Science and Technology Policies in Developing Countries (Cambridge, Mass.: Oelgeschlager, Gunn and Hain, 1980): Chs. 4, 6.

Ziauddin Sardar. Science and Technology in the Middle East: A Guide to Issues, Organizations, and Institutions (London: Longman, 1982): 3-79.

Clement Henry Moore. Images of Development: Egyptian Engineers in Search of Industry (Cambridge, Mass.: MIT Press, 1980): Chs. 1, 2, 4, Conclusion.

REQUIRED READING

(11) December 8 Development of Regional Institutions

Shireen Hunter, ed. Gulf Corporation Council: Problems and Prospects (Washington, D.C.: Center for Strategic and International Studies, 1984): Intro., Chs. 1, 2, 3, 4.

Michele Achilli and Mohamed Khaldi, eds. The Role of the Arab Development Funds in the World Economy (St. Martin's Press in Assoc. with ICEI, 1984): Chs. 1, 2, 5, 6, 7.

Ibrahim Ibrahim, ed. Arab Resources: The Transformation of a Society, Hisham M. Nazer, "Institution-Building in Developing Countries," and Ibrahim M. Oweiss, "The Arab Development Funds and Arab Foreign Aid" (Washington, D.C.: Center for Contemporary Arab Studies, 1983).

Traute Wohlers-Scharf. Arab and Islamic Banks: New Business Partners for Developing Countries (Paris: Development Center of the Organization for Economic Co-Operation and Development, 1983): Part I.

POLITICS, TECHNOLOGY, AND DEVELOPMENT IN THE MIDDLE EAST

Fall 1986

RECOMMENDED READING

(1) September 15 Introduction: Contemporary Conflicts and Competing Ideologies

Mary B. Anderson and Peter Buck. "Essay Review: Scientific Development: The Development of Science, Science and Development, and the Science of Development," Social Studies of Science, 10 (2) May 1980: 215-230.

William Quandt. "Riyadh Between the Superpowers," Foreign Policy (44) Fall 1981: 37-56.

(2) September 22 Islam and Politics in Historical and Contemporary Perspectives

Wilfred Cantwell Smith. Islam in Modern History (Princeton: Princeton University Press, 1957): Ch. 4.

Hamid Enayat. Modern Islamic Political Thought (Austin: University of Texas Press, 1982): Ch. 3.

Morroe Berger. Islam in Egypt Today: Social and Political Aspects of Popular Religion (Cambridge, Eng.: Cambridge University Press, 1970): Ch. 2.

(3) September 29 Decolonization, Nationalism, and the Cold War

Rashid Khalidi. "Arab Views of the Soviet Role in the Middle East," The Middle East Journal, 39 (4) Autumn 1985: 716-732.

Malcolm H. Kerr. The Arab Cold War: Gamal 'Abd al-Nasir and His Rivals, 1958-1970 (London, Eng.: Oxford University Press, 1971): Chs. 1, 2, 3.

(4) October 6 State Building and Contending Institutions of Authority

J.C. Hurewitz. Middle East Politics: The Military Dimension (New York: Praeger Press, 1969): Chs. 2, 3, 4, 10, 15.

(5) October 20 Inter-State Migration and Interdependence

Karl W. Deutsch. Nationalism and Social Communication: An Inquiry into the Foundations of Nationality, 2nd ed. (Cambridge, Mass.: MIT Press, 1966): Chs. 1, 2, 3, 7, 8.

(6) October 27 Development in the Urban Context

(No recommended reading for Week 6)

(7) November 3 The Middle East as a Source of Capital for International Investment

M.H. Pesaran. "The System of Dependent Capitalism in Pre- and Post-Revolutionary Iran," International Journal of Middle East Studies, 14 (1982): 501-522.

(8) November 17 The Middle East as a Context for International Business

Friedrich Schneider and Bruno S. Frey. "Economic and Political Determinants of Foreign Direct Investment," World Development, 13 (2): 162-175.

(9) November 24 Role of Technology in Middle East Development

Technology Transfer to the Middle East (Washington, D.C.: US Congress, Office of Technology Assessment, September 1984): Ch. 12.

(10) December 1 Development of Scientific and Technological Institutions

Ziauddin Sardar. Science and Technology in the Middle East: A Guide to Issues, Organizations, and Institutions (London: Longman, 1982): 81-121.

Norman Clark. "The Economic Behavior of Research Institutions in Developing Countries--Some Methodological Points," Social Studies of Science, 10 (1) 1980: 75-93.

(11) December 8 Development of Regional Institutions

(No recommended reading for Week 11)

Near Eastern History 383

INTRODUCTION TO MEDIEVAL ISLAMIC SOCIAL HISTORY

I. Week of April 1 **Organizational Meeting**

II. April 8 **Patterns of Social Organization**

Reading:
- •Claude Cahen, "L'Histoire économique et sociale de l'orient musulman médieval," Studia Islamica 3 (1955), pp. 93-115 [reprinted in Cahen, Les Peuples musulmans dans l'histoire médieval, pp. 209-229].
- •Roy P. Mottahedeh, Loyalty and Leadership in an early Islamic Society.
- •EI (new ed.), " 'Ā'ila."
- •A. L. Udovitch, "Formalism and Informalism in the Social and Economic Institutions of the Medieval Islamic World," in A. Banani & S. Vryonis (eds.), Individualism and Conformity in Classical Islam, pp. 61-81.

III. April 15 **The Basic Strata of Islamic Societies, I: Middle & Upper Strata**

Reading:
- •EI (new ed.), "dihkān," "kātib."
- •S. D. Goitein, "The Rise of the Middle Eastern Bourgeoisie in Early Islamic Times," Journal of World History 3 (1957), pp. 583-604 [reprinted in Goitein, Studies in Islamic History and Institutions, pp. 217-241].
- •Richard Bulliet, The Patricians of Nishapur, pp. 1-81.
- •Carl Petry, The Civilian Elite of Cairo during the Later Middle Ages.

IV. April 22 **The Basic Strata of Islamic Societies, II: Lower Strata**

Reading:
- •EI (new ed.), "'Abd," "Ghulām."
- •R. Brunschvig, "Metiers vils en Islam," Studia Islamica 16 (1962), pp. 41-60.
- •S. D. Goitein, "The working people of the Mediterranean area during the high Middle Ages," in his Studies in Islamic History and Institutions, pp. 255-278.
- •C. Cahen, "Fiscalité, Propriété, Antagonismes Sociaux en Haute-Mésopotamie au temps des premiers 'Abbasides d'après Denys de Tell-Mahré," Arabica 1 (1954), pp. 136-152.
- •Lambton, A. K. S., "Aspects of Agricultural Organisation and Agrarian History in Persia," in B. Spuler (ed.), Handbùch der Orientalistik I.VI.6.1 ("Wirtschaftsgeschichte des vorderen Orients in islamischer Zeit"), pp. 160-187.

V. April 29 **Nomads in Middle Eastern Societies**

Reading:
- •EI (new ed.), "Badw."
- •Pick one of: (a) Alois Musil, The Manners and Customs of the Rwala Bedouins, Donald P. Cole, Nomads of the Nomads, or Robert Montagne, La civilisation du désert

  or (b) Fredrik Barth, Nomads of South Persia, or John Frödin, "Les Formes de la vie pastorale en Turquie," Geografiska Annaler 25, 26

(1943-44), pp. 219-272.
or (c) Sechin Jagchid and Paul Hyer, Mongolia's Culture and Society, pp. 1-162, and Dennis Sinor, "Horse and Pasture in Inner Asian History," Oriens Extremus 19 (1972), pp. 171-184.

•Fred M. Donner, "Some Reflections on the Role of Nomadic Groups in the Fertile Crescent and the Arabian Peninsula," (unpublished typescript).

VI. May 6 — Non-Muslim Communities under Islamic Rule

Reading:
•EI (new ed.), "Dhimma."
•S.D. Goitein, "Minority Selfrule and Government Control in Islam," Studia Islamica 31 (1970), pp. 101-116.
•Pick one of: (a) Mark Cohen, Jewish Self-Government in Medieval Egypt.
(b) J.-M. Fiey, Chrétiens syriaques sous les Abbassides.
(c) J.-M. Fiey, Chrétiens syriaques sous les Mongols.
(d) S. D. Goitein, A Mediterranean Society, vol. I.

VII. May 13 — Conversion to Islam

Reading:
•Richard Bulliet, Conversion to Islam in the Medieval Period.
•Claude Cahen, "Considerations sur l'utilisation des ouvrages de droit musulman par l'historien," Atti del III Congresso di studi Arabi e Islamici, Ravello, 1966 (Naples, 1967), pp. 239-247 [reprinted in Cahen, Les Peuples musulmans dan l'histoire médiéval, pp. 209-229].

VIII. May 20 — Women in Islamic Society

Reading:
•Elizabeth Fernea and Basima Q. Bezirgan, Middle Eastern Muslim Women Speak, chapter 2, "The Koran on the Subject of Women," pp. 7-26.
•John L. Esposito, "Women's Rights in Islam," Islamic Studies 14 (1975), pp. 99-114.
•J.N.D. Anderson, "The Islamic Law of Marriage and Divorce," in Abdulla M. Lutfiyya and Charles W. Churchill (eds.), Readings in Arab Middle Eastern Societies and Cultures, pp. 492-504.
•Barbara C. Aswad, "Key and Peripheral Roles of Noble Women in a Middle Eastern Plains Village," Anthropological Quarterly 40 (1967), pp. 139-152.
•Safia K. Mohsen, "The Legal Status of Women among Awlad 'Ali," Anthropological Quarterly 40 (1967), pp. 153-166.
•Amina Farrag, "Social Control amongst the Mzabite Women of Beni-Isguen," Middle Eastern Studies 7 (1971), pp. 317-327.
•Cynthia Nelson, "Public and Private Politics: Women in the Middle Eastern World," American Ethnologist 1 (1973), pp. 551-563.
•Elizabeth and Robert Fernea, "Variation in Religious Observance among Islamic Women," in Nikki Keddie (ed.), Scholars, Saints, and Sufis, pp. 385-401.
•Ian C. Dengler, "Turkish Women in the Ottoman Empire: The Classical Age," in Lois G. Beck and Nikki Keddie (eds.), Women in the Muslim World, pp. 229-244.

IX. May 27 **Technology and Society in the Islamic World**

Reading:
- Richard Bulliet, The Camel and the Wheel.
- Andrew Watson, "A Medieval Green Revolution," in Abraham L. Udovitch (ed.), The Islamic Middle East, 700-1900, pp. 29-58.
- Husam Q. El-Samarraie, Agriculture in Iraq during the 3rd Century A.H.
- Robert Fernea, "Conflict in Irrigation," Comparative Studies in Society and History 6 (1963-64), pp. 76-83.
- David Ayalon, Gunpowder and Firearms in the Mamlûk Kingdom. A Challenge to a Medieval Society.

X. June 3 **Historical Demography of the Islamic Middle East**

Reading:
- Charles Issawi, "The Area and Population of the Arab Empire," in Abraham L. Udovitch (ed.), The Islamic Middle East, 700-1900, pp. 375-396.
- Basim Musallam, Sex and Society in Medieval Islam.
- Lawrence I. Conrad, The Plague in the Early Medieval Near East.
- Michael W. Dols, The Black Death in the Middle East.
- (recommended: William McNeill, Plagues and Peoples.)

Reserve Reading

All (or almost all) works listed above are on JRL reserve, except those articles in journals normally kept in RR5 reserve (e.g., Studia Islamica, etc.). In addition, a number of other works of potential interest, some of which may be useful for doing papers, have been placed on reserve.

Books for Purchase

A few copies of the following works have been ordered and should be in stock at CTS Co-op bookstore, should you wish to purchase them:

Richard Bulliet, The Camel and the Wheel.
Richard Bulliet, Conversion to Islam in the Medieval Period.
Roy Mottahedeh, Loyalty and Leadership in an early Islamic Society.
Basim Musallam, Sex and Society in Islam.

Course Requirements

1. Come to classes!
2. Do the reading!
3. Speak up in discussion!
4. Report periodically in a more formal fashion on a specific problem or bit of reading (assigned as we go along), and help steer discussion on the issues raised.
5. Prepare a paper (ca. 15 pages) on a topic of your choice, chosen in consultation with Mr. Donner. Papers will be due at end of quarter. Submission of preliminary outlines, drafts, etc., is strongly encouraged.
6. A brief book review (500 word maximum) will be assigned early in the quarter.

NEHIST 212

THE ORIENT TRADE from Roman Times to 1800

Fred M. Donner
702-9544

Spring Quarter, 1987

305 Oriental Institute

The course is intended to provide students with a broad overview of some of the main patterns of Eurasian commerce from roughly the first century B.C. until about 1800. Clearly no single individual can hope to master all details of this vast body of information, and it is hoped that each student will pursue his or her interest in a particular region, period, or problem by undertaking to read more fully in that subject, so that the knowledge of various members of the seminar will complement that of their fellows. Your specific area of interest should, logically, become the subject of both your quarter paper, and of the oral class presentation given in the second half of the quarter. (See below for details of these two course requirements.)

In addition to the narrower economic issues raised in any consideration of commerce and its history, it is hoped that the study of commerce may provide as well a vehicle for the discussion of some larger historical issues. Among these are the relationship between commercial activity and cultural change (e.g., religious conversion), political integration and hegemony, and general economic prosperity. Conversely, the impact of cultural factors, of political and military developments, and of non-commercial economic factors (e.g., monetary policy) on commerce will be considered.

The attached bibliography includes only a small fraction of those works available in English that deal with the "Orient trade" in some way. You are encouraged to seek out further bibliography, particularly in researching the topic chosen for your paper.

Course Requirements and Grades

1. Attendance at all scheduled class discussions.
2. Partcipation in class discussions. Speak up!
3. A quarter paper, of about 15 pages in length (ca. 3000 words), on a topic of your choice dealing with some issue within the broad range of the seminar. Papers are due at the end of week 10 of the course (Friday, June 5, 1987). You are strongly encouraged to:
   (a) consult closely with Prof. Donner when choosing the topic of your paper,
   (b) seek additional bibliography relevant to your paper topic, and
   (c) submit a rough draft of part or all of your essay sometime during the quarter, so that you have an opportunity to benefit from another reader's reactions to it, and so that you are sure to give yourself enough time to revise your essay before submitting the final draft. Note that week eight of the quarter is designated "paper-writing week", and no class sessions are to be held that week.
4. An oral presentation, of about 30 minutes' length, on any topic of interest to you; this can be the subject of your quarter paper, or can be something entirely different, if you prefer. This oral presentation will be scheduled for some time between about week 4 and the end of the seminar.

Reserve Readings and Books for Purchase

The attached book list includes items placed on reserve or otherwise readily available. Readings with "(RR5)" , etc., after the call number are available in the standing reserve collections on the designated floor of Regenstein Library. Books with no additional designation after their call numbers are in the Regenstein main reserve room.

A limited number of books, forming the main readings for the course, have been ordered and should be available for purchase at the Chicago Theological Seminary Co-op Bookstore (in CTS, corner of 58th St. and University Ave.). These books are marked by an asterisk (*) to the left of the author's name in the reading list.

Class Discussion Schedule

It is hoped that classes can be scheduled twice weekly, on Tuesdays and Thursdays, for 90 minutes. The dates in the schedule below are given accordingly; please modify them if class must be scheduled for other days of the week.

Week & Date — Topic and Reading to be completed before each Session

1. March 31 **Organizational Meeting**

April 2 **Caravan Cities**

Rostovtzeff, Caravan Cities, pp. 1-35, and either pp. 37-53 (Petra), pp. 55-90 (Jerash), or pp. 91-119 (Palmyra and Dura).

2. April 7 **Roman Commerce with the Orient/Markets**

Jones, "Asian Trade in Antiquity" in Richards, Islam and the Trade of Asia, pp. 1-11.

Polanyi, Trade and Market in the Early Empires, pp. 3-63.

April 9 **Roman Maritime Commerce with the Orient**

Charlesworth, Trade and Trade-Routes, pp. 1-111; OR

Warmington, The Commerce between the Roman Empire and India, 1-140.

3. April 14 **Central Asian Route**

Boulnois, The Silk Road, pp. 1-117.

April 16 **Sasanian Commerce**

Whitehouse, "Sassanian Maritime Trade"

4. April 21 **Early Southeast Asian Commerce**

Hall, Maritime Trade and State Development in Early Southeast Asia, pp. 1-135.

April 23 **Byzantine Commerce**

Lopez, "Silk Industry in the Byzantine Empire"

Lopez, "The Dollar of the Middle Ages"

Runciman, "Byzantine Trade and Industry"

5. April 28 **Rise of Islam/Pirenne Thesis**
Hodges and Whitehouse, Muhammad, Charlemagne, and the Origins of Europe

April 30 **Islamic Commerce**
Goitein, "The Unity of the Mediterranean World in the 'Middle Middle Ages" OR "Medieval Tunisia: the Hub of the Mediterranean"
Udovitch, "Commercial Techniques in Medieval Islamic Trade"
Goitein, "The Beginnings of the Karim Merchants..." OR
Stillman, "The Eleventh-Century Merchant House of Ibn 'Awkal"

6. May 5 **Later East Asian Commerce**
Hall, Maritime Trade and State Formation..., 136-260.

May 7 **Chinese Commerce**
Hudson, "The Medieval Trade of China"
Jung-pang Lo, "Chinese Shipping and East-West Trade from the Tenth to the Fourteenth Century," Sociétés et Compagnies de Commerce en Orient et dans l'Ocean Indien, pp. 167-176.
Wang, Gungwu, " 'Public' and 'Private' Overseas Trade in Chinese History," Sociétés et Compagnies..., pp. 215-226.

7. May 12 **Venetian Commerce/Technology**
McNeill, Venice, the Hinge of Europe, 1-100.

May 14 **The "Commercial Revolution"**
Lopez, The Commercial Revolution of the Middle Ages, 56-167.
Lopez, "European Merchants in the Medieval Indies"
Inalcik, "The Ottoman Empire and International Trade"

8. May 19, 21 **PAPER-WRITING WEEK. NO CLASSES.**

9. May 26 **Portuguese Commerce in the Indian Ocean**
Parry, The Establishment of the European Hegemony, 7-43.

May 28 **Dutch and English Companies**
Furber, Rival Empires of Trade in the Levant, 1-184.

10. June 2 **Asian Traders in the age of the European companies**
Curtin, Cross-Cultural Trade in World History, 158-206.
Boxer, "A Note on Portuguese Reactions to the Revival of the Red Sea Spice Trade and the Rise of Atjeh, 1540-1600"
Louise Sweet, "Pirates or Polities? Arab Societies of the Persian or Arabian Gulf," Ethnohistory 11 (1964), pp. 262-280.

June 4 **Summing Up**
Charles Issawi, "The Decline of Middle Eastern Trade, 1100-1850"

NEHIST 212

THE ORIENT TRADE from Roman Times to 1800

A. General Works

Boulnois, Luce, The Silk Road HD9926.C5B76
Curtin, Philip D., Cross-Cultural Trade in World History
De Somogyi, Joseph, A Short History of Oriental Trade HF3764.D46
Hicks, John, A Theory of Economic History HC26.H63
Polanyi, Karl, Trade and Market in the Early Empires HC31.P76
Simkin, C.G.F., The Traditional Trade of Asia HF3764.S58 (Harp)
Toussaint, Auguste, History of the Indian Ocean DS335.T73

B. The "Four Empires" Age (to ca. 300 A.D.)

Boulnois, pp. 1-117.
Charlesworth, M. P., "Roman Trade with India: A Resurvey," in P.R. Coleman-Norton (ed.), Studies in Roman Economic and Social History in Honor of Allan Chester Johnson, pp. 131-143. DG107.C7
Charlesworth, M. P., Trade and Trade-Routes of the Roman Empire, pp. 1-111. DG107.C5
Groom, Nigel, Frankincense and Myrrh HD9769.I533.A6740
Hourani, George F., "Did Roman Commercial Competition Ruin South Arabia?", JNES 11 (1952), pp. 291-295. DS41.J86 (RR5)
Hirth, Friedrich, China and the Roman Orient DS6.H67
Miller, J. Innes, The Spice Trade of the Roman Empire, 29 B.C.-A.D. 641 HD9210.R62M64 (Harp)
Rostovtzeff, Michael, Caravan Cities DS49.R83
Seligman, C. G., "The Roman Orient and the Far East," in Smithsonian Institution Annual Reports, 1938, pp. 547-567. Q11.S66
Simkin, pp. 1-48.
Tibbetts, G. R., "Pre-Islamic Arabia and Southeast Asia," Journal of the Malayan Branch of the Royal Asiatic Society 29 (1956), pp. 182-208. AS492.S65A18
Warmington, E. H., The Commerce between the Roman Empire and India, pp. 1-140. Nfa35.928W
Wheeler, R. E. Mortimer, Rome beyond the Imperial Frontiers, pp. 115-175. DG107.W56

Primary Sources in Translation:

Hirth, Friedrich, China and the Roman Orient DS6.H67
Isidore of Charax, Parthian Stations (transl. W. Schoff) PA4215.I4S8
Schoff, Wilfred H. (transl.), The Periplus of the Erythraean Sea HF386.P4
(Most other classical sources are found in RR5 reserve in the Loeb editions)

C. Medieval Commerce, ca. 300-1200 A.D.

Adelson, Howard L., Medieval Commerce, pp. 7-104. HF395.A23

Boulnois, pp. 118-176.

Cambridge Economic History, vol. 2 HC240.C2.vol. 2

Chaudhuri, K. N., Trade and Civilisation in the Indian Ocean. An Economic History from the Rise of Islam to 1750.

Chittick, N., "East African Trade with the Orient," in D. S. Richards (ed.), Islam and the Trade of Asia, pp. 97-104. HF3760.8.Z7A8.I8

Citarella, Armand O., "The Relations of Amalfi with the Arab World before the Crusades," Speculum 42 (1967), pp. 299-312. CB351.A1S7 (RR3)

Fischel, Walter J, "The region of the Persian Gulf and its Jewish Settlements in Islamic Times," Alexander Marx Jubilee Volume, pp. 203-230. BM40.M4J6

Goitein, S.D., "The Beginnings of the Karim Merchants and the Character of their Organization," in his Studies..., pp. 351-360. DS38.G6

______, "From Aden to India, Specimens of the Correspondence of India Traders of the Twelfth Century," JESHO 23 (1980), pp. 43-66. HC411.A1J8 (RR5)

______, "From the Mediterranean to India," Speculum 19 (1954), pp. 181-197. CB351.A1S7 (RR3)

______, "Letters and Documents on the India Trade in Medieval Times," in his Studies..., pp. 329-350. DS38.G6

______, Letters of Medieval Jewish Traders DS135.L6G62

______, "Medieval Tunisia: the Hub of the Mediterranean," in his Studies..., pp. 308-328. DS38.G6

______, Studies in Islamic History and Institutions DS38.G6

______, "Two eyewitness reports of an expedition of the king of Kish...," BSOAS 16 (1954), pp. 247-257. PJ3.L8 (RR5)

______, "The Unity of the Mediterranean World in the "Middle" Middle Ages," in his Studies..., pp. 296-307. DS38.G6

Hall, Kenneth, "International Trade and Foreign Diplomacy in early Medieval South India," JESHO 21 (1978), pp. 75-98 HC411.A1J8 (RR5)

Hall, Kenneth, Maritime Trade and State Development in Early Southeast Asia

Hodges, Richard, and David Whitehouse, Mohammed, Charlemagne, and the Origins of Europe 0000.000

Hourani, George F., Arab Seafaring in the Indian Ocean V45.H841

Hudson, G. F., "The Medieval Trade of China," in D.S. Richards (ed.), Islam and the Trade of Asia, pp. 159-167. HF3760.8.Z7.A818

van Leur, Jacob Cornelis, Indonesian Trade and Society, pp. 44-144 DS613.7.L6

Lewis, Bernard, "The Fatimids and the Route to India," Revue de la Faculte des Sciences Economiques de l'Universite d'Istanbul 11 (1949-50), pp. 50-54. HB1.I83

Lopez, Robert S., The Commercial Revolution of the Middle Ages, 950-1350 HF395.L848

______, "The Dollar of the Middle Ages," Journal of Economic History 11 (1951), pp. 209-234. HC10.J86

______, "European Merchants in the Medieval Indies," Journal of Economic History 3 (1943), pp. 164-184. HC10.J86

______, "Silk Industry in the Byzantine Empire," Speculum 20 (1945), pp. 1-42. CB351.A1S7 (RR3)

______, "The Trade of Medieval Europe: the South," Cambridge Economic History, volume 2, pp. 257-354. HC240.C2 vol. 2

McNeill, William H., Venice, the Hinge of Europe, 1081-1797. DG675.6.M19

Di Meglio, R. R., "Arab Trade with Indonesia and the Malay Peninsula from the 8th to the 16th Century," in D.S. Richards (ed.), Islam and the Trade of Asia, pp. 105-135. HF3760.8.Z7A8.18

Mookerji, Radhakumud, A History of Indian Shipping HE879.M82

Pirenne, Henri, Mohammed and Charlemagne D199.P67.1955

Prins, A.H.J., "The Persian Gulf Dhows," Persica 2 (1965-1966), pp. 1-18. DS251.P47

Richards, D. S. (ed.), Islam and the Trade of Asia HF3760.8.Z7A8.18

Runciman, Steven, "Byzantine Trade and Industry," Cambridge Economic History, volume 2, pp. 86-118. HC240.C2 vol. 2

Scanlon, George T., "A Note on Fatimid-Saljuq Trade," in D. S. Richards (ed.), Islamic Civilization, 950-1150 A.D., pp. 265-274. DS38.6.182

Simkin, pp. 49-180.

Sinor, Dennis, "The Historical Role of the Turk Empire," Journal of World History 1 (1953), pp. 427-434. CB3.C2

Spuler, Bertold, "Trade in the Eastern Islamic Countries in the early centuries," in D.S. Richards (ed.), Islam and the Trade of Asia, pp. 11-20. HF3760.8.Z7A8.18

Stern, S. M., "Ramisht of Siraf, a merchant millionaire of the twelfth century," JRAS 1967, pp. 10-14. AS122.L84 (RR5)

Stillman, Norman, "The Eleventh-century Merchant House of Ibn 'Awkal," JESHO 16 (1973), pp. 15-88. HC411.A1J8 (RR5)

Tibbetts, G. R., "Early Muslim Traders in South-East Asia," Journal of the Malaya Branch of the Royal Asiatic Society 30 (1957), pp. 1-45. AS492.S65A18

Udovitch, A. L., "Commercial Techniques in Early Medieval Islamic Trade," in D. S. Richards (ed.), Islam and the Trade of Asia, pp. 37-62. HF3760.8.Z7A8.18

Villiers, Alan, "Sailing with Sindbad's Sons," National Geographic Magazine 94.5 (November, 1948), pp. 675-688 G1.N27

Whitehouse, David, and Andrew Williamson, "Sasanian Maritime Trade," Iran 11 (1973), pp. 29-49. DS251.158

Williamson, Andrew, "Sohar and the sea trade of Oman in the tenth century A.D.," Proceedings of the Seminar for Arabian Studies 7 (1974), pp. 78-96.

Wolters, O. W., Early Indonesian Commerce, pp. 1-48, 71-85, 139-158. HF408.W86

Primary Sources in Translation:

Adelson, pp. 105-190.

Ahmad ibn Majid al-Najdi, Kitab al-fawa'id...(G. R. Tibbetts, Arab Navigation in the Indian Ocean before the Coming of the Portuguese) VK144.A294.1971

Chau Ju-kua, Chau-fan-chi ("His work on the Chinese and Arab Trade in the 12th and 13th centuries entitled Chau-fan-chi, translated by F. Hirth and W. W. Rockhill") HF408.C5.1970

Cosmas Indicopleustes, The Christian Topography of Cosmas... (transl. J. McCrindle) G161.H2.v.98

Lopez, Robert, and Irving W. Raymond, Medieval Trade in the Mediterranean World. Illustrative documents translated with introductions and notes. HF395.L85

D. Venice, The Mongols, and European Hegemony

Ashtor, Eliyahu, The Levant Trade in the Later Middle Ages
Boxer, C. R., Four Centuries of Portuguese Expansion JV 4211. B78. 1969
______, "A Note on Portuguese Reactions to the Revival of the Red Sea Spice Trade and the Rise of Atjeh," Journal of Southeast Asian History 10 (1969), pp. 415-428 DS 501. J 83
Cahen, Claude, Pre-Ottoman Turkey, pp. 163-168, 317-325. DR 481. C 171 (Harp)
Carswell, John, "China and Islam in the Maldive Islands," Transactions of the Oriental Ceramic Society (London), 1975-77, pp. 121-198. NK 3700. O 69
Chaudhuri, K. N., Trade and Civilisation in the Indian Ocean..., pp. 63-97.
Furber, Holden, Rival Empires of Trade in the Orient, 1600-1800 HF 481. F94
Inalcik, Halil, "Bursa and the Commerce of the Levant," Journal of the Economic and Social History of the Orient 3 (1960), pp. 131-147. HC 411. A1J8 (RR5)
______, "The Ottoman Empire and International Trade," in his The Ottoman Empire. The Age of Grandeur, 1300-1600, pp. 121-139. DR 486. I 35
Issawi, Charles, "The Decline of Middle Eastern Trade, 1100-1850," in D. S. Richards (ed.), Islam and the Trade of Asia, pp. 245-266. HF 3760. 8. Z7A8. 18
Lane, Frederic, "The Economic Meaning of War and Protection," in his Venice and its History, pp. 383-398. HC 307. V55L26
______, "The Mediterranean Spice Trade: its Revival in the Sixteenth Century," in his Venice and its History, pp. 25-34. HC 307. V55L26
______, "Venetian Shipping during the Commercial Revolution," in his Venice and its History, pp. 3-24. HC 307. V55L26
______, Venice and its History HC 307. V55L26
McNeill, William H., Venice, the Hinge of Europe, 1081-1797 DG 675. 6. M19
Meilink-Roelofsz, M.A.P., "Trade and Islam in the Malay-Indonesian Archipelago Prior to the Arrival of the Europeans," in Richards, Islam and the Trade of Asia, pp. 137-157.
Parry, John H., The Establishment of the European Hegemony, 1415-1715 JV 61. P259
Serjeant, Robert B., The Portuguese off the South Arabian Coast DS 247. A14S48
Simkin, pp. 127-180.
Steensgaard, Niels, The Asian Trade Revolution of the Seventeenth Century HF 495. S81. 1974

University of California, Davis
Dept. of Economics

Economy of the Middle East

Econ. 170

TuTh 2-3:30
Office Hours: Tu 10-11;
Th 4-5

The course will deal mostly with the post WW II period and will combine lectures with discussion. The requirements include a paper and a final. The paper will be due on Nov. 6 and the final will be on Th Dec. 12, 10:30 -12:30. A 5-page outline of the paper will be due on Oct. 24. The topic will be determined in consultation with me. The grade will be based on the paper and the final with equal weights.

The main reference will be my ECONOMIC AND POLITICAL CHANGE IN THE MIDDLE EAST, Pacific Books, 1987 (to be refered below as Tuma '87)

Other references will be listed below and put on reserve.
The following journals should be good supplements for data and analysis: Middle East Economic Digest (MEED); Internaltional Journal of Middle Eastern Studies (IJMES); Middle East Economic Survey (MEES); OPEC Bulletin.

I suggest that each student "adopt" one Middle Eastern country and build strong background with regard to that country. The recommended readings include items which you are asked to read selectively. This means you consult that reference regarding the general or theoretical issue under disucssion and those sections relating to your adopted country.

The course outline is as follows:

1. Course objectives, coverage, and methodology: A profile of the Middle East.
   Issawi, in U.S. Congress, 1980, p 7-24
   Eckaus, Ibid., p. 55-90
   Tuma, '87, ch. 1

2. The Socio-Political Context of Development:
   Tuma, '87 ch. 2
   Udovitch, 1976, ch. 5-7; slections by Burger, Vatikiotis, Kadourie;
   Hudson, ARAB POLITCS, ch. 1-3;
   Ajami, FOREIGN AFFAIRS, 57 (2) W '79;

Gendzier, MEJ 30, (4) ;
Harik, IJMES 3 (72) 303-23;
Lenczowski, FOREIGN AFFAIRS 57 (4) Sp.'79;
Waterbury and Mallakh, 1978, pp. 27-100;

3. The Demographic Context:
Tuma, '85, ch. 3;
Choucri, U.S. Congress, 1980, pp.25-54;
Lapham, MESA Bulletin, XI, 2, 1977, 1-28;

4. The Infrastructure Context:
Tuma, '85, 4 ch.;
Daret and Hartman, J. COMPARATIVE ADMINISTRATION,3(4) 1972, 405-434;
Waterbury, GOVERNMENT AND OPPOSITION, 11(4) 1976, 426-45;
Koenigsbergr, 1971, selectively;
Udovitch, 1976, ch. V (again);
Wohler-Scharf, '84, selectively;

5. Science and Technology Context:
Tuma, '85 ch. 5;
Clawson, et al., 1971, selectively;
Qubain, 1966, selectively;
El Ghannam, 1971, selectively;
Zahlan, 1970 and 1978, selectively;
Sardar, 1977, selectively;
U.S. House of Representatives, TECHNOLOGY TRANSFER , 1976;

6. Developments in Agriculture
Tuma, '85, ch. 6;
Clawson. et al., 1971, selectively;
Springborg, MEJ 31(1), Sp. 1977;
El Sherbini, 1979, selectively;
El Ghonemy, 1979;

7. Developments in Industry
Tuma, '85 , ch. 7;
MEED Special Reports on individual countries;
Wilson, 1979, selectively;
Finger,1971, selectively;
Tuma, MEJ 33(3) 1979;
Penrose, "Industrial Policy" in Kelidar, 1979;
Aliboni, 1979, selectively;

8. Developments in Trade
Tuma, '85, ch. 8;
Preston, 1970, selectively;
Wilson, 1977, ch. 3-6;
U.S. Congress, 1980, 247-81;
Musrey, 1969, selectively;
MEED Special Reports;

9. The Oil Factor
Tuma, '85 ch. 10;
U.S. Congress, 1980, [selection by David Curry and by Wald , 306-12
and 400-23 [to check pages]
El Serafy, J. ENERGY AND DEVELOPMENT IV(2) Sp. 1979
Jaidah, Ibid, ;
Anthony, 1975, selectivley,
Al Sowayegh, '84. selectively

10. The Prospects
Tuma, '85, ch. 9.
Contributions by students in general discussion.

University of California, Davis
Department of Economics
ECONOMICS 170

Fall 1985 Elias Tuma

REFERENCES

AJAMI, Fouad — "The End of Pan Arabism" Foreign Affairs 57, 2, Winter 1979.

CLAWSON, M., LANDSBERG, H., & ALEXANDER, L. — The Agricultural Potential of the Middle East, New York: American Elsevier Publishing Co., 1972.

DARET, Brenda & HARTMAN, Harritt — "On 'Proteksia' Orientations Toward the Use of Personal Influence in Israeli Bureaucracy" J. Comparative Administration 3(4) Feb. 1972.

EL-GHANNAM, M.A., Education — In the Arab region as viewed from the Marrakesh Conference, Unesco, 1971.

EL-GHONEMY, M. Riad — Agrarian Reform and Rural Development in the Near East, Rome: FAO, 1979.

EL-SERAFY, Salah — "The Oil Price Revolution of 1973-74" Journal of Energy and Development IV, #2, Spr. 1979.

EL-SHERBINI, A.A., ed., — Food Security Issues in the Arab Near East Pergamon Press, for ECWA, 1979.

FINGER, Nachum — The Impact of Government Subsidies on Industrial Management. The Israeli Experience. Praeger, 1971.

GENDZIER, Irene — "Psychology and Colonialism: Some Observations" Middle East Journal, 30, #4, 1976.

HARIK, Iliya F. — "The Ethnic Revolution and Political Integration in the Middle East" International Journal of Middle Eastern Studies 3, 1972.

HUDSON, Michael C. DS 62.4 H821 — Arab Politics: The Search for Legitimacy, New Haven: Yale University Press, 1977.

JAIDAH, Ali M. — "Downstream Operations and the Development of OPEC Member Countries," Journal of Energy and Development IV, #2, Spr. 1979.

KELIDAR, Abbas, ed., — The Integration of Iraq, London: Croom Helm, 1979.

KOENIGSBERGER, Otto H., et. al., — Infrastructure Problems of the Cities of Developing Countries, Ford Foundation, 1971.

LAPHAM, Robert J. — "Population Policies in the Middle East & North Africa" _Middle East Studies Association Bulletin_ XI, #2, 1977.

LENCZOWSKI, George — "The Arc of Crisis: Its Central Sector" _Foreign Affairs_ 57, 4, Spr. 1979.

MUSREY, Alfred G. — _An Arab Common Market_, Praeger, 1969.

PRESTON, Lee E. — _Trade Policies in the Middle East_, Washington: American Enterprise Institute, 1970.

QUBAIN, Fahim H. — _Education and Science in the Arab World_, Johns Hopkins Press, 1966.

SARDAR, Ziaddin — _Science, Technology, & Development in the Muslim World_, London: Croom Helm, 1977.

SPRINGBORG, Robert — "New Pattern of Agrarian Reform in the Middle East," _Middle East Journal_ 31, #1, Apr. 1977.

TUMA, E.H. — "Strategic Resources and Viable Interdependence: The Case of Middle Eastern Oil," _Middle East Journal_ 33, (3), 1979.

UDOVITCH, A.L., ed., — _The Middle East, Oil, Conflict, and Hope_. Lexington, 1976.

UPHOFF, Norman T. & ILCHMAN, Warren F., eds. — _The Political Economy of Development_, Berkeley: University of California Press, 1972.

U.S. Congress, Joint Economic Committee — _The Political Economy of the Middle East: 1973-78_, Washington, D.C.: U.S. Government Printer, April 1980.

U.S. House of Representatives, Committee on Science and Technology — _Technology Transfer to the Middle East OPEC Nations and Egypt_, Washington, Sept. 1976.

WATERBURY, John JA8 G6 — "Corruption, Political Stability & Dev.: Comp. Evidence from Egypt & Morocco" _Gov't. & Opposition_ 11(4) Aut. '76, 426-45.

WATERBURY, John & EL MALLAKH, Ragael HC 407.7 W371 — _The Middle East in the Coming Decade: From Wellhead to Wellbeing?_ New York: McGraw-Hill, 1978.

WHELAN, John — _The Rise of Arab Banks_, Beckenham Kent, UK: Croom Helm Ltd. Press, 1985.

WILSON, Rodney — _Trade & Investment in the Middle East_, New York: Holmes & Meier, 1977.

WILSON, Rodney — *The Economies of the Middle East*, New York: Holmes & Meier, 1979.

WILSON, Rodney — *Banking and Finance in the Arab Middle East*, New York: St. Martin's Press, 1983.

WOHLER-SCHARF, Traute — *Arab and Islamic Banks*, OECD, 1984.

ZAHLAN, A.B. — *Science & Higher Education in Israel*, Beirut: The Institute of Palestine Studies, 1970.

ZAHLAN, A.B., ed. — *Technology Transfer & Change in the Arab World*, Pergamon Press, for the U.N., 1978.

University of California, Davis
Department of Economics
ECONOMICS 170

Fall 1985 Elias Tuma

REFERENCES

AJAMI, Fouad — "The End of Pan Arabism" *Foreign Affairs* 57, 2, Winter 1979.

CLAWSON, M., LANDSBERG, H., & ALEXANDER, L. — *The Agricultural Potential of the Middle East*, New York: American Elsevier Publishing Co., 1972.

DARET, Brenda & HARTMAN, Harritt — "On 'Proteksia' Orientations Toward the Use of Personal Influence in Israeli Bureaucracy" *J. Comparative Administration* 3(4) Feb. 1972.

EL-GHANNAM, M.A., Education — *In the Arab region as viewed from the Marrakesh Conference*, Unesco, 1971.

EL-GHONEMY, M. Riad — *Agrarian Reform and Rural Development in the Near East*, Rome: FAO, 1979.

EL-SERAFY, Salah — "The Oil Price Revolution of 1973-74" *Journal of Energy and Development* IV, #2, Spr. 1979.

EL-SHERBINI, A.A., ed., — *Food Security Issues in the Arab Near East* Pergamon Press, for ECWA, 1979.

FINGER, Nachum — *The Impact of Government Subsidies on Industrial Management. The Israeli Experience*. Praeger, 1971.

GENDZIER, Irene — "Psychology and Colonialism: Some Observations" *Middle East Journal*, 30, #4, 1976.

HARIK, Iliya F. — "The Ethnic Revolution and Political Integration in the Middle East" *International Journal of Middle Eastern Studies* 3, 1972.

HUDSON, Michael C. DS 62.4 H821 — *Arab Politics: The Search for Legitimacy*, New Haven: Yale University Press, 1977.

JAIDAH, Ali M. — "Downstream Operations and the Development of OPEC Member Countries," *Journal of Energy and Development* IV, #2, Spr. 1979.

KELIDAR, Abbas, ed., — *The Integration of Iraq*, London: Croom Helm, 1979.

KOENIGSBERGER, Otto H., *et. al.*, — *Infrastructure Problems of the Cities of Developing Countries*, Ford Foundation, 1971.

LAPHAM, Robert J.	"Population Policies in the Middle East & North Africa" Middle East Studies Association Bulletin XI, #2, 1977.
LENCZOWSKI, George	"The Arc of Crisis: Its Central Sector" Foreign Affairs 57, 4, Spr. 1979.
MUSREY, Alfred G.	An Arab Common Market, Praeger, 1969.
PRESTON, Lee E.	Trade Policies in the Middle East, Washington: American Enterprise Institute, 1970.
QUBAIN, Fahim H.	Education and Science in the Arab World, Johns Hopkins Press, 1966.
SARDAR, Ziaddin	Science, Technology, & Development in the Muslim World, London: Croom Helm, 1977.
SPRINGBORG, Robert	"New Pattern of Agrarian Reform in the Middle East," Middle East Journal 31, #1, Apr. 1977.
TUMA, E.H.	"Strategic Resources and Viable Interdependence: The Case of Middle Eastern Oil," Middle East Journal 33, (3), 1979.
UDOVITCH, A.L., ed.,	The Middle East, Oil, Conflict, and Hope. Lexington, 1976.
UPHOFF, Norman T. & ILCHMAN, Warren F., eds.	The Political Economy of Development, Berkeley: University of California Press, 1972.
U.S. Congress, Joint Economic Committee	The Political Economy of the Middle East: 1973-78, Washington, D.C.: U.S. Government Printer, April 1980.
U.S. House of Representatives, Committee on Science and Technology	Technology Transfer to the Middle East OPEC Nations and Egypt, Washington, Sept. 1976.
WATERBURY, John JA8 G6	"Corruption, Political Stability & Dev.: Comp. Evidence from Egypt & Morocco" Gov't. & Opposition 11(4) Aut. '76, 426-45.
WATERBURY, John & EL MALLAKH, Ragael HC 407.7 W371	The Middle East in the Coming Decade: From Wellhead to Wellbeing? New York: McGraw-Hill, 1978.
WHELAN, John	The Rise of Arab Banks, Beckenham Kent, UK: Croom Helm Ltd. Press, 1985.
WILSON, Rodney	Trade & Investment in the Middle East, New York: Holmes & Meier, 1977.

WILSON, Rodney — The Economies of the Middle East, New York: Holmes & Meier, 1979.

WILSON, Rodney — Banking and Finance in the Arab Middle East, New York: St. Martin's Press, 1983.

WOHLER-SCHARF, Traute — Arab and Islamic Banks, OECD, 1984.

ZAHLAN, A.B. — Science & Higher Education in Israel, Beirut: The Institute of Palestine Studies, 1970.

ZAHLAN, A.B., ed. — Technology Transfer & Change in the Arab World, Pergamon Press, for the U.N., 1978.

NEHist 382

EARLY ARABIC HISTORIOGRAPHY

Week I. Organizational Meeting.

Week II. General Overview.

Reading: Look at/handle Carl Brockelmann, Geschichte der arabischen Litteratur (PJ 7510 .B85 in RR5).
Look at/handle Fuat Sezgin, Geschichte des arabischen Schrifttums (PJ 7510 .S52 in RR5, also in Oriental Institute Archives).
Read H.A.R. Gibb, "Ta'rikh," in EI (1), Supplement.
Read A. A. Duri, The Rise of Historical Writing among the Arabs, transl. L. Conrad (Princeton, 1983).
Read Nabia Abbott, Studies in Arabic Literary Papyri, I: Historical Texts (Chicago, 1957), introduction only (PJ 7595 .A2 vol. I, also in OI).
Skim Franz Rosenthal, The Technique and Approach of Muslim Scholarship (Rome, 1947) (DS 38 .R78).

Week III. Early Critiques of Legal and Historical Sources.

Reading: Ignaz Goldziher, Muslim Studies (London, 1967), vol. 2, pp. 17-251 on hadith (BP25 .G601 vol. 2; also in OI)
Joseph Schacht, The Origins of Muhammadan Jurisprudence (Oxford, 1956) (DS39 .S3)
Julius Wellhausen, Prolegomena zur altesten Geschichte des Islams (Berlin, 1899) (= Skizzen und Vorarbeiten vol. 6, part 1) (DS42 .5 .W45).

Week IV. Recent Skeptical Writings.

Reading: Patricia Crone and Michael Cook, Hagarism (Cambridge, 1977), chapters 1 and 2 (BP55 .C92).
Patricia Crone, Slaves on Horses (Cambridge, 1980), chapter 1 (DS38 .5 .C760).
John Wansbrough, The Sectarian Milieu (Oxford, 1978) (BP191 .W25).

Week V. Isnads.

Reading: Sezgin, GAS I, introduction to chapter on hadith.
Look again at Schacht, Origins, pp. 138-159.
Joseph Schacht, "A Revaluation of Islamic Traditions," Journal of the Royal Asiatic Society (1949), pp. 143-154 (AS122 .L84 in RR5).
Josef Horovitz, "Alter und Ursprung des isnad," Der Islam 8 (1918), pp. 39-47 (YH 3405, or BP1 .I8 in RR5).
G. H. A. Juynboll, "The Date of the Great Fitna," Arabica 20 (1973), pp. 142-159 (YJ 1761).
J. Robson, "Al-Djarh wa l-ta'dil," EI (2) (BP40 .E61 in RR5, also in OI).
J.M.B. Jones, "Ibn Ishaq and al-Waqidi," BSOAS 22 (1959), pp. 41-51 (YJ 1763).
Donald R. Hill, The Termination of Hostilities in the Arab Conquests (London, 1971) (DS38 .1 .H64).

Week VI. Form Criticism and Chronology Problems.

Reading: Klaus Koch, The Growth of the Biblical Tradition (New York, 1969) (BS486 .K763).

Albrecht Noth, Quellenkritische Studien zu Formen, Themen, und Tendenzen fruhislamischen Geschichtsuberlieferung (Bonn, 1973) (DS38 .16 .N9).

Fred M. Donner, The Early Islamic Conquests (Princeton, 1981), pp. 111-142 (DS38 .1 .D660, also in OI).

J.M.B. Jones, "The Chronology of the Maghazi," BSOAS 19 (1957), pp. 245-280 (YJ 1762).

Week VII. Tribal Materials and Oral Tradition.

Reading: Werner Caskel, "Aijam al-'Arab--Studien zur altarabischen Epik," Islamica 3, fascicule 5 (Erganzungsheft), pp. 1-99 (1930) (YC 3325).

Eugen Mittwoch, "Aiyam al-'Arab," EI (1).

August Fischer, "Kais-'Aylan," EI (1).

Egbert Meyer, Der historische Gehalt der Aiyam al-'Arab (Wiesbaden, 1970) (DS231 .M61).

Fred M. Donner, "The Bakr b. Wa'il Tribes and Politics in Northeastern Arabia on the Eve of Islam," Studia Islamica 51 (1980), pp. 5-38 (YD 2552).

Jan Vansina, Oral Tradition. A Study in Historical Methodology (Chicago, 1965) (D16. V27).

Week VIII. The Sira and Religious Materials.

Reading: Rudolf Sellheim, "Prophet, Chalif, und Geschichte," Oriens 18-19 (1965-66), pp. 33-91 (YS 4650).

Franz Rosenthal, "The Influence of the Biblical Tradition on Muslim Historiography," in Bernard Lewis and Peter M. Holt (eds.), Historians of the Middle East (London, 1962) (DS32 .5 .L84 vol. 4).

W. Montgomery Watt, "The Materials used by Ibn Ishaq," in Lewis and Holt, pp. 23-34.

P. Jensen, "Das Leben Muhammeds und die David-Sage," Der Islam 12 (1922), pp. 84-97 (YJ 1764).

C. H. Becker, "Prinzipielles zu Lammens' Sirastudien," Der Islam 4 (1913), pp. 263-269 (YB 4680).

Islamic Spain, North Africa and Sicily

Peter von Sivers

SYLLABUS

(1) Description of the Course

During the classical Islamic period (c. 600-1500 AD) the area comprising Spain, North Africa and Sicily was known under the name of "Maghrib" (West) and as such developed a distinct historical identity, setting it apart from the experience of historical evolution in the "Mashriq" (East). This course deals with the history of western Islamic lands and the territories adjacent to these lands in West Africa and Europe.

The purpose of the course is to introduce you to a civilization which displayed singular political power and cultural achievement. Like Christianity, the great adversary of Islam during this period, it was founded on revealed religion and Greek philosophy. But unlike Christianity, whose western portion experienced a painful transition from the sophistication of the Roman empire to the rustication of the Germanic kingdoms, western Islamic countries displayed from an early date onwards a high level of complexity. During the time from the seventh to the thirteenth centuries when Christian Europe had barely begun to recover from economic recession and political decentralization the western Islamic states were affluent and cosmopolitan. A sequence of powerful empires came into existence, that is, the Umayyad, Fatimid, Almoravid and Almohad realms, all of which encouraged trade and, in varying degrees, agricultural development and urbanization. The growing of oranges, rice, sugar cane and silk worms go back to the skills which farmers cultivated during the time of these empires, as does the manufacturing of steel and paper. The swords of Toledo were eagerly sought after by the knights of Europe and Arab horses and Merino wool played an important part in medieval economy. Living standards in tenth century Cordoba were far above those of Venice or Pisa in Italy, the leading Christian cities at that time. Muslim merchants traveled regularly back and forth to Cairo, India and across the Sahara. A brisk trade of West African gold and Indian spices formed the basis for considerable fortunes. In the field of culture the Christian world owes its rediscovery of the writings of Aristotle to Muslim philosophers, especially Ibn Rushd (Averroes) and a large number of scientific works in Arabic found their way to Europe through Jewish translators in Spain and Sicily. Altogether, western Islam was one of the most developed areas of the world during the period from c. 600 to 1500 and exerted a decisive and stimulating influence on Europe.

This course will be comparative in its approach and frequent references to Spanish, Portuguese, French, Italian and West African history will be necessary in order to put the history of western Islam into proper focus. The nature of the course as a lecture survey, however, limits the materials which can be profitably analyzed in class. Therefore the emphasis in the lectures will be on social, economic and cultural developments rather than a detailed enumeration of political, dynastic or military events. You are expected to familiarize yourself with a basic outline of these latter events through the readings assigned for this course.

(2) Requirements

(a) For a variety of historical reasons the number of English speaking scholars who have done research on western Islam has remained small. Therefore good basic texts are either absent or available only intermittently. The little that exists can be consulted in the reserve section of Marriott Library. Since I find work with books on reserve cumbersome and frustrating I have decided to make a term paper the basic requirement of this course. By doing such a paper, of about 20 pages, on a topic of your choice you will be able to check out all necessary materials and engage in specialized research on a subject which allows you to acquire in depth knowledge at least in one area of western Islamic history. This term paper is due by Thursday of exam week. During the quarter I expect frequent consultations and I will not accept any paper that has not been discussed with me prior to submission.

(b) For each week specific readings have been assigned and you should make a strenuous effort to keep up with these readings. Only if you are current with your readings will you be able to fully absorb and remember what I present in the lectures. Two short (15 minute) exams are scheduled to ensure that you do your reading assignments. I shall announce the dates of these exams one week ahead of time.

(c) There will be a midterm at a date also announced well ahead of time. This midterm will cover all reading and class materials up to the time of the examination.

(d) The term paper will be worth 50 percent of the grade, the midterm 30 and the short exams 10 each.

(e) Should you be unable, for some grave reason, to take the exams on the scheduled dates I expect notification prior to the date of the exam.

(f) You are encouraged to ask questions of make contributions to the materials discussed in class. Lectures and dialogues should alternate as much as possible.

(g) In the course of the quarter I would like very much to see each of you personally and discuss any individual problems you might have with the course, its content and its handling. My office is in Carlson Hall and I can be called there or at home during the day and evening.

(3) Lecture Schedule

Part I: The Emergence of Western Islam (642-827)
- Week 1 - General Introduction: The Origins of the Islamic Community
- Week 2 - The Era of Conquest: North Africa and Spain
- Week 3 - The Arabization of Berber Society
- Week 4 - Early Autonomy in the Maghrib

Part II: The Imperial Period of Maghribi History (827-1212)
- Week 5 - The Aghlabid and Fatimid Realms
- Week 6 - The Umayyad Caliphate of Spain
- Week 7 - The Almoravids
- Week 8 - The Almohads

Part III: Christian Ascendancy and Islamic Defense (1212-1500)
Week 9 - The Almohad Successor States
Week 10 - Thirteenth and Fourtheenth Century Culture
Week 11 - Iberian Expansion against Western Muslims; Conclusion

(4) Reading Assignments

I shall pass out a detailed list of weekly reading assignments corresponding to the above lecture schedule during the first week of classes.

(5) Bibliography

The following selected bibliography contains the most important studies on western Islamic history and culture, regardless of the language in which they are written. The books by Laroui, Ahmad, Watt, Burckhardt and Ibn Khaldun which are on reserve are not included in this bibliography.

The bibliography is designed to give you a general idea of what is available on a given topic that you might be interested in for your term paper. I shall pass out a list with suggested paper topics during the first week of classes. If you are interested in a topic other than one taken from the list of suggestions you are most welcome to discuss it with me.

Literature (books, articles) beyond this bibliography can be found in the Index Islamicus (Marriott Library, Middle East Section on fifth floor, book table at far end to the right after entering), in the bibliographies published by Heggoy and Lawless, and at the end of Julien (on reserve).

General and Period from 642 to 1212
Abun-Nasr, Jamil, A History of the Maghrib (Cambridge, 1971);
Barbour, Nevill, Morocco (London, 1965);
Bosch Vilà, Jacinto, Los Almoravides (Tetuán, 1956);
Bovill, E.W., The Golden Trade of the Moors (London, 1968);
Brignon, Jean and others, Histoire du Maroc (Casablanca, 1967);
Diehl, CharlesH., L'Afrique byzantine (New York, reprint, 1968);
Eickhoff, Ekkehard, Seekrieg und Seepolitik zwischen Islam und Abendland (Berlin, 1966);
Holt, Peter M. and others, eds., The Cambridge History of Islam, vol. 2 (Cambridge, 1970);
Hopkins, J.F.P., Medieval Muslim Government in Barbary (London, 1958);
Huici Miranda, Ambrosio, Historia politica del imperio Almohade (Tetuán, 1956-57);
Idris, Hady R., La Berberie orientale sous les Zirides (Paris, 1962);
Levtzion, Nehmeia, Ancient Ghana and Mali (London, 1973);
Mauny, Raymond, Tableau géographique de l'Ouest africain au Moyen Age (Dakar, 1961);
Robert, D.S. and J. Devisse, Tegdaoust I. Recherches sur Aoudaghost (Paris, 1970);

Muslim Spain, Portugal and Sicily
Arié, Rachel,
Amari, Michele, Storia dei musulmani di Sicilia (Rome, reprint, 1933-39);
Dufourq, Charles-Emmanuel, L'Espagne catalane et le Maghreb (Paris, 1966);
Lévi-Provençal, Evariste, Histoire de l'Espagne musulmane (Paris, 1944-53);

Lèvi-Provençal, Evariste, L'Espagne musulmane au Xe siècle (Paris, 1932);
Livermore, H.V., The Origins of Spain and Portugal (London, 1971);
Luzatto, Gino, An Economic History of Italy (New York, 1961);
Menendez Pidal, Ramòn, The Cid and His Spain (London, 1934);
Vicens Vives, Jaime, An Economic History of Spain (Princeton, 1966);

Period from 1212 to 1600

Barbour, Nevill, "North Africa", in Bertold Spuler, ed., The Muslim World: A Historical Survey, vol. 3 (Leiden, 1969);
Bradford, Ernle, The Sultan's Admiral: The Life of Barbarossa (London, 1970);
Earle, Peter, Corsairs of Malta and Barbary (London, 1970);
Geertz, Clifford, Islam Observed (New Haven, Conn., 1968);
Monlaü, Jean, Les Etats barbaresques (Paris, 1964);

Islamic Art and Architecture

Bargebuhr, Frederick P., The Alhambra (Berlin, 1968);
Hill, Derek, Islamic Architecture in North Africa (Hamden, Conn., 1976);
Hoag, J., Western Islamic Architecture (New York, 1963);
Kuehnel, Ernst, Maurische Kunst (Berlin, 1924);
Marçais, Georges, L'architecture musulmane d'Occident (Paris, 1924).

History 472 **THE OTTOMAN EMPIRE AND OTHER MUSLIM STATES** Dr. Goldschmidt

Schedule of Classes and Reading Assignments (fall 1986)

This course will, I hope, be taught in a way that will maximize the learning experience of students who are developing a serious commitment to the use of their minds and to the study of Middle East history. It is not a course for the faint-hearted, nor will it be a rehash of History 181, a course that most of you have taken, as it is the prerequisite stated in the catalog. Most of you who have not will have taken other Middle East courses. If you have not, and if you do not feel ready for a challenging course amid high-powered classmates, consider replacing History 472 with something else. Now, while drop-add is free and before you buy the books.

The readings will often demand much time and attention. Class time will be devoted to discussing both the primary and secondary historical source materials. I will give brief, impromptu lectures when I think that you need my help to grasp an historical problem, or to answer your questions, which are always welcome. The best time to take notes is when you do the reading assignments, not during class (past students have objected when I told them to listen and not take notes, so I warn you now). I expect you to complete the assignments by the dates on which they are due to be discussed and may direct questions about the readings to individuals. Class attendance and substantive participation in discussion will count 25% of your grade, as will your independent study project, your midterm, and the final examination. If you know that you will miss a class, please call ahead (863-0086) to tell me so. Also if you know you will be coming late.

In the midterm and final examination, each student may choose whether to do the take-home exercise (normally handed out in the class preceding the test) or to take a "group oral" exam, usually involving 3-4 students, to be held at a mutually acceptable time and place. Requests for make-ups or time extensions will be granted under extraordinary and extenuating circumstances. Every student must do at least one thing in writing.

One condition that tends to promote learning is a sense of asabiyah (group solidarity) among the members of the class. I will try to build it by addressing you by name; circulating a sheet to collect and circulate your names, addresses, and phone numbers reasonably early in the term; and finding ways of bringing you together socially if other demands on my time and energy don't overwhelm me. If you wish, you may choose a facilitator from among yourselves to convene such a gathering. Good rapport with your instructor also helps the learning process. I will try to meet with you as individuals or small groups at mutually convenient times and places. You, too, may take the initiative. My office, 614 Liberal Arts (Oswald) Tower, is where you can find me every MW 2-3:15 PM and Th 8:30-9:30 AM, unless I announce otherwise. You may call my home (237-3517) at times other than 6:30-7 PM or after 10 PM. If I'm out when you call, leave your name with my wife, son, or answering machine, letting her/him/it know whether, how, and when you want me to call you back. You can also leave notes on the message board affixed to my office door, or in my mailbox in 615 LAT.

Buy The Ottoman Centuries and the Middle East Studies Handbook. I have photocopied anything typed on this syllabus in boldface; everything also is on reserve in the ground floor of West Pattee Library.

Here, at last, is the syllabus:

27 August	INTRODUCTION TO THIS COURSE
29	STUDYING THE MIDDLE EAST DURING THE ERA OF TURKISH RULE **Kelly, Islam, ch. 5** **Kritzeck, pp. 261-266; Lewis, Islam, II, 278-284**
3 September	THE EARLIEST TURKISH EMPIRES Setton, History of the Crusades, I, ch. v or Saunders, History of the Mongol Conquests, chs. 1-2 or Kwanten, Imperial Nomads, chs. 1-2 [no primary source assignment; meet me in 614 LA Tower to discuss your independent study project]
5	THE TRANSITION FROM EARLY TURKS TO MONGOLS Saunders, ch. 3; or Kwanten, chs. 3-4 **Lewis, Islam, I, 68-76** [See me in my office about your project, if you have not already done so]
8	CHINGIS KHAN Saunders, ch. 4; or Kwanten, skim ch. 5, read pp. 105-124 **Spuler, History of the Mongols, pp. 17-45**
10	THE MONGOL EMPIRE UNDER CHINGIS' SUCCESSORS Saunders, ch. 5; or Kwanten, pp. 124-140; or Setton, II, ch. xxi **Spuler, pp. 45-64**
12	THE MONGOL EMPIRE'S RELATIONS WITH CHRISTENDOM AND ISLAM Saunders, chs. 6-7; or Kwanten, ch. 7 **Spuler, pp. 64-114**
15	THE DECLINE OF THE MONGOLS Saunders, chs. 8 & 10; or Kwanten, chs. 9-11 **Spuler, pp. 115-161**
17	LIBRARY ORIENTATION **Map due** You are required to attend this meeting, to be held in the lecture room of the Reference Dep't, 1st floor E. Pattee.
19	MAMLUK EGYPT AND SYRIA Setton, Crusades, II, ch. xxii; or III, ch. xiv; **or Cambridge History of Islam, I, 201-230** **Lewis, pp. 97-100; Kritzeck, pp. 298-336**
22	INTRODUCTION TO THE LATER MUSLIM EMPIRES **Kelly, Islam, ch. 6** **Kritzeck, pp. 274-284**
24	THE ORIGIN OF THE OTTOMAN TURKS Kinross, Ottoman Centuries, pp. 15-43 **Gibbons, Foundations of the Ottoman Empire, pp. 19-24** **Travels of Ibn Battuta, II, 448-457**

26	THE RISE OF THE OTTOMANS TO POWER Kinross, pp. 45-79 **Lewis, <u>Islam</u>, I, 135-144**
29	MEHMED THE CONQUEROR Kinross, pp. 83-158 **Lewis, <u>Islam</u>, I, 144-148;** Saunders, <u>Eve</u>, 22-26, 95-99
1 October	**Progress Reports on Independent Study Projects** Submit preliminary list of primary & secondary sources
3	SULEYMAN THE MAGNIFICENT: I Kinross, pp. 161-215 Saunders, <u>Eve</u>, 20-22, 99-103
6	SULEYMAN THE MAGNIFICENT: II Kinross, pp. 215-255 Saunders, <u>Eve</u>, pp. 103-105; Vucinich, pp. 127-130, 143-147
8	SEEDS OF OTTOMAN DECLINE: I Kinross, pp. 259-318 **Kritzeck, pp. 352-360**
10	SEEDS OF OTTOMAN DECLINE: II Kinross, pp. 319-357 **Kritzeck, pp. 361-365**
13	THE OTTOMAN EMPIRE IN THE 18TH CENTURY Kinross, pp. 361-413 Saunders, <u>Eve</u>, pp. 124-127; or Vucinich, pp. 151-153; or **Landen, <u>Emergence</u>, pp. 16-21** [Students observing Yom Kippur are excused from attending this class, but should arrange to meet me at another time to discuss the readings]
15	OTTOMAN CULTURE AND GENERAL REVIEW **R. Lewis, <u>Everyday Life in Ottoman Turkey</u>, chs. 4-5; or** **B. Lewis, <u>Istanbul</u>, chs. v-vi** **<u>Selected Letters of Lady Mary Wortley Montagu</u>, pp. 90-99**
17	Class cancelled due to MIDTERM EXAMINATION and the annual meeting of Middle East Institute in Washington, DC (17-18 October 1986). If you wish to accompany me there, try to take a group oral exam some time before we leave Thursday.
20	OTTOMAN AND SAFAVID SLIDE ORGY Take-home examinations are due at 12:20 PM
22	SAFAVID IRAN **<u>Cambridge History of Islam</u>, I, iii, 5 or** <u>Cambridge History of Iran</u>, VI, pp. 189-372 Saunders, <u>Eve</u>, pp. 31-47

24	IRAN UNDER NADER SHAH AND THE QAJARS **Cambridge History of Islam, I, iii, 6** **or Keddie, Scholars, chs. 8-9** **Landen, pp. 13-16, 76-91**
27	BACKGROUND TO MODERN EGYPT **Goldschmidt, Modern Egypt, ch. 1** no primary source assignment
29	BEGINNINGS OF OTTOMAN WESTERNIZATION Kinross, pp. 417-436 **Landen, pp. 29-33**
31	MAHMUD II Kinross, pp. 437-471 **Landen, pp. 33-38**
3 November	THE TANZIMAT ERA **Kinross, pp. 471-499; and Keddie, ch. 2** **Landen, pp. 38-46**
5	THE NEW OTTOMANS AND THE 1876 CONSTITUTION Kinross, pp. 501-530 **Landen, pp. 94-106**
7	**Progress Reports on Independent Study Projects** Submit detailed outline of paper
10	EARLY WESTERNIZATION IN EGYPT AND SYRIA **Goldschmidt, ch. 2** **al-Jabarti's Chronicle, pp. 40-42** **Landen, pp. 46-62**
12	FROM MEHMET ALI TO ISMA'IL IN EGYPT **Goldschmidt, ch. 3** **Landen, pp. 65-75**
14	THE URABI REVOLUTION AND THE BRITISH OCCUPATION **Goldschmidt, ch. 4** **Landen, pp. 154-163**
17	EUROPEAN IMPERIALISM AND THE MUSLIM REACTION **Kelly, chs. 7-8** **Landen, pp. 106-109**
19	BEGINNINGS OF NATIONALISM IN THE ARAB EAST **Hourani, chs. 3-4** **Abu-Lughod, Arab Rediscovery of Europe, pp. 98-101** **Keddie (ed.), Islamic Response to Imperialism, pp. 123-129**
21	**Class cancelled due to annual meeting of Middle East Studies Association in Boston (20-23 November 1986). Let me know if you wish to accompany me there.**

24	EGYPTIAN NATIONALISM **Goldschmidt, ch. 5; Hourani, ch. 8** **Landen, pp. 110-116**

This class will not meet on Wednesday and Friday, 26-28 November, due to Thanksgiving vacation.

1 December	ABDULHAMID II Kinross, pp. 533-581 Vucinich, pp. 130-135; **Landen, 178-180**
3	THE YOUNG TURKS Kinross, pp. 583-609 **Landen, pp. 117-125, 187-191**
5	EARLY ARAB NATIONALISM **Hourani, pp. 260-283** Haim, Arab Nationalism, nos. 2-5
8	THE DEVELOPMENT OF ARAB NATIONALISM **Hourani, pp. 283-307** Haim, nos. 1 & 6; **Landen, pp. 125-126**
10	WORLD WAR I AND THE BEGINNINGS OF THE PALESTINE QUESTION **Landen, pp. 192-197; INDEPENDENT STUDY PROJECT DUE**
12	SUMMATION AND REVIEW Kinross, pp. 615-622

FINAL EXAMINATION (each student may choose between the take-home exercise and a group oral exam, to take place during the final examination period)

NEW YORK INSTITUTE OF TECHNOLOGY
(Dept. of Soc. & Pol. Sci.)

Prof. A. J. Abraham
(212 399-837/Rm. 401 B)

Hist. of Modern Lebanon

This course will survey the history of modern Lebanon from the great Ottoman conquest to the present. The intended audience for the course is college-wide; and there is no prerequisite.

Course requirements include a term paper and a comprehensive final exam. Reading assignments will be selected from the required and reserved texts as well as the reading list.

Required Texts:

Abraham, A.J., Lebanon at Mid-Century, Maronite-Druze Relations in Lebanon 1940-1860: A Prelude to Arab Nationalism, Wash.: Univ. Press of America, 1981.

____________, Lebanon: A State of Siege (1975-1984), IN.: Wyndham Hall Press, 1984.

Salibi, K.S., The Modern History of Lebanon, Conn.: Greenwood Press, 1965.

On Reserve (for background information):

Hitti, P.K., Lebanon in History, N.Y.: St. Martin's Press, 1957.

Holt, P.M., Egypt and the Fertile Crescent, 1516-1922, N.Y.: Longmans Green & Co., 1966.

COURSE OUTLINE

1. Introduction: Christianity and Islam in the Lebanon, co-existance and co-operation.
2. In the Porte's embrace: The Ottoman conquest of the Near East (1516); and the Lebanese province of the Turkish Empire.
3. The rise of the Mani dynasty: The first attempt at independence

from the Porte undertaken by Fakhr al-Din al-Mani II.

4. The Shihabi era: Neutral Lebanon (Shihabi domestic and foreign policy).
5. The Maronite-Druze Civil Wars of the ninteenth century.
6. The Mutasarrifiyah of Jabal Lubnan: Five power rule and the origins of the Confessional System.
7. W.W. I and the Mandate system: French rule in Lebanon and the origins of the Lebanese Formula.
8. Independence, the National Pact, and the rise of modern political parties.
9. Modernization through human resource development: The success story of the Maronite community and its neighbors.
10. Crisis and Accomodation: The 1958 altercation and the PLO presence in Lebanon.
11. The Civil War and its aftermath (1975-present).
12. Term papers (discussion).
13. Comp. Final Exam (2 hr.).

A. J. Abraham

READING LIST

HISTORY OF MODERN LEBANON

GENERAL:

Hitti, P.K., Lebanon in History, N.Y.: St. Martin's Press, 1957.

Holt, P.M., Egypt and The Fertile Crescent, 1516-1922, N.Y.: Longmans Green & Co., 1966.

Salibi, K.S., The Modern History of Lebanon, Conn.: Greenwood Press, 1965.

Tibawi, A.L., A Modern History of Syria, N.Y.: St. Martin's Press, 1969.

Introduction:

Abraham, A.J., Islam and Christianity: Crossroads in Faith, IN.: Wyndham Hall Press, 1986.

Dib, Rev. Pierre, History of The Maronite Church, Wash.: The Maronite Seminary.

Hitti, P.K., Lebanon in History, N.Y.: St. Martin's Press, 1957.

__________, Origins of The Druze People And Religion, N.Y.: AMS Press, 1966.

In the Porte's embrace:

Holt, P.M., Egypt and The Fertile Crescent, 1516-1922, N.Y.: Longmans Green & Co., 1966.

The Mani dynasty/ the Shihabi era:

Harik, I.F., Politics And Change in a Traditional Society, Lebanon, 1711-1845, N.J.: Princeton Univ. Press, 1968.

Polk, W.R., The Opening of South Lebanon, 1788-1840, Mass.: Harvard Univ. Press, 1963.

The Maronite-Druze Civil Wars of the nineteenth century:

Abraham, A.J., Lebanon at Mid-Century, Maronite-Druze Relations in Lebanon, 1840-1860: A Prelude to Arab Nationalism, Wash.: Univ. Press of America, 1981.

The Mutasarrifiyah of Mount Lebanon:

Spagnolo, J.P., France and Ottoman Lebanon, 1861-1914, London: Ithaca Press, 1977.

World War I and the French Mandate:

Abouchdid, E.E., Thirty Years of Lebanon and Syria (1917-1947), Beirut: Sader Rihani Pub. Co., 1948.

Hourani, A.H., Syria and Lebanon: A Political Essay, London: Oxford Univ. Press, 1946.

Longrigg, S.H., Syria And Lebanon Under French Mandate, N.Y.: Oxford Univ. Press, 1958.

Modern Politics/Modernization:

Binder, L. (ed.), Politics in Lebanon, N.Y.: John Wiley, 1966.

Entelis, J.P., Pluralism and Party Transformation in Lebanon: al-Kata'ib 1936-1970, Lieden Brill, 1974.

Hudson, M.C., The Precarious Republic: Political Modernization in Lebanon, N.Y.: Random House, 1968.

Salem, E.A., Modernization Without Revolution: Lebanon's Experience, Bloomington: Indiana Univ. Press, 1973.

Sayigh, Y.A., Entreprereurs of Lebanon: The Role of The Business Leader in a Developing Economy, Mass.: Harvard Press, 1962.

Suleiman, M.W., Political Parties in Lebanon: The Challenge of a Fragmented Political Culture, N.Y.: Cornell Univ. Press, 1967.

Crisis and Accomodation:

Agwani, M.S. (ed.), The Lebanese Crisis, 1958: A Documentary Study, N.Y.: Asia Pub. House, 1967.

Khoury, E.M., The Crisis in The Lebanese System: Confessionalism and Chaos, Wash.: Amer. Enterprise Instit., 1976.

__________, The Operational Ability of The Lebanese Political System, Beirut: Catholic Press, 1972.

Meo, L.M.T., Lebanon, Improbable Nation, Conn.: Greenwood Press, 1965.

Qubain, F.I., Crisis in Lebanon, Wash.: Middle East Institute, 1958.

Stewart, D., Trouble in Beirut, London: Wingate, 1959.

The Lebanese Civil War (1975-   ):

Abraham, A.J., Lebanon: A State of Siege (1975-1984), IN.: Wyndham Hall Press, 1984.

Ajami, F., The Vanished Imam, Musa Sadr and the Shia of Lebanon,

Azar, E.E. (ed.), Lebanon And The World In The 1980's, Md.: Univ. of Maryland Press, 1983.

Ball, G.W., error and betrayal in Lebanon, Foundation for Middle East Peace, 1984.

Barakat,H., Lebanon in Strife: Student Preludes to Civil War, Austin: Univ. of Texas Press, 1977.

Cobban, H., The Making of Lebanon, Colorado: Westview Press, 1985.

Deeb, M.K., The Lebanese Civil War, N.Y.: Praeger, 1980.

Gabriel, P.L., In the ashes, Penn.: Whitmore Pub. Co., 1978.

Gemayel, A., peace and unity, Gt. Brit.: Colin Smyth, 1984.

Gilmour, D., Lebanon, The Fractured Country, N.Y.: St. Martin's Press, 1984.

Gordon, D.C., Lebanon: The Fragmented Nation, CA.: Hoover Instit. Press, 1980.

______, The Republic of Lebanon, Nation in Jeopardy, Colorado: Westview Press, 1983.

Haley, P.E. & Snider, L.W., Lebanon in Crisis: Participants And Issues, N.Y.: Syracuse Univ. Press, 1979.

Joumblatt, K., I Speak For Lebanon, London: Zed Press, 1982.

Khalidi, W., Conflict And Violence In Lebanon; Confrontation In The Middle East, MA.: Harvard Univ., Center for Int'l. Affairs, 1979.

Mallison S.V. & Mallison, W.T., Armed Conflict in Lebanon, Wash.: Amer. Educational Trust, 1983.

Owen, R. (ed.), Essays on the Crisis in Lebanon, London: Ithaca Press, 1976.

Odeh, B.J., Lebanon: Dynamics of Conflict,

________, Class And Confessionalism, A Modern Political History, London: Zed Press, 1984.

Petran, T., The Struggle Over Lebanon,N.Y.: Monthly Review Press,1985.

Rabinovich, I., The War For Lebanon, N.Y.: Cornell Univ. Press, 1984.

Randal, J.C., Going All The Way: Christian Warlords, Israeli Adventurers, And The War in Lebanon, N.Y.: Vintage Books, 1983.

Sahliyah, E., The Lebanon War: Implications For the PLO, Colorado: Westview Press, 1985.

Salibi, K.S., Crossroads to Civil War: Lebanon 1958-1976, N.Y.: Caravan Books, 1976.

Schiff, Z. & Yaari, E., Israel's Lebanon War, N.Y.: Simon and Schuster, 1984.

Timerman, J., The Longest War, Israel in Lebanon, N.Y.: Alfred A. Knopf, 1982.

Vocke, H., The Lebanese War, N.Y.: St. Martin's Press, 1978

HISTORY 288

PALESTINE AND THE ARAB-ISRAELI CONFLICT

Joel Beinin
History Corner, Room 326
Office hours: Tuesday 2:00-4:00

Autumn 1986
Wednesday
2:15-4:05

Week 1: Introduction to the Course (Oct. 1)

Reading
BEFORE THE FIRST MEETING OF CLASS
Sarah Graham-Brown, Palestinians and Their Society, 1880-1946, pp. 1-30 and browse through the photos.

Questions
1) What images of Palestine and Palestinians do you receive from the photos?
2) How are these different from or similar to images you (or others) may already have had about Palestine?
3) To what extent are the photos an "objective" rendering of the realities of Palestinian society? Does the fact that they record what actually was in front of the camera necessarily make them "objective?"
4) What does it mean to be "objective?"

Week 2: Political and Labor Zionism (Oct. 8)

Reading
Amos Elon, The Israelis: Founders and Sons, pp. 33-186
*Arthur Hertzberg (ed.), The Zionist Idea, pp.201-26; 331-50; 353-54; 360-66.

Questions
1) What are the basic assumptions of Zionist thinking about the Jews and their status in the world?
2) What are the differences between Herzl and the labor Zionists?
3) What were the goals and accomplishments of the labor Zionist movement during the 2nd and 3rd aliyot (waves of immigration)? How did these Zionists see themselves? How did they see the Palestinians?
4) How does Elon, as a native born Israeli, view the Zionist founders and their activity?

Week 3: A British View (Oct. 15)

Reading
Christopher Sykes, Crossroads to Israel (all)

Questions

1) Who is Christopher Sykes? (Look him up in Contemporary Authors if you don't know.)
2) What are the Husayn-McMahon correspondence, the Sykes-Picot Treaty, and the Balfour Declaration? Why did the British make these commitments? Are they consistent?
3) What can you learn about the "official mind" of the British administration from Sykes' account of the mandate?
4) What is Sykes' view of Weizmann, Ben Gurion, Begin and the Palestinian Arab political leaders?
5) How does Sykes view the American and Soviet roles towards the end of the mandate?

Week 4: Revisionist Zionism (Oct. 22)

Reading

Menachem Begin, The Revolt (all)

Questions

1) What are Begin's views on the Soviet Union, armed struggle, the Jewish religion, Arabs, the British?
2) What were the relations between the Irgun and the Haganah in the King David Hotel, Dir Yasin and Altalena incidents?
3) How important was the Irgun to achieving Zionist aims in Palestine?
4) Was the Irgun a terrorist organization? the Haganah?
5) By now you should have some idea of the map of political forces within the yishuv (Jewish community in Palestine). Come prepared to talk about it.

Week 5: Palestinian Perspectives (Oct. 29)

Reading

William Quandt, Fu'ad Jabber, Ann M. Lesch, The Politics of Palestinian Nationalism, pp. 7-42
Edward Said, The Question of Palestine, pp.ix-114
Maxime Rodinson, Israel: A Colonial Settler State?, pp. 27-96

Questions

1) Why did the Palestinians fail to attain their objectives during the Mandate period?
2) How does Said explain why we have not heard his version of the story very often?
3) What are his basic premises?
4) What is the role of intellectuals in society according to Said?
5) Is Israel a colonial settler state?

PAPER IS DUE MONDAY, NOV. 3.
BE SURE TO MEET THIS DEADLINE
SO YOU HAVE TIME TO READ FOR NEXT CLASS

Week 6: Regionalization of the Conflict, 1948-1967 (Nov. 5)

Reading
Maxime Rodinson, Israel and the Arabs , Chapters 3-5, 7-8
Nadav Safran, Israel: The Embattled Ally, pp.334-413

Questions
1) Who is Nadav Safran? Who is Maxime Rodinson?
2) What is the status of Palestinians who are citizens of Israel?
3) How did Israel regard and respond to Arab violations of the 1949 truce agreements?
4) Compare the discussion of the "Lavon affair" by Safran and Rodinson and the significance each attributes to it.
5) How did the U.S. view the Arab-Israeli conflict in the 1950s?
6) What are the reasons for the outbreak of the 1956 and 1967 wars?

Week 7: The Palestinian Arab National Movement (Nov. 12)

Reading
Helena Cobban, The Palestinian Liberation Organization, pp. 1-192
Yehoshafat Harkabi, "The Palestinian National Covenant" and "The Weakness of the Fedayeen" from Palestinians and Israel, pp. 49-69, 107-114

Questions
1) How did the PLO originate?
2) How did it change after the 1967 war?
3) What are the component elements of the PLO?
4) What does the PLO want?
5) Is the PLO a terrorist organization?

MONDAY NOV. 17 -- MOVIE "Stranger at Home"

Week 8: Israel and the Occupied Territories (Nov. 19 --I will be out of town on the 19th. Class will be rescheduled.)

Reading
Noam Chomsky, The Fateful Triangle, The United States, Israel, and the Palestinians, pp. 54-63, 103-146
Naseer Aruri (ed) Occupation: Israel Over Palestine, (Chapters by Ibrahim Matar, Sheila Ryan and Salim Tamari)
Yigal Allon, "Israel: The Case for Defensible Borders," Foreign Affairs 55 (no. 1, Oct 1976):38-53
Menachem Milson, "How to Make Peace with the Palestinians," Commentary, May 1981, pp.25-35
H. Cobban, The Palestinian Liberation Organization, pp. 168-184

Questions
1) What are Israel's objectives in the occupied territories? How have they changed over time?
2) What are the differences between Labor and the Likud on this issue?

3) How have different forces in Israel pursued their objectives?
4) What has happened to the lands of these territories?
5) Who represents politically the Palestinians of the occupied territories?

Week 9: The American Decade, 1967-1976 (Nov.26)

Reading
William Quandt, Decade of Decisions, pp. 105-127, 287-300
N. Safran, Israel: The Embattled Ally, pp. 414-598
N. Chomsky, The Fateful Triangle, pp. 9-54, 64-80
M. Rodinson, Israel and the Arabs, pp. 243-276 [Recommended: read to p. 300 if you have time]

Questions
1) What were the policy objectives of Israel, Egypt, Syria, the U.S. and the U.S.S.R. from 1967-73?
2 Why did Egypt attack Israel in 1973 and what what were the results of the war?
3) How can the Kissinger and Rogers approaches to Israel be characterized. Which has been the dominant one in American policy towards Israel? Why? How was this manifested in the diplomatic activities of the 1970s?

Week 10: Camp David (Dec. 3)

Reading
N. Safran, Israel: The Embattled Ally, pp. 599-622
M. Rodinson, Israel and the Arabs, pp. 300-313
William Quandt, Camp David: Peacemaking and Politics, pp.6-29, 168-205, 320-339, 376-387
Joel Beinin, "The Cold Peace," MERIP Reports, no. 129, pp. 3-9

Questions
1) To what extent does American domestic policy influence Middle East policy?
2) What are the provisions of the Camp David Agreements and why did they or did they not fail?

Week 11: Israel's Lebanon War, 1982 (Dec. 10)

Reading
Robert Tucker "The Case for the War," Commentary, October 1982, pp. 19-30
Martin Peretz, "Lebanon Eyewitness," The New Republic, Aug. 2, 1982, pp. 15-23
N. Chomsky, The Fateful Triangle, 181-409

Questions
1) How did the Palestinians get to Lebanon and what were they doing there?
2) Why did Israel invade Lebanon in 1982?
3) Who wins the exchange between Martin Peretz and Noam Chomsky?
4) Did the Israeli invasion achieve its objectives?

COURSE REQUIREMENTS

1) Each participant in the colloquium is required to read all the assignments carefully and thoughtfully and to participate actively in the weekly discussions. i.e. **CLASS PARTICIPATION AND PREPAREDNESS COUNTS.** (20%)

2) On Monday, November 3, a 6-7 page paper characterizing and analyzing the arguments of the four positions examined in the first five weeks of the course will be due. (30%)

3) Each student will be responsible for one oral class presentation initiating a discussion of the readings. This presentation will be based on a 3-4 page written analysis and critique of the readings to be handed in on the day the oral presentation is made. Neither the oral presentation nor the written analysis should simply summarize the material in a narrative fashion. Try to analyze the underlying structure of the arguments, why they are made in the way they are, and what their strengths and weaknesses are. Feel free to criticize the readings or to make any other remarks which will stimulate discussion. Plan to come to see me before your presentation, preferably after you have done at least part of the reading for which you are responsible. (20%)

4) A final paper is due on Wednesday December 17. This will be a 7-8 page review essay based on Book Two of *Israel: The Embattled Ally* and the sections of *Decade of Decisions*, *Camp David*, *Israel and the Arabs* and *The Fateful Triangle* which you have read for weekly assignments during the second half of the course. This should be a comparative and analytical essay in which you point out the different approaches of the authors toward American policy in the Arab-Israeli conflict and argue their relative merits. Feel free to include material you have learned from other readings (with appropriate references). If you are not clear about how to write this kind of essay, look at some of the reviews in *The New York Review of Books* and/or discuss the assignment with the instructor.

> **DO NOT SIMPLY RECAPITULATE THE ARGUMENTS OF THE AUTHORS. THIS ASSIGNMENT IS DIFFERENT THAN THE FIRST ESSAY. IT IS DESIGNED TO LET YOU SHOW THAT YOU CAN THINK ABOUT WHAT THE AUTHORS YOU HAVE READ SAY AND SUPPORT YOUR THINKING WITH WHAT YOU HAVE LEARNED IN THE COURSE.** (30%)

TEXTS AVAILABLE FOR PURCHASE

The following texts will be available for purchase in the Bookstore. They are also on library reserve.

Sarah Graham-Brown, _Palestinians and their Society, 1880-1946_
Nadav Safran, _Israel: The Embattled Ally_
Christopher Sykes, _Crossroads to Israel: 1917-1948_
Edward Said, _The Question of Palestine_
Maxime Rodinson, _Israel: A Colonial Settler State?_
Maxime Rodinson, _Israel and the Arabs_
William Quandt, Fuad Jabber and Ann Mosely Lesch, _The Politics of Palestinian Nationalism_
Noam Chomsky, _The Fateful Triangle: The United States, Israel and the Palestinians_
Amos Elon, _The Israelis: Founders and Sons_
Naseer Aruri (ed) _Occupation: Israel Over Palestine_
Menachem Begin, _The Revolt_
Helena Cobban, _The Palestinian Liberation Organization_
William Quandt, _Decade of Decisions: American Policy Toward the Arab-Israeli Conflict, 1967-1976_

Donna Robinson Divine
Wright 106

SMITH COLLEGE

Government 348a

THE ARAB-ISRAELI DISPUTE
Fall 1985

1. Introduction

2. Focus of the Dispute: The Land and Its Peoples

Peter Beaumont, Gerald H. Blake, J. Malcolm Wagstaff, The Middle East: A Geographical Survey, pp. 404-425.
Edward W. Said, The Question of Palestine
Hillel Halkin, "Whose Palestine"

3. The Initial Jewish Claims and Their Context: Classical Zionism

Arthur Herzberg, The Zionist Idea, pp. 178-231; 247-277; 352-396; 556-572.
Walter Laqueur, A History of Zionism, pp. 3-136.
Haim Nachman Bialik, "In the City of Slaughter"
"The Scholar"
Walter Laqueur and Barry Rubin, editors, The Israel-Arab Reader, Documents 1, 3, 4.

4. The Contemporary Jewish Claims and Their Context

Menachem Begin, The Revolt, pp. 1-58.
Walter Laqueur, A History of Zionism, pp. 209-270.
David J. Schnall, "Religion, Ideology and Dissent in Contemporary Israeli Politics," Tradition, Vol. 18, No. 1 (Summer 1979):13-34
Benjamin Z. Kedar, "Masada: The Myth and the Complex," Jerusalem Quarterly, 24 (Summer 1982):57-63.

5. The Initial Arab Claims and Their Context

Walter Laqueur and Barry Rubin, editors, The Israel-Arab Reader, Documents 2.
Yehoshua Porath, The Emergence of the Palestinian-Arab National Movement 1918-1929, pp. 1-31; 70-123.
George Antonius, The Arab Awakening, pp. 79-183.
Kenneth W. Stein, "Legal Protection and Circumvention of Rights for Cultivators in Mandatory Palestine," in Palestinian Society and Politics, edited by Joel S. Migdal, Chapter 7.

6. The Contemporary Arab Claims and Their Context: Palestinian Arab Nationalism

Fawaz Turki, The Disinherited.
Helena Cobban, The Palestine Liberation Organization.
Walter Laqueur and Barry Rubin, editors, The Israel-Arab Reader, Documents 29, 32, 33, 37, pp. 366-399; 518-545.

7. Co-existence, Combat and Futile Diplomacy

Walter Laqueur, A History of Zionism, pp. 270-599.
J. C. Hurewitz, The Struggle for Palestine.
Walter Laqueur and Barry Rubin, editors, The Israel-Arab Reader, Documents 5, 6, 7, 8, 9, 10, 11 and Part II.

8. The First War

Nadav Safran, Israel The Embattled Ally, pp. 41-64.
Dov Joseph, The Faithful City, pp. 28-187.
Dominique Lapierre and Larry Collins, O Jerusalem, pp. 243-343.
Walter Laqueur and Barry Rubin, editors, The Israel-Arab Reader, Document 26.

9. Confrontations with Arab States

Nadav Safran, From War to War, pp. 266-382.
Walter Laqueur and Barry Rubin, editors, The Israel-Arab Reader, pp. 196-244; 414-460; 461-480; 487-498.

10. Confrontations with Palestinian Arabs

Ibrahim Abu-Lughod, "The Meaning of Beirut, 1982," Race and Class, Volume XXIV, Number 4 (Spring 1983):345-360.
"Israel in Lebanon: Excerpts from the McBride Report," Race and Class, Volume XXIV, Number 4 (Spring 1983):465-471.
Itamar Rabinovich, "Seven Wars and One Peace Treaty," in The Arab-Israeli Conflict: Perspectives, edited by Alvin Z. Rubinstein, pp. 41-68.
Walter Laqueur and Barry Rubin, editors, The Israel-Arab Reader, pp. 670-675.

11. Politics: The Great Powers

William Quandt, A Decade of Decisions.
Alan J. Kreczko, "Support Reagan's Initiative," Foreign Policy, No. 49 (Winter 1982-83):140-153
Ian S. Lustick, "Israeli Politics and American Foreign Policy," Foreign Affairs, Vol. 61, No. 2 (Winter 1982/83):379-399
Steven L. Spiegel, The Other Arab-Israeli Conflict, pp.
Walter Laqueur and Barry Rubin, editors, The Israel-Arab Reader, pp. 584-591; 608-616; 656-662.

12. Politics: The Great Powers

Galia Golan, "The Soviet Union and the Arab-Israeli Conflict"
John Norton Moore, ed., The Arab-Israeli Conflict, Vol. III, Documents Nos. 24, 35, 37, 38, 51, 152, 153.
Galia Golan, "The Soviet Union and the Israeli Action in Lebanon," International Affairs, Vol. 59, No. 1 (Winter 1982/83):7-16.
Karen Dawisha, "The USSR in the Middle East: Superpower in Eclipse?," Foreign Affairs, Vol. 61, No. 2 (Winter 1982/83):438-452
Robert O. Freedman, Soviet Policy Toward the Middle East Since 1970, pp. 345-405.

13. Consequences: Political, Social, Econmic

J. David Bleich, "Judea and Samaria: Settlement and Return," Tradition, Vol. 18, No. 1 (Summer 1979):44-78
Ehud Sprinzak, "Gush Emunim: The Tip of the Iceberg," Jerusalem Quarterly, 21 (Fall 1981):28-47
Fawaz Turki, "The Future of a Past: Fragments from the Palestinian Dream"
Arthur Hertzberg, "Israel and the West Bank," Foreign Affairs, Vol. 61, No. 5 (Summer 1983):1064-1077
Salim Tamari, "The Palestinians in the West Bank and Gaza: The Sociology of Dependency," in The Sociology of the Palestinians, edited by Khalil Nakhleh and Elia Zureik
Gush Emunim, "Opinion Paper," in Israel in the Middle East, pp. 267-269.
Eqbal Ahmad, "Israel and the Palestinians," Race and Class, Volume XXV, Number 4 (Spring 1984):1-20.
Eli Rekhess, "The Politicization of Israel's Arabs," in Every Sixth Israeli, edited by Alouph Hareven, pp. 135-142.
George Kanazi, "The Problem of Identity in the Literature of the Israeli Arabs," in Every Sixth Israeli, edited by Alouph Hareven, pp. 143-162.
Raphael Vurdi, "Israeli Administration and Self-Rule in the Territories: The Israeli Perspective," in Governing Peoples and Territories, edited by Daniel J. Elazar, pp. 171-180.
Emile A. Nakhleh, "Israeli Administration and Self-Rule in the Territories: The Inhabitants' Perspective," in Governing Peoples and Territories, edited by Daniel J. Elazar, pp. 181-192.
Daniel J. Elazar, ed., Governing Peoples and Territories, pp. 249-278.
David Newman, "The Evolution of a Political Landscape: Geographical and Territorial Implications of Jewish Colonization in the West Bank," Middle Eastern Studies, 21 (April 1985):192-205.

History 334/534
Arab-Israeli Conflict

General Instructions
Fall 1986

Gifford B. Doxsee
7-9 TTh-Bentley 306

I. Course Objectives: (1) To survey briefly the history of the Arab and the Jewish peoples before 1900; (2) to examine the origins of Zionism and Arab nationalism before 1914; (3) to analyze the effects of the First World War and the Peace Settlement on the Palestine Question; (4) to examine British, Arab and Zionist policies during the era of the British Mandate, 1920-1948; (5) to study the causes and results of Arab-Israeli Wars in 1947-1949, 1956, 1967, and 1973; (6) to explore the contemporary situation, including the roles of Lebanon and of the Great Powers in the conflict and to place the Arab-Israeli struggle in global perspective.

II. Texts: The Israel-Arab Reader, ed. by Walter Laqueur and Barry Rubin, Rev. edition, Penguin, 1984.
Grose, Peter, A Changing Israel, Vintage Paper, 1985.

Required for Graduate Students, optional for others:
Khouri, Fred J., The Arab-Israeli Dilemma, Syracuse, 2nd ed., 1976.
OR Sachar, Howard M., A History of Israel from the Rise of Zionism to Our Time, Knopf, 1976.

Optional for all students:
John Bartholomew and Sons, Bartholomew's Map of the Middle East.

III. Course Requirements: Map assignment and short library assignment
Mid-term and final examinations
Course project: book reports (two) or term paper

Graduate students will meet separately with the instructor to discuss the graduate component of the course.

IV. Grading. The course grade will be computed approximately as follows:

	For students doing book reports:	For students doing paper:
mid-term examination	30 per cent	25 per cent
final examination	40 per cent	35 per cent
book reports	20 per cent	30 per cent
*Instructor's evaluation	10 per cent	10 per cent

*Instructor's evaluation is based on regularity of attendance, participation in class discussion, evidence of interest, and overall effort.

V. Attendance Policy: Be in class regularly. The instructor will take attendance and will keep a record of absences.. The content of lectures, films, and class discussions is important and will be included in examinations. More than two unexcused absences will affect adversely the instructor's evaluation segment of the course grade.

VI. The Current Situation. An important purpose of this courrse is to provide historical background for understanding the contemporary Middle East. To keep abreast of current developments, students are required to read on a regular basis a daily newspaper of recognized excellence. To this end,

The Christian Science Monitor, Box 125, Astor Station, Boston, MA 02123 is highly recommended. The Monitor has long been noted for its extensive coverage of the Middle East and for its objectivity. It is available at reduced rates for university students, professors, and teachers. The cost of a subscription can be further reduced by sharing with a roommate, classmate, or friend.

COURSE OUTLINE AND SYLLABUS

Reference Tools: Bartholomew's Map of the Middle East.
Atlases of Israel, the Middle East, and the world are available in the reference room of the Alden Library, fourth level.
Encyclopedias, biographical dictionaries, Yearbooks, and bibliographical references for Israel, the Arab World, Judaism, Islam, Zionism, etc. are also available in the Alden Library reference room. Consult these!

Suggested Background Reading:
Coon, Carleton S., Caravan: The Story of the Middle East.
Fisher, Sydney N., The Middle East: A History, 3rd ed.
Gibb, H. A. R., Mohammedanism. Fazlur Rahman, Islam.
Weizmann, Chaim, Trial and Error (autobiography), especially Chapters 1 and 2.

Weekly Syllabus and Assignments

Week of:

Sept. 8 Introduction. Course objectives. Essential terms and concepts.

*The Christian Science Monitor. Read in library. Note carefully all articles on the Middle East and on U. S. foreign policy.
Goitein, D. S., Jews and Arabs: Their Contacts Through the Ages.
Works cited above by Coon, Fisher, Gibb, and Weizmann.

Sept. 15 Historical Background. The Emergence of Zionism and Arab Nationalism.
*Laqueur & Rubin, Docs. 1-4
*Begin reading for book reports or research paper.
Antonius, George, The Arab Awakening.
Laqueur, Walter, A History of Zionism.
Zeine Zeine, Arab-Turkish Relations and the Emergence of Arab Nationalism

Sept. 22 The Impact of the First World War and the Peace Settlement.
*Laqueur & Rubin, Docs. 5-11
*Map Assignment, due Thursday, Sept. 25.
Leonard Stein, The Balfour Declaration.
Tibawi, A. L., Anglo-Arab Relations and the Question of Palestine.

Sept. 29 The Era of Hopeful Illusions, 1922-1936.
*Library Assignment due, Thursday, October 2.
*Laqueur & Rubin, Docs. 12-18
Lesch, Ann Mosely, Arab Politics in Palestine, 1917-1939, 1979.
Porath, Y., The Emergence of the Palestinian-Arab National Movement, 1918-1929, London: Frank Cass, 1974.
Porath, Y., The Palestinian Arab National Movement, 1929-1939: From Riots to Rebellion. London: Frank Cass, 1977.

Oct. 6 The Collapse of the British Mandate in Palestine, 1936-1948.
*First book report or working bibliography for paper due, Thursday.
*Text of the 1939 Malcolm MacDonald White Paper.
*Comprehensive review for mid-term examination.
*Laqueur & Rubin, Docs. 17-25.

MID-TERM EXAMINATION

Oct. 13 The Establishment of the State of Israel, 1947-1949.
*Laqueur & Rubin, Part III.

Snetsinger, John, Truman, The Jewish Vote and the Creation of Israel.
Wilson, Evan, Decision on Palestine.

Oct. 20 From Israel's Independence to the Suez Crisis, 1948-1956.
*Laqueur & Rubin, Part IV.

*Intensive work on course projects.
Love, Kennett, Suez, The Twice-Fought War.
Sachar, Howard M., From the Ends of the Earth: Peoples of Israel.
Jones, Christina H., The Untempered Wind: Forty Years in Palestine.

Oct. 27 Great Power Rivalry: The Arab Cold War; the June War of 1967.
*Laqueur & Rubin, Documents, Part V.

Abu-Lughod, Ibrahim, ed., The Arab-Israeli Confrontation of 1967.
Abu-Lughod, Ibrahim, ed., The Transformation of Palestine.
Kerr, Malcolm H., The Arab Cold War, 1958-1970.
Safran, Nadav, From War to War. Safran, The U.S. and Israel.
Polk, William R., The U. S. and the Arab World.

Nov. 3 The October War of 1973 and Its Aftermath
*Laqueur & Rubin, Documents, Part VI.
*Richardson, The West Bank, A Portrait.
Cooley, John K. Green March, Black September.
Lustick, Ian, Arabs in the Jewish State.
Quandt, William B., et al., The Politics of Palestinian Nationalism.
The Yom Kippur War by the Insight Team of the London Sunday Times.

Nov. 10 War in Lebanon, Sadat's Peace Initiative, & The Camp David Accords
*Laqueur & Rubin, Documents, Part VII.
*Heller, A Palestinian State, Implications for Israel.
*Course Projects due, Tuesday, Nov. 12.

Nov. 17 The Current Situation and Future Outlook
*Complete all assignments. Review for final.

FINAL EXAMINATION: Thursday, Nov. 20, 7 P.M.

UNIVERSITY OF WISCONSIN-RIVER FALLS   Prof. Stephen Feinstein

History 345/545 History of the Arab-Israeli Conflict

Purpose of the Course:

As the Arab-Israeli conflict enters its fourth decade of actual physical encounters, it has become increasingly more important, especially for Americans who have perceived a huge "stake" in the Middle East for political economic, strategic and most importantly, energy reasons. This is a topic which is between history and current events, being in the news every day. The purpose of the course, therefore, is to examine the origins and basis of the conflict in great detail. In this process, arguments of both sides. Arab and Israeli, as well as Palestinian Arab, will be examined. Emphasis will be on themes such as Zionism, British policy in Palestine, Jewish aims and ideals, Arab reactions, wars, conflict, terrorism as well as an examination of those displaced in the conflict, the Palestinian refugees.

Class Format:

This class will attempt to bring together various means to develop an understanding of the material. These techniques will include lectures, clas discussions of the reading materials and some films.

Textbooks:

There are two texts, available from the textbook library. The first is to be read completely and will be the basis of daily class sessions. The second is to be read partially, as indicated on the class topic/reading page of the syllabus:

Howard M. Sachar. A History of Israel (Random House)
Quandt, Jabbar and Lesch. The Politics of Palestinian Nationalism. (California).

Outside Reading:

In addition to the materials in the textbook library the following reading requirements are part of the course:

Outside Reading #1:

Fawaz Turki, The Disinherited (Monthly Review Press pb) Available in the University bookstore.

Write a 5-8 page analytical book report on this work, analyzing the nature of the arguments and the validity of the material as you see it.

Outside Reading #2.

Pick a book on your own from the library related to the Arab-Israeli conflic This can be on topics such as military conflict, ideological development, terrorism, politics or domestic development of Israel. Then write a 5-8 page book report on this book, again relating the material to the overall issue of the conflict,

Examinations:

There will be two examinations, a mid-term and a final.

Geography:

Since the Arab-Israeli conflict conjures up names and places which may be unfamiliar, please study the enclosed list of items and locate them on the enclosed map. A short map test will be given on the grography of the conflict after one week of the class.

Office:

My office is in 355 Fine Arts. I am in every day--hours will be announced in class or are posted on my door. If you have difficulty with names, reading or studying, please see me before examinations.

Grading:

Grading is based on the following system: 90-100=A; 80-89=B 70-79=C; 60-69=D; below 59 is an F. There is equal weight in the course to examinations and reports. Therefore, exams are 50% and papers are 50%.

Tentative Lectures and Readings

1. Aspects of the conflict--Introduction. Who are the antagonists? Aims?

2. The Jewish "Problem" in Western Civilization and Eastern Civilizations. READ: Sachar, Chapter 1.

3. Zionism, Herzl, the Yishuz. READ: Sachar, Chapters 2, 3, 4.

4. The Balfour Declaration and the Mandate for Palestine. READ: Sachar, Chapters 5 and 6.

5. Building the Jewish National Home. READ: Sachar, Chapter 7.

6. Arab-Jewish Confrontation: 1917-1939. READ: Sachar, Chapter 8 & Quandt et al., Part 1, pages 1-42.

7. Palestine in World War II & the Impact of the Holocaust. Biltmore program. READ: Sachar: Chapters 9-11.

8. Palestinian and Arab Nationalism Under the Mandate. READ: Quandt et al: pgs. 1-42.

9. Partition and Birth of Israel: READ: Sachar, Chapter 12.

****MIDTERM EXAMINATION****

10. War of Independence and Statebuilding. READ: Sachar, Chapter 13.

11. Israel's Internal structure. READ: Sachar: Chapters 14. 15.

12. Film: The Illegals

13. The Kibbutz and implications for Middle Eastern agriculture.

14. The Search for Security: 1948-1967. General problems. READ: Sachar, Chapters 16 and 19. Quandt et al., pp. 43-64.

15. Sinai War, 1956. READ: Sachar, Chapter 17.

16. Ideological problems inside Israel. READ: Sachar, Chapter 18-120.

17. The Six-Day War, 1967. READ: Sachar, Chapter 21.

18. Film: Life of Golda Meir.

19. From Six Day War to the Yom Kippur War, 1967-73. READ: Sachar, Chapters 22-24.

20. Palestinian Arab Zionism and resistance. READ: Quandt et al, pp. 43-124 Also, Turki, The Disinherited--all.

21. Black September, Terrorism and the aftermath. Politics of the PLO and other groups.

22. Film on PLO.

23. Great Powers and the Middle East/The United Nations/Geneva Conference and Camp David Agreements. READ: Sachar, Chapter 25.

24. The Energy issue and the Arab Israeli Conflict.

25. Repercussions of the Arab-Israeli dispute in American Politics & Conclusions.

GEORGETOWN UNIVERSITY
Department of History

Arab-Israeli Conflict
History 144-417

Summer 1986
Professor John Ruedy

Required Readings

Available for purchase

Fred Khouri	The Arab-Israeli Dilemma
Howard Sachar	A History of Israel from the Rise of Zionism to Our Times
Pamela Ann Smith	Palestine and the Palestinians

Library Reserve

Ann Mosely Lesch	Arab Politics in Palestine, 1917-1939
Wm. Quandt et al	The Politics of Palestinian Nationalism
John Ruedy	"Dynamics of Land Alienation"
Nadav Safran	From War to War
Seth Tillman	The United States in the Middle East

Topics

9 June — Introduction. Points of view.

10 June — Political, social and economic background of Palestine before Zionism; the emergence of Arab nationalism to 1916

Required: Khouri, Ch. I; Smith, Ch. I & II.

Collateral: Moshe Ma'oz, Studies on Palestine During the Ottoman Period;
Joel S. Migdal, ed., Palestinian Society and Politics. Introduction and Ch. I;
George Antonius, The Arab Awakening, Chs. I-XII;
James Reilly, "Peasantry of Late Ottoman Palestine," Journal of Palestine Studies, Vol. X, No. 4;
Saul S. Friedman, Land of Dust
Roger Owen, Studies in the Social and Economic History of Palestine, Introduction & Ch. I.

12 June — The origins and early development of Zionism: the Balfour Declaration

Required: Sachar, Chs. I-V

Collateral: M. Halpern, The Idea of the Jewish State;
Arthur Hertzberg, The Zionist Idea
Walter Laqueur, A History of Zionism

16 June — The Mandate between the World Wars - an overview

Required: Khouri, pp. 16-27
Sachar, Ch. VI
Ruedy, all
Smith, Ch. III

Collateral: Aharon Cohen, Israel and the Arab World;
Christopher Sykes, Crossroads to Israel;
Esco Foundation, Palestine, A Study of Jewish, Arab and British;
Antonius, Chs. XIV, XV;
Kenneth Stein, The Land Question in Palestine, 1917-1939;
William R. Polk, Backdrop to Tragedy, pp. 33-106

18 June — Growth of the yishuv; the Palestinian resistance

Required: Sachar, Chs. VII-IX;
Lesch, all

Collateral: Esco Foundation, Vol. I, Ch. VI; Vol. II, Ch. X;
Maxine Rodinson, Israel: A Settler Colonial State;
Y. Porath, Palestine Arab Nationalism, (2 volumes);
George Antonius, The Arab Awakening
Neville Mandel, The Arabs and Zionism Before World War I
Shai Lachman, "Arab Rebellion and Terrorism in Palestine," in Elie Kedourie and Sylvie G. Haim, Zionism and Arabism in Palestine and Israel
Roger Owen, Ch. II
Rosemary Sayigh, Palestinians: From Peasants to Revolutionaries, Ch. I

19 June — The birth of Israel

Required: Khouri, p. 27 through Ch. V;
Sachar, Chs. X-XIII

Collateral: J.C. Hurewitz, The Struggle for Palestine;
Dan Kurzman, Genesis 1948;
Jon and David Kimche, A Clash of Destinies;
J. Bowyer Bell, Terror Out of Zion;
Menachem Begin, The Revolt;
Wm. R. Polk, pp. 106-130

23 June — Evolution of Israeli society after 1948

Required: Khouri, Ch. VI;
Sachar, Chs. XIV, XV, XVIII, XX;

Collateral: Leonard Fein, Politics of Israel;
S. N. Eisenstadt, Israeli Society;
Don Peretz, The Government and Politics of Israel

24 June — Mid-term examination

26 June — Evolution of Palestinian society after 1948

Required: Smith, Ch. VI
Khouri, Ch. VI and pp. 293-99

Collateral: Don Peretz, Israel and the Palestine Arabs;
Jacob Landau, The Arabs in Israel;
Sabri Jiryis, The Arabs in Israel;
Ian Lustick, Arabs in the Jewish State;
Fawzi el Asmar, To be an Arab in Israel;
Sayigh, Ch. III

30 June — The Arab-Israeli conflict and the great powers; the 1956 and 1967 wars

Required: Khouri, Ch. VII, pp. 299-308, Ch. VIII;
Safran, Chs. I, II, III, VI and VII;
Sachar, Ch. XXI

Collateral: Elmer Berger, The Covenant and the Sword;
Peter Calvocoressi, Suez Ten Years After;
Malcolm Kerr, The Arab Cold War;
Hal Kosut, Israel and the Arabs: The June 1967 War
Donald Neff, Warriors for Jerusalem

1 July — The re-emergence of the Palestinian resistance

Required: Khouri, pp. 356-61;
Quandt, Palestinian Nationalism, Parts I and II

Collateral: John Cooley, Green March, Black September;
Gerard Chaliand, The Palestinian Resistance;
Michael Curtis, ed., The Palestinians: People, History and Politics;
Issa Sharabi, "The Development of the Palestinian Entity-Consciousness." Journal of Palestine Studies, Summer 1979, Winter 1980, Spring 1980;
Helena Cobban, The Palestinian Liberation Organization, Chs. II, III, VII, VIII, IX
Sayigh, Ch. IV and Epilogue

3 July — The 1973 War and its aftermath

Required: Khouri, Ch. X;
Sachar, Chs. XXII and XXIV

Collateral: Tillman, Chs. III, IV, V;
London Sunday Times Insight Team, The Yom Kippur War;
Safran, Israel: The Embattled Ally

7 July — The Egyptian-Israeli peace

Required: Khouri, Ch. XI
Tillman, Ch. I, VII

Collateral: Cyrus Vance, Hard Choices
Ismail Fahmy, Negotiating for Peace in the Middle East
Moshe Dayan, Breakthrough
William Quandt, Camp David: Peacemaking and Politics

8 July — Lebanon, the Palestinians, and Israel; Prospects

Required: Khouri, Ch. XII, XIII
Ilya Harik, Lebanon: Anatomy of Conflict
Other readings to be announced

Collateral: Ze'ev Schiff, "Motivation and Interest in Israel's Middle East Policy," The Middle East Journal, Spring 1984
Itamar Rabinovich, The War For Lebanon, 1970-1983;
Jonathan Randall, Going All the Way

10 July — Final examination

SEMINAR: ARAB NATIONALISM - 1

NE Hist 484 — Autumn 1987
W 2:00-5:00 — R. Khalidi

This seminar is part of a two-quarter sequence exploring facets of Arab nationalism in the nineteenth and twentieth centuries. The focus of the seminar this quarter is the antecedents and rise of Arabism, and the development of the Arab movement until 1920. Its sequel, NE Hist 485, will cover the development of Arab nationalism during the following decades.

Members of the seminar will examine the ideas and writings of Arab and Islamic thinkers who influenced the genesis of Arab nationalism, as well as those of later authors, some of them not well known, who contributed to the development of Arab nationalist ideology. External influences on the shaping of Arab nationalism will also be assessed.

Although ideology will be one concern of the seminar, most attention will be paid to the development of Arab nationalism as a discrete political force starting in the early years of this century, to the social make-up of the movement at this stage, and to the historical and historiographical controversies which have developed around this period. The impact of the Ottoman constitutional period (1908-1914), the World War I years, and the brief life of the Arab government in Damascus (1918-1920) will also be subjects of study.

Unanswered questions on these topics include the relationship of Arab nationalism to the Islamic tradition; the influence of _salafi_ thinking and of Western models and ideas on the growth of Arabism; the extent of the adherence of elites in the Arab _mashriq_ to Arabism; the nature of the relationship between Arabism and Ottomanism before 1918, and the extent to which developments before 1920 prefigured the later growth of local nationalisms in different parts of the Arab world.

REQUIREMENTS: It is highly preferable, but not required, that students have a reading knowledge of Arabic. Knowledge of other Middle Eastern languages, particularly Turkish (modern or Ottoman), would be useful. In addition to a research paper of under 40 pages due at the end of the quarter on a topic to be agreed upon with the instructor, students will make a presentation to the class on an important figure in Arab nationalism, or a key work in Arabic on the subject.

TEXTS: The following works are on reserve in Regenstein Library, as are other works in Arabic listed separately. Additional readings, primarily articles or passages of works in Arabic by key contemporary figures, will be distributed to the class during the quarter as indicated below.

Antonius, George. *The Arab Awakening*. London, 1939.
Arjomand, Said, ed. *From Nationalism to Revolutionary Islam*. Albany, 1984.
Buheiry, Marwan, ed. *Intellectual Life in the Arab East 1890-1939*. Beirut, 1981.
Cleveland, William. *The Making of an Arab Nationalist*. Princeton, 1971.
----------. *Islam Against the West. Austin, 1985*.
Dawn, C. Ernest. *From Ottomanism to Arabism*. Urbana, 1973.
Haim, Sylvia, ed. *Arab Nationalism: An Anthology*. Berkeley, 1976.
Haddad, William, and William Ochsenwald, eds. *Nationalism in a Non-National State*. Columbus, 1977.
Hourani, Albert. *Arabic Thought in the Liberal Age 1789-1939*. 2nd ed., Cambridge, 1983.
---------. *The Emergence of the Modern Middle East*. London, 1981.
Khalidi, Rashid. *British Policy towards Syria and Palestine 1906-1914*. London, 1980.
Khoury, Philip. *Urban Notables and Arab Nationalism*. Cambridge, 1983.
Saab, Hassan. *Arab Federalists of the Ottoman Empire*. Amsterdam, 1958.

READINGS:

Week	Date	Subject / Readings
I	9/30	Introduction
II	10/7	Islamic roots of Arabism: Hourani, *Arabic* preface and chs. 1-6; Haim, Intro., 1 and 2. [Readings in Arabic from *al-'Urwa al-wuthqa*].
III	10/14	*al-Nahda* and early Arab nationalism: Antonius, 1-100; Hourani, *Emergence*, 193-215. [Arabic readings: Kawakibi, Sulayman al-Bustani].
IV	10/21	Arabism as a political movement: Haddad, Khalidi in Haddad and Ochsenwald; R. Khalidi & Seikaly in Buheiry. [Arabic readings: al-'Uraisi].
V	10/28	Arabism and the *salafi* movement: Hourani, *Emergence*, 90-102; Commins in IJMES 18, 4 (Nov. 86); Escovitz in IJMES 18, 3 (Aug. 86). [Arabic readings: Rashid Rida].
VI	11/4	Arabism and Ottomanism: Dawn, 122-206; Khoury to 67; Cleveland, *Making*, Intro, 1-59; Cleveland, *Islam*, intro and 1-44; Khalidi, "Reassessment" (to be distributed) [Arabic readings: Muhammad Kurd 'Ali, Rafiq al-'Azm].
VII	11/11	Social Dimensions of Arabism: Khoury, 67-74; Khalidi in Arjomand; "Reassessment"[Arabic readings: selections from the press].
VIII	11/18	Interaction with the West: Khalidi, *British*; Antonius, 101-276 [Arabic readings: selections from the press].
IX	11/25	The Arab state in Damascus: Antonius, 276-324; Khoury, 75-100 [Arabic readings: al-Husri].
X	12/2	Conclusions

ارسلان ، شكيب
رشيد رضا او اخاء اربعين سنه
القاهرة ،١٩٣٧ .

الافغاني ،جمال الدين ،والشيخ محمد عبده
العروة الوثقى
بيروت ،١٩٨٠ (الطبعة الثانية) .

ايبش ،يوسف ،اعداد
رحلات رشيد رضا
بيروت ،١٩٧٩ .

امين ،جلال
المشرق العربي والغرب
بيروت ،١٩٧٩ .

برو ،توفيق علي
العرب والترك في العهد الدستوري العثماني ١٩٠٨ - ١٩١٤ .
القاهرة ١٩٦٠ .

البستاني ،سليمان
عبرة وذكرى او الدولة العثمانية قبل الدستور وبعده
بيروت ،١٩٧٨ (الطبعة الثانية)

التميمي ،رفيق ومحمد بهجت
ولاية بيروت
بيروت ١٩١٧ ٢ ج ،الطبعة الثانية ١٩٧٩ .

الحصري ،ساطع
يوم ميسلون ،صفحة من تاريخ العرب الحديث
بيروت ،١٩٤٧ .

الحصري ، ساطع
البلاد العربية والدولة العثمانية
بيروت ، ١٩٦٠ .

الحصري ، ساطع
نشوء القومية
القاهرة ، ١٩٥٥ .

(داغر اسعد)
ثورة العرب
القاهرة ،مطبعة المقطم ١٩١٦ .

دروزة ،محمد عزة
نشأة الحركة العربية الحديثة
صيدا ،الطبعة الثانية ١٩٧١ .

رافع ،عبد الكريم
العرب والعثمانيون ١٥١٦ - ١٩١٦ .
دمشق ١٩٧٤ .

رضا ،رشيد
مختارات سياسية من مجلة المنار
اعداد وجيه كوثراني
بيروت ،١٩٨٠ .

رضا ،محمد رشيد
تاريخ الاستاذ الامام الشيخ محمد عبده
القاهرة ،١٩٣١ .

سعيد ،امين
الثورة العربية الكبرى
القاهرة ،١٩٣٤ ٣ ج .

عبد الهادي ،عوني
اوراق خاصة ، اعداد خيرية قاسمية
بيروت ،١٩٧٤ .

العريسي،عبد الغني
مختارات المفيد
اعداد ناجي علوش
بيروت ،١٩٨١ .

عمارة ،محمد
العرب يستقظون (٢) العروبة في العصر الحديث
بيروت ،١٩٨١ (الطبعة الثانية) .

عمارة ،محمد ،اعداد
الاعمال الكاملة لعبد الرحمن الكواكبي
بيروت ،١٩٧٥ .

فريد ،محمد
تاريخ الدولة العلية العثمانية
بيروت ،١٩٨١ (الطبعة الثالثة) .

قاسمية ،خيرية
الحكومة العربية في دمشق بين ١٩١٨ – ١٩٢٠ .
القاهرة ،١٩٧١ .

كوثراني ،وجيه
الاتجاهات الاجتماعية والسياسية في جبل لبنان والمشرق العربي
بيروت ،١٩٧٦ .

كوثراني ،وجيه
بلاد الشام : السكان ،الاقتصاد والسياسة الفرنسية في مطلع القرن العشرين:
قراءة في الوثائق
بيروت ،١٩٨٠ .

اللجنة العليا لحزب اللامركزية بمصر
المؤتمر العربي الاول
القاهرة ،١٩١٣ .

ليفين ،ز.د
الفكر الاجتماعي والسياسي الحديث في لبنان وسوريا ومصر
بيروت ،١٩٧٨ .

موسى ،سليمان
الحركة العربية : سيرة المرحلة الاولى للنهضة العربية الحديثة ١٩٠٨ – ١٩٢٩ .
بيروت ،١٩٧٠ .

MODERN ARAB HISTORY

NE Hist 219 Autumn 1987
TTh 10:00-11:30 Pick 218 R. Khalidi

This course is part of a two-quarter sequence (each segment of which can be taken separately) intended to provide an introduction to modern Arab history from the eighteenth century until modern times for both undergraduates and graduates. In scope this course will cover the Arab heartland which comprised part of the Ottoman Empire until World War I, with some attention to North Africa and Arabian peninsula. The second quarter will cover the entire Arab world during the period after World War I.

The course will focus on the apparent decline of state and society in the Middle East and the expansion of Western influence, starting in the 18th century. Among topics to be examined will be the changing place of the region in the world economy; traditional forms of the Middle Eastern state at the outset of the modern era; explanations for its seeming decline; the extent to which this took place in a "stagnant" society; indigenous reactions to this process, including Western-style reforms, nationalism, and a re-emphasis on the religious tradition; the absorption of the region into formal and informal spheres of European dominion; and the varying responses within the society to foreign domination.

The readings are intended to be accessible to students who are unfamiliar with the Islamic tradition or other aspects of the history of the region, although the course is primarily directed at those with some exposure to these subjects. An attempt will be made to examine different generations of recent scholarship, and to assess differing historiographical approaches to central problems of modern Arab history over the past few decades. In particular, the much-debated question of whether change in this region was internally generated, externally stimulated, or a combination of both, will be considered in light of the various works to be read.

REQUIREMENTS for the course will differ for undergraduates and graduates. UNDERGRADUATES will be expected to write an essay of under ten pages examining a limited number of works (preferably NOT the required readings) dealing with a discrete problem in the literature, AND a term paper of under 20 pp. on a subject to be chosen in consultation with the instructor. The former is due at the end of the first week in November, the latter at the end of the quarter. GRADUATES will be expected to write a research paper of under 40 pp. based on primary as well as secondary sources. If possible some of these should be in Middle Eastern languages. The paper is due at the end of the quarter. A selected bibliography of secondary works will be distributed to the class early in the quarter.

<u>TEXTS</u>: Books marked with a * are available at the Seminary Coop book shop. All readings are on reserve in Regenstein Library.

F. Rahman. <u>Islam</u>. Rev. ed. U. of Chicago Press ppbk., 1979. *
S. Fisher. <u>The Middle East: A History</u>. 3rd ed., Knopf, 1979.*
H.A.R. Gibb and H. Bowen. <u>Islamic Society and the West</u>. Vol. I, parts 1 and 2. Oxford University Press, 1950, 1957.
W. Polk and R. Chambers. <u>Beginnings of Modernization in the Middle East</u>. University of Chicago Press, 1968.
G. Antonius. <u>The Arab Awakening</u>. Lippincott, 1939 (several paperback editions since, but now out of print).
A. Hourani, <u>Arabic Thought in the Liberal Age 1798-1939</u>, rev. ed. Cambridge University Press ppbk., 1983. *
L.C. Brown. <u>International Politics and the Middle East</u>. Princeton University Press ppbk., 1984. *

Hourani, Brown and Fisher contain useful bibliographies. For texts of many documents see J.C. Hurewitz, <u>The Middle East and North Africa in World Politics: A Documentary Record</u>. 2 vols. Yale University Press, 1975 and 1979.

READING ASSIGNMENTS: Lectures and discussion will range well beyond these readings, and the following headings are only an approximate indication of the topics to be covered. Other readings will be recommended from time to time.

Week	Dates	Subject	Readings
I	9/29-10/1	Islam & the Middle Eastern state:	Rahman, all.
II	10/6-8	The West & the Middle East:	Fisher, 160-377.
III	10/13-15	A traditional approach to the subject:	Gibb & Bowen, part 1: 201-34; 258-75; 292-313; part 2: 59-69 [Part 1: 173-99, 235-58 and 276-92 recommended].
IV	10/20-22	The modernization paradigm:	Polk and Chambers, Intro. and articles by Hourani, Chevalier, Berque, Maoz, Shamir and Issawi [Baer, Salibi & Marsot recommended].
V	10/27-29	Arab nationalism, a self-view:	Antonius, all.
VI	11/3-5	Intellectual trends:	Hourani, preface to 323.
VII	11/10-12	The Middle East & the World:	Brown, to 138.
VIII	11/17-19	Religion and nationalism.	
IX	11/24	The Arab world in 1914.	
X	12/1-3	Conclusions.	

[During the last three weeks students will choose their own readings in relation to their paper topics.]

UNIVERSITY OF WISCONSIN
Department of History
Semester II, 1983-84

story 371 | The Modern Arab World | Prof. Humphreys

urse Description:

A survey of the political, social, and cultural evolution of the Arab lands from the mid-eighteenth century down to the present. For the most part we will be dealing with the eastern Arab countries, with particular focus on Egypt, and the Palestine conflict. The course attempts to address a series of problems: the decay of established political and economic structures in the 19th century; attempts at military and administrative modernization by Middle Eastern states in the early and mid-19th century; the growing European presence in all domains of life down to World War I; the emergence of new ideologies as a response to internal weakness and foreign pressure; the collapse of the Ottoman Empire and the emergence of "independent" Arab states under French and British tutelage; the struggle for national independence after World War II; the quest for Arab unity; the impact of the Arab-Israeli conflict; ecnomic growth and social destablization after World War II; the reassertion of Islam as a political ideology in the region.

ctures and Class Format:

Lectures are on Tuesdays and thursdays, 2:25-3:40. The lectures do not repeat the readings, and you are responsible for their contents. Portions of many meetings wil be devoted to the discussion of particular problems in the readings. For this and other reasons, the readings must obviously be done on time, as assigned.

itten Assignments:

Three Credits: mid-term examination (20%); final examination (40%); essay, 7-10 pp., on one of a choice of topics supplied by the instructor or individually negotiated with him (40%).

Four Credits: as above, but with the addition of a 3-5 page book review, on a book chosen from a list supplied by the instructor. In this case, the percentage value of each unit is as follows: mid-term (20%), final exam (30%); essay (30%); book review (20%).

equired Readings:

To purchase:
Arthur Goldschmidt, Concise History of the Middle East (Westview pb.)
A.H. Hourani, Arabic Thought in the Liberal Age (Cambridge, pb.)
Fouad Ajami; The Arab Predicament (Cambridge pb.)
Charles Issawi, An Economic History of the Middle East and North Africa (Columbia, hard cover - OPTIONAL)

On reserve: Helen C. White, 3-hours.
A.H. Hourani, Arabic Thought...
Ch. Issawi, Economic History of the Middle East and North Africa.

1. (Jan 24) Introduction to the Course

2. (Jan 25) What is an Arab? A Geographic and Ethnographic Survey.

3. (Jan 31) The rise of the Islamic State

4. (Feb 2) Politics and Society in Medieval Islam: Themes and Structures

   Readings, sessions 1-4: Goldschmidt, 1-110.

5. (Feb 7) The Ottoman Empire: the Classical Phase, 1300-1700

6. (Feb 9) The Ottoman Empire and the Rise of Europe in the 18th Century

   Readings, sessions 5-6: Goldschmidt, 111-143.

7. (Feb 14) Egypt in the 18th Century: an Autonomous Military Oligarchy

8. (Feb 16) Egypt, 1798-1854: the Destruction of the Late Ottoman System System and the Foundations of the Modern Egyptian State.

9. (Feb 21) Egypt, 1854-1382: Rapid Modernization, Dependency, and Crisis.

10. (Feb 23) Patterns of Ottoman Reform, 1789-1875.

11. (Feb 28) The Discovery of Europe: New Trends in Intellectual Life down to 1870.

    Reading, sessions 7-11: Goldschmidt, 145-165, Hourani, iv-x, 34-102

12. (March 1) The Rethinking of Islam, 1870-1925.

    Reading, session 12: Hourani, 103-192

13. (March 6) Egypt under British Rule, 1882-1914: Europeanization and Nationalis

    Reading, session 13: Goldschmidt, 165-166, Hourani, 193-209.

14. (March 8) The Genesis of Arab Nationalism, 1875-1914

    Reading, session 14: Hourani, 245-286, Goldschmidt, 166-180.

15. (March 13) MID-TERM EXAM

16. (March 15) The Arab Lands and the World Economy: the 19th Century

17. (March 27) The Arab Lands and the World Economy: the 20th Century

    <u>Reading</u>, <u>sessions 16-17</u>: Issawi, pp. 1-43, 62-169.

18. (March 29) World War I: the Collapse of Ottoman Power.

19. (April 3) World War I: Franco-British Policy, the Arab Revolt, and the Balfour Declaration

    <u>Reading</u>, <u>sessions 18-19</u>: Goldschmidt, 181-190, 227-235, Hourani, 286-291

20. (April 5) Palestine under British Mandate, 1920-1939.

21. (April 10) Establishment of the State of Israel and the Origin of the Palestinian Problem, 1939-1949.

    <u>Readings</u>, <u>sessions 20-21</u>: Goldschmidt, 235-262.

22. (April 12) Arab Nationalism, 1920-1952: Ideological Development and Early Practical Initiatives.

    <u>Reading</u>, <u>session 22</u>: Hourani, 291-323

23. (April 17) Egypt under the Constitutional Monarchy, 1919-1952: the Struggle for Independence.

24. (April 19) The Era of Egyptian Paramounty: Nasser, 1952-1970.

    <u>Reading</u>, <u>sessions 23-24</u>: Goldschmidt, 213-226, 263-278, Hourani, 209-221, 324-340.

25. (April 24) Egypt since the Revolution: Essays in Economic Development and Social Mobilization.

26. (April 26) NO CLASS

27. (May 1) The Emergence of the PLO, 1967-1983.

28. (May 3) The Breakdown of a Consensus System: the Lebanese Civil War.

    <u>Reading</u>, <u>sessions 25-27</u>: Goldschmidt, 279-316, Ajami, 1-135

29. (May 8) The Reassertion of Islam, 1967-1984: Religion as Revolutionary Ideology.

    Reading, session 28: Goldschmidt, 317-340, Ajami, 137-200, Hourani, 341-373

30. (May 10) Recapitulation and Conclusions

History 547
Iran Since 651

Spring 1976
Peter von Silvers

COURSE SYLLABUS

(1) Description

In this class we shall study Iranian history from the Arab-Muslim conquest to the origin of the Safavids. The roughly eight and a half centuries which our course will cover are almost entirely dominated by the phenomenon of nomads on horseback as founders of more or less (usually less) solid states. Admittedly, in the ancient world equestrian nomads were by no means unknown, especially in the Fertile Crescent. But the appearance of far-flung states founded by nomads whose place of origin was thousands of miles removed from the centers of their conquests has to be dated from the relatively late period of the fifth century A.D. when the stirrup and firm saddle were invented, probably in Iran or central Asia. These technological improvements gave cavalries the decisive edge ove the hitherto invincible traditional infantries and inaugurated the period of nomadic empires in history. The nomadic period came eventually to an end only with the advent of the "gunpowder states" (Marshal G.S. Hodgson) of which the Safavid realm was a typical example and in which infantries equipped with artillery and muskets regained equal status with mounted foces.

Iranian history during the age of horseback nomads had its share of successive, inherently unstable but frequently surprisingly efflorescent, states. Large cavalry forces do not lend themselves to strict centralized organization as the Arabs found out only one century after the conquest of Iran and even though Arab-Muslim centralization continued for another century,the provinces (including Iran) eventually reverted to a status of autonomy. This cycle of cavalry conquest, imperial organization and provincial decentralization was repeated three times in Iranian history, with the successive realms of the Saljugs, Mongols and Timurids. Each of these realms and the various ephemeral provincial states interspersed between them provide the matter for our lectures: we shall look at their military and administrative frameworks, economic underpinnings and technological and cultural achievements in order to explain the shortlivedness as well as theeffflorescence of their power and glory during classical Islamic times.

(2) Requirements

(a) The class shall meet four times a week, on M. Tu, W and Th. You are urged to attend classes regularly. Please inform me if you are sick or otherwise have to miss several lectures so that arrangements can be made for you to catch up.

(b) The basic text for this class is Alessandro Bausani, The Persians (London, Elek, 1962). This text alone is not sufficient for a full understanding of Iranian history between 650 and 1500. I have, therefore, assigned a number of additional books to the Reserve Section of the library. Please make a conscientious effort to keep up with your basic and supplementary readings.

(c) I shall distribute outlines on Thursday of every week containing a survey of the materials to be presented in the lectures of the following week. In each of the outlines a section is included which contains the reading assignment of the day.

(d) There will be four take-home tests, spaced on the average every two weeks. The dedaline of each of these essay tests will be one week after the announcement of the essay questions. (Esceptions will be allowed only under grave circumstances.) There will be no midterm in this class.

(e) You will have the choice of several questions in the aforementioned essay tests. There is no limit to the length of the essay, although it seems reasonable to assume a minimum of two or three pages on which a sufficiently detailed answer can be formulated. The tests will be based on the texts on reserve and on any additional materials you might need to search for in the library.

(f) The final exam will be comprehensive and will cover both the lectures and assigned readings. The exam will iclude short identification and detailed essay questions. You will have a choice of several questions.

(g) In this relatively small upper division class I want all of you to participate vigorously. If you have questions or comments please raise your hand. If you want to discuss matters further with me please come and see me in my office. My office hours are on Mondays, 2-3 p.m. in my history office, Carlson 301, and on Tuesdays, 2-3 p.m. in my Middle East office. I can always be reached at the following phone numbers: 581-8312 (History Department office). 581-6181 (Middle east Center) and 359-9659 (home).

Should I still be elusive after you have tried numbers please leave a note in the Department of History or Middle East Center.

(3) Class schedule

Week 1	- March 29	-	General orientation meeting
	March 30	-	Sassanid Iran
	March 31	-	Iran and Byzantium
	April 1	-	The Origins of the Islamic Community
Week 2	- April 5-8	-	The Islamic Conquest of Iran
Week 3	- April 12-15	-	Abaasid Iran
Week 4	- April 19-22	-	The Autonomous Dynasties of Iran
Week 5	- April 26-29	-	Buyid Rule in Iran and Iraq
Week 6	- May 3-6	-	The Coming of the Turks: Qarakuanids and Ghaznawids
Week 7	- May 10-13	-	Saljuq Iran
Week 8	- May 17-20	-	The Mongol Invasion
Week 9	- May 24-27	-	Ilkhanid Iran
Week 10	- June 1-3	-	Timur's Invasion and the Realms of the Turkmen

(4) Selected bibliography

(a) General and caliphal period

H.F. Amedroz, "The Vizier Abu'l-Fadl Ibn al-Anud from the 'Tajaraib al-umam' of Abu ali Miskawaih", Der Islam 3 (1912), 323-51

A.J. Arberry, ed., The Legacy of Persia (Oxford, 1955)
Idem, Shiraz: Persian City of Saints and Poets (U. of Oklahoma Press, 1964)

Jean Aubin, "Elements pour L'etude des agglomerations urbaines dans L'Iran medieval', The Islamic City, A. Hourani, ed., 65-75

W. Barthold, "Zur Geschichte der Saffariden", Noeldeke Festschrift, vol. 1, 171-91

C.E. Bosworth, "The Armies of the Saffarids", BSOAS 31 (1968), 534-54

(4) Selected bibliography con't

Idem, "The Heritage of Rulership in Early Islamic Iran and the Search for Dynastic Connections with the Past", Iran 11 (1973), 51-62

Idem, "On the Chronology of the Ziyarids in Gurgan and Tabaristan", Der Islam 40 (1964), 25-34

Idem, Sistan under the Arabs (Rome, 1968)

E.G. Browne, A Literary History of Persia (London, 1902)

Claude Cahen, "L'emigration de persane des origines de l'Islam aux Mongoles", La Persia nel medioevo, 181-94

The Cambridge History of Iran (2 vols. published so far)

Ellwell-Sutton, L.P, A guide to Iranian Area Study (Ann Arbor, 1952)

Mostefa K. Fateh, "Taxation in Persia: A Synopsis from the Early Times to the Conquest of the Mongols", BSOAS 4 (1926-28), 723-43

M. Forstner, "Ya qub b. al-Laith under Zunbil", ZDMG 120 (1970), 69-83

R.N. Frye, Bukhara: The Medieval Achievement (U. of Oklahoma, 1965)

H.A.R. Gibb, The Islamic Conquests in Central Asia (London, 1923)

Hasan Hadi, Persian Navigation (London, 1928)

Muhammad Ishaq, "A Scholar Prince of Sistan" J. As. Soc. Pak. 10 (1965), 55-65

Farhad Nomani, "The Origin and Development of Feudalism in Iran, 300-1600 A.D.", Tahqiqate eqtosadi 9 (1972), 5-61

F. Omar, "The Nature of the Iranian Revolts in the early Abbasid Period", IC 1 (1974), 1-9

Jan Rypka, History of Iranian Literature (Dordrecht, 1968)

P. Schwarz, Iran in Mittelalter (Stuttgart, 1896-1936)

B. Spuler, "Afghanistans Geschichte und Verwaltung in fruehislamischer Zeit", Caskel Festschrift, 351-59

(4) Selected bibliography con't

Idem, Iran in fruehislamischer Zeit (Wiesbaden, 1952)

E.M. Wright, "Babak of Badhdh and al-Afshin during the Years AD 816-41", MW 38 (1948), 43-59, 124-31

(b) Buyids

H. Busse, Chalif und Grosskoenig: Die Buyiden in Iraq, 945-1055 (Beirut, 1969)

V.F. Minorsky, La domination des Dailamites (Paris, 1932)

R. Mottahadeh, "Administration in Buyid Qazwin", Islamic Civilization 950-1150, 33-46

(c) Saljuqs

C.E. Bosworth, The Ghaznawids (Edinburgh, 1963)

R. Bulliet, The Patricians of Mishapur (Harvard UP, 1972)

Heribert Horst, Die Staatsverwaltung der Grosseldschuken... Wiesbaden, 1964)

R. Schnyder, "Political Centres and Artistic Powers in Saljuq Iran", Islamic Civilization 950-1150 (Oxford, 1973)

(d) Mongls, Turkmen

R. Grousset, L'empire des steppes (Paris, 1939).

Karl Jahn, "Paper Currency in Iran: A Contribution to the Cultural and Economic History of iran in the Mongol Period", J. Asian Mist. 4 (1970), 101-35

Owen Lattimore, Inner Asian Frontiers of China (New york, 1940)

V. Minorsky, "The Aq-Qoyunlu and Land Reforms", BSOAS 17 (1955), 449-62

Idem, "The Qara-Qoyunlu and the Qutb-Shahs", BSOAS 17 (1955), 50-73

J.J. Saunders, A History of the Mongol Conquests (London, 1971)

John M. Smith, "Mongol Manpower and Persian Population", JESHO 18 (1975), 271-300

MIDDLE EAST LANGUAGES AND CULTURES
COLUMBIA UNIVERSITY
PROFESSOR E. YAR-SHATER

PERSIAN HISTORY II

Political, Social, and Cultural History from the Advent of Islam to Modern Time
(W4468x)

I. Introductory Remarks

(a) a general view of Persian history
(b) geographical, economic, and human factors influencing the course of Persian history
(c) distinctive features of life and culture in Islamic Persia
(d) landmarks of Persian history
(e) transcription of Persian words

Required readings:

Arberry, A.J. Classical Persian Literature (London: Allen and Unwin, 1958 (Arberry), pp. 7-29.

Ghirshman, R. Iran (London: Penguin Books, 1954), pp. 20-26, 350-57.
Yarshater, E. "Cultural Development in Iran," in Iran: Past, Present and Future (Jane W. Jacqz, ed.) Aspen Institute: 1976, pp. 704-19

II. Sources of the Islamic History of Persia: A Bibiographical Survey

(a) general
(b) histories
(c) literary works
(d) other written documents
(e) archeological and numismatic evidence

Required readings:

Arberry, pp. 139-63.

III. Transiton from Zoroastrian Persia to Islamic Persia

(a) Islam and its tenets
(b) the conquest of Persia by the Arab armies
(c) the new social order and values
(d) transformation of the Persian society
(e) elements of continuity

Required readings:

Browne, E.G. A Literary History of Persia, 4 vols. (Cambridge University Press, 1928) (Browne), vol. I, pp. 185-247.

Recommended readings:

Bulliet, Richard W. Conversion to Islam in the Medieval Period (Cambridge MA, 1979), Introduction and first chapter.

IV. The Persian Elements in Islamic History and Culture

(a) the Abbasid caliphs and the Persians
(b) Persian viziers and administrators
(c) cultural contributions
(d) religious and philosophical thought

Required readings:

Browne, vol. I, pp. 251-70.

Recommended readings:

Mottahedeh, Roy. "The Abbasid Caliphate in Iran," in The Cambridge History of Iran (Cambridge University Press, 1975), vol. IV, pp. 57-89.

V. Resurgence of Persian Nationalism and the Renaissance of Persian Culture

(a) religio-political movements of the first two centuries
(b) Ya'qub of Sistan and the establishment of local dynasties
(c) the Samanids and the emergence of a new Persian literature
(d) new recensions of Persian national history

Required readings:

Browne, vol. I, pp. 308-90.

Recommended readings:

Bosworth, C.E. "The Tahirids and Saffarids," in The Cambridge History of Iran, vol. IV, pp. 90-135.
Fry, R.N. "The Samanids," ibid., pp. 136-161.
Lazard, Gilbert. "The Rise of the New Persian Language," ibid., pp. 595-632.
Yarshater, Ehsan. "Iranian National History," in The Cambridge History of Iran, vol. III (1), pp. 359-83, 393-411.

VI. Turkic Invasions and Turkic Dynasties of Persia

(a) Turkish elements in Persian history
(b) the culture of the Muslim Turks
(c) the Ghaznavids, the Seljuqs, the Atabegs, and the Khwarezm-shahs
(d) the achievements of the Turkish dynasticss and their impact on Persian life

Required readings:

Bosworth, C.E. "The Early Ghaznavids," in The Cambridge History of Iran, vol. IV, pp. 163-97.
Gibb, F.J. A History of Ottoman Poetry, 6 vols. (London: Luzac and Co., reprinted 1958), vol. I, pp. 12-32 and vol. II, Introduction.

VII. The Vizier Nizam al-Mulk and his Manual of Good Government

(a) the theory of government underlying the state
(b) justice as the leading principle
(c) religious orthodoxy
(d) socio-political attitudes

Required readings:

Lambton, A.K.S. "The Internalstructure of the Saljuq Empire," in The Cambridge History of Iran, vol. V, pp. 203-282.
al-Mulk, Nizam. The Book of Government, tr. Hubert Darke (London: Routledge & Kegan Paul, 1960), pp. 12-23, 33-62, 103-06, 193-212, 238-50.

VIII. Social Customs and Traditons: Kaykavus's Mirror for Princes

(a) social structure
(b) social etiquette
(c) court customs and ceremonies

Required Readings:

Kaykavus ibn Eskandar. A Mirror for Princes, tr. R. Levy (London: Cresset Press, 1951), pp. 49-77, 85-90, 182-219.

IX. Religious Thought and Practice

(a) Islam in Persia
(b) development of Shi'ism
(c) the Isma'ilis
(d) religious philosophy-Avicenna and Ghazzali

Required Readings:

Bausani, A. "Religion in the Saljuq Period," in The Cambridge History of Iran, vol. V, pp. 283-303.
Browne, vol. I, pp. 279-307, 391-415.

X. The Sufi Movement and its Development in Persia

(a) the origins of Sufism
(b) Sufi orders
(c) the importance of Persian mystical literature
(d) some outstanding Persian Sufis

Required readings:

Attar, Farid al-Din. Muslim Saints and Mystics, tr. A.J. Arberry (Chicago, 1966), pp. 1-12, 100-123.

Browne, vol. I, pp. 416-44, (optional: vol. II, pp. 489-526).
Nicholson, R. Divan-e Shams-e Tabrizi (Cambridge, 1989), the Introduction.

XI. The Mongol and Tatar Invasions and their Aftermath

(a) the collapse of the Islamic state of Persia and the fall of Baghdad
(b) the Persification of the Mongol rulers
(c) Ghazan, the reformer-king
(d) Timur and his successors
(e) Turkoman successor-states

Required readings:

Browne, vol. II, pp. 426-66.

XII. The Course of Persian Literature from Rudaki to Hafiz

(a) forms of Persian poetry
(b) conventionalism and freedom in Persian poetry
(c) Persian epic literature
(d) Persian lyrics
(e) satire and skepticism
(f) major Persian literary figures

Required readings:

Arberry, A.J. (ed.). The Legacy of Persia (Oxford, 1953) (Legacy), pp. 199-229.
Yarshater, Ehsan. "Persian Literature," in The Cambridge History of Islam, 2 vols. (Cambridge University Press, 1970), vol. II, pp. 671-82.
"Some Common Characteristics of Persian Poetry and Art," Studia Islamica 16 (1962), pp. 61-71 (mimeographed).

Recommended readings:

Arnold, Matthew. Sohrab and Rustum, any edition.
Fitzgerald, Edward. The Rubaiyat of Omar Khayyam, any edition.
Sa'di. Kings and Beggars, tr. A.J. Arberry (London, 1943).

XIII. The Safavids vs. the Ottomans

(a) the dynasty of saint-kings
(b) Shi'ism as the state religion
(c) Shah Abbas the Great
(d) the fall of the Safavids and the emergence of Nadir Shah

Required readings:

Sykes, Sir Percy. A History of Persia, 2 vols. (MacMillan and Co., 1915), vol. II, pp. 158-83.
or: Browne, vol. IV, pp. 32-120.

XIV. Artistic Developments

(a) a general view of Persian art
(b) visual arts
(c) music
(d) artistic impulse and Islamic restriction

Required readings:

Ettinghausen, Richard. "The Immanent Features of Persian Art," in Highlights of Persian Art, Ettinghausen and Yarshater, eds. (Bibliotheca Persica, 1979), pp. xiii-xviii.

________. "World Awareness and Human Relationships in Persian Painting," ibid., pp. 243-72.

Grabar, Oleg. "Iranian Architecture: The Evolution of a Tradition," ibid., pp. 135-64.

Ross, Dennison (ed.). Persian Art (London, 1930), pp. 25-36, 60-73, 74-85, 94-100.

Hist. - M.E.
Professor E. Yar-Shater
Gr. W4474y

Political, Cultural and Social History of Iran in the 20th Century

The proposed course has been prompted by the overwhelming interest that students in my history courses have exhibited for a course dealing with the eventful history of Iran since the turn of the century. The period has seen a sharpened awakening of Persia to the requirements of modern times, an accelerated reaction to the impact of the West; the Constitutional Revolution of 1905-1911; the demises of the Qajar dynasty (1796-1921); the rise of Reza Shah (1925-1944), the reign of his son, Mohamed Reza Sha (1944-1979); a serious oil crisis under the nationalist leader, Mosaddeq; and, finally, the events leading to the 1979 Revolution and the establishment of the Islamic Republic of Iran.

The period is rich not only in political events but also in social and cultural ones. This was the period which saw the conscious efforts at modernization and the introduction of new technologies; the development of new genres in Persian literature; the currency of modernist, Western-inspired painting, sculpture and urban architecture; attempts at the secularization and the decline of the clerical establishments; land reform and the restructuring of political power bases; polarization of the urban society; and, at the end, the resurgence of religious revivalist forces.

Up to three years ago, it appeared proper to cover this period as part of another course that I give, namely Social, Cultural and Political History of Iran in Modern Times (1500-1925). The rapid succession of events in Iran, however, the downfall of the Pahlavi regime, and the militancy of Islamic fundamentalist forces, along with a number of other political and social monuments have made it impractical to deal with all the pertinent data concerning this period in a one semester course. All the more so since it is now possible to deal with the Pahlavi period, a period of intense, if not entirely successful, modernization, oil wealth and change of mores -- with a better perspective. Furthermore, the Islamic revivalist zeal has brought to the fore a number of issues in religious and social history of modern Iran, which I find to be often the focus of my students' interest.

Synopsis

The topics to be covered in this course are as follows:

1. Political and social background: the conditions which prevailed in Persia at the turn of the century leading to the Constitutional Revolution of 1906; the Qajar political system of government; Anglo-Russian rivalries in Iran; concessions made to the foreign powers detrimental to the sovereignty and economic independence of Iran; the religious establishment; contacts with the West; patriotic press and poetry of the period; cultural developments.

2. Major advocates of reform: Sayyed Jamal al-Din al-Afghani, the pan-Islamist; Mirza Malkom Khan, the advocate of law and political reform; Mirza Hosein Moshir al-Dowleh, the progressive statesman.

3. The course of the Constitutional Revolution: anti-government demonstrations; the granting of the charter of the Constitution by Mozaffar al-Din Shah (1907); the role of the Shi'ite ulema and the liberals; the uneasy

course of the parliamentary regime; Mohammad Ali Shah's coup d'etat; the gathering storm of the revolutionary forces; the banishment in 1911 of Mohammad Ali Shah and the re-establishment of the parliamentary regime.

4. Parliamentary rule under Ahmad Sha (1911-1921): the ineffectual rule of Ahmad Shah; tension between the democratic and royalist forces; the effects of World War I; the deterioration of political, social, and economic conditions; the Bolshevik Revolution and the cancellation of Tsarist claims on Iran; expansion of British influence and the Treaty of 1919; the nationalist outrage, and the premiership of Sayyed Zia al-Din; Reza Shah assumes effective power.

5. Towards a strongman's rule: the accession of Reza Shah (1925); reformist measures taken by Reza Khan; the establishment of internal security; the pacification of the tribes; cancellation of the capitulations; adoption of modernizing measures.

6. The reign of Reza Shah: the establishment of a national state; reform of the standing army; judicial reforms and the introduction of new civil and penal laws; reform of the educational system; improvement of communications; unveiling of women; tension between the church and the state; decline of the Shi'ite ulama.

7. World War II and the collapse of Persian neutrality: the forced abdication of Reza Shah; the pursuant period of active freedom and political debates; the formation of growth of the Tudeh (Communist) Party; the early phase of Mohammad Reza Shah's rule; the Azerbaijan crisis; the premiership of Qavam al-Saltaneh, and the inclusion of communist ministers in the cabinet; Russian demand for the concession of oil exploration in Iran; the emergence of Mossadeq's leadership of a nationalist movement.

8. The United States and Iran: the withdrawal of the British from India and the expansion of the American role in the Middle East; American economic aid to Iran; the American stand on the question of Azerbaijan and the demise of the autonomous Republic of Azerbaijan; the oil crisis.

9. The premiership of Dr. Mossadeq: the nationalization of the British Anglo-Iranian Oil Company; the National Front and clashes with the Tudeh Party; failure of the oil policies; the overthrow of Dr. Mossadeq.

10. The second phase of Mohammad Reza Shah's rule: the consolidation of royal and autocratic powers; relations with the United States, the Russians and the British; the "White Revolution" of 1963 and the land reform; the sharp rise in oil prices in the early 1970s; the new wealth and its effect on the political and social fabric of Persian society; the military build-up; gradual alienation of the educated classes and of the traditional ulama; increasing popular dissatisfaction; the engage literature of the period as a mirror of social change.

11. Khomaini versus the Pahlavi regime: Khomaini and the "White Revolution"; the years of exile; the fundamentals of Khomaini's political thought; Islamic covert activities against the regime; the Palestinian connection; the impact of American human rights policies in the late 1970s; the gathering storm; Bakhtiar's permiership and the departure of the royal family from Iran; the collapse of the Pahlavi regime.

12. The Islamic Republic of Iran: the transitional phase of Bazargan's government; the emergence of the clergy as factual rulers; anti-Israeli policies; persecution of the Baha'is; violence and xenophobia; the Hostage Crisis; the Irano-Iraqi War; the second majlis of the Islamic Republic.

13. The Shi'ite ulama as rulers: a consideration of the Shi'ite religious and political doctrines from the eighth century to the present; Shi'ite esoteric and revolutionary sects; the doctrine of the velayat-e faqih; the tensions between Islamic revivalism and the requirements of modern times; cultural trends in the Islamic Republic; the Islamic press.

14. Women's rights since the Constitutional Revolution: traditional status of women; women's rights and duties in Shi'ite law; women and laws of property, marriage, and guardianship; unveiling of women in 1938; women's progressive societies; political franchise in 1963; reform of marriage law; women and the educational system; women's status in the Islamic Republic.

BIBLIOGRAPHY

INTRODUCTORY

Algar, Hamid — Mirza Malkum Khan: A Study in the History of Iranian Modernism (University of California Press, Berkeley, 1973)

Algar, Hamid — Religion and State in Iran, 1785-1906, Role of the Ulama in the Qajar Period (University of California Press, Berkeley, 1969)

Alexander, Yonah & Nanes, Allan (ed.) The United States and Iran (University Publications of America, Frederick, Md., 1980)

Bakhash, Shaul — Iran: Monarchy, Bureaucracy, & Reform under the Qajars: 1858-1896 (Ithaca Press, London, 1978)

Browne, Edward G. — A Year Amongst the Persians (Adam & Charles Black, London, 1893)

Cottam, Richard — Nationalism in Iran (University Pittsburgh Press, Pittsburgh, 1964, 1979)

Kazemi, Farhad — Poverty and the Revolution in Iran: the Migrant Poor, Urban Marginality, and Politics

Keddie, Nikki — Sayyid Jamal ad-Din "al-Afghani" (University of California Press, Los Angeles, 1972)

Keddie, Nikki — Women in the Muslim World (Harvard University Press, Cambridge, 1978)

Mahbubi, Ardakani, H., — Tarikh-e Mo'assesat-e Tamaddoni-ye Jadid dar Iran (The History of Modern Institutions in Iran) (Tehran University Press, No. 1879, 1975)

CONSTITUTIONAL MOVEMENT

Adamiyat, Faridun, — Ideologi-ye Nihzat-e Mashrutiyyat-e Iran (Ideology of the Constitutional Revolution (Teharan Payam, 1355/1976)

Browne, Edward G., — The Persian Revolution of 1905-1909 (Barnes & Noble, New York, 1966)

Kasravi, Ahmad, — Tarikh-e Mashruta-ye Iran (History of the Persian Constitutional Revolution, 3 Vols (Tehran, 1353/1974)

PAHLAVI PERIOD

Abrahamian, Ervand — Iran Between Two Revolutions (Princeton University Press, Princeton, 1982)

Banani, Amin — Modernization and Iran, 1921-1941 (Stanford University Press, Stanford, 1961)

Halliday, Fred — Iran: Dictatorship and Development (Penguin Books, New York, 1979

Lenczowski, George (ed.) — Iran Under the Pahlavis (Hoover Institution Press, Stanford, California, 1978)

Saikal, Amin — The Rise and Fall of the Shah (Princeton University Press, Princeton, 1980)

Upton, Joseph M. — The History of Modern Times: an Interpretation (Harvard University Press, Cambridge, 1961)

OPPOSITION AND REVOLUTION

Akhavi, Shahrough — Religion and Politics in Contemporary Iran (State University of New York Press, Albany, 1980)

Algar, Hamid (trans.) Khumayni, Ruh Allah — Islam and Revolution: Writings and Declarations of Iman Khomeni (Mizan Press, Berkeley, California, 1981)

Arjomand, Said Amir (ed.) — From Nationalism to Revolutionary Islam (MacMillan)

Bill, James — "Power and Religion in Revolutionary Iran", Middle East Journal, Vol. 36, No. 1, Winter 1982

Fischer, Michael M.J. — Iran: From religious Dispute to Revolution (Harvard University Press, Cambridge, 1980)

Keddie, Nikki — Roots of Revolution (Yale University Press, New Haven, 1981)

Khomeini, Ruhollah — Islamic Government (Manor books, Inc., New York, 1979)

UNIVERSITY OF WISCONSIN-MADISON
Department of History

Semester I Year 1986-87

COURSE NO.	COURSE TITLE	INSTRUCTOR
573	**Undergraduate Studies in Africa, Asia, and Latin America: THE IRANIAN REVOLUTION**	**Humphreys**

COURSE DESCRIPTION

This course represents an effort to identify the character and the causes of the Iranian Revolution of 1978-1980. We will try to view this event from both an internal perspective (the dynamics of Iranian society and culture in the 20th century) and an external one (the relations of Iran with foreign powers, in particular Russia, Great Britain, and the United States). Among topics to be investigated: the conflict between monarchical absolutism and constitutionalism in modern Iran; the social values and political orientations developed within Shi'ite thought; the economic stresses created by imperialism and modernization in the late 19th and 20th centuries; secularist alternatives to Shi'ite ideology; the quest for cultural authenticity -- Westernization, traditionalism, nostalgia, and disorientation. The Revolution itself calls for an investigation of three issues: 1) the abrupt collapse of the monarchy; 2) the assertion of political leadership by the Shi'ite clergy; 3) the focusing of popular wrath against external enemies, in particular the United States.

LECTURES

The class will meet on Tuesdays, 2:25 - 4:25.

Except for the first three weeks or so, in which I will try to provide you with a general background in modern Iranian history and Shi'ite Islam, the classes will be in a discussion/colloquium format rather than lectures.

WRITTEN ASSIGNMENTS AND EXAMINATIONS

No examinations or research papers. Students will be asked to keep a journal based on the assigned readings and class discussions. Periodically (at the end of September, October, and November) they will be asked to submit a concise essay (ca. 5 pp.) based on this journal and addressing some aspect of the Iranian Revolution. These will be critiqued for style and content by me, but not graded. At the end of the term, students will submit a longer essay (10-12 pp.) based on this earlier work, in which they will try to define and bring together the various levels of significance of the Revolution.

GRADING SYSTEM

A-F

REQUIRED READINGS

Nikki Keddie, Roots of Revolution: an Interpretive History of Modern Iran
Shaul Bakhash, The Reign of the Ayatollahs
Roy Mottahedeh, The Mantle of the Prophet
Gary Sick, All Fall Down: America's Tragic Encounter with Iran
Selected Readings, History 573 (Available at Kinko's, 626 University Ave.)

History 573 Humphreys

COURSE SCHEDULE

Sept. 2 Introduction to the Course
A Geographic and Ethnographic Overview of Iran

Sept. 9 Traditional Conceptions of Politics and Society in Iran

Readings: Keddie, 1-39 (chs. 1-2)
Nizam al-Mulk, Book of Government (Selected Readings)

Sept. 16 Imperialism and the Constitutional Revolution

Readings: Keddie, 40-78 (chs. 3-4)
Treaties and Concessions regarding Iran, 1890-1914 (Selected Readings)

Sept. 23 Iran under Reza Shah

Readings: Keddie, 79-112 (ch. 5)
Treaties and Agreements regarding Iran, 1917-1941 (Selected Readings)

Sept. 30 Muhammad Reza Shah and the White Revolution

Readings: Keddie, 113-182 (chs. 6-7)
Treaties and Agreements regarding Iran, 1943-1946 (Selected Readings)

Oct. 7 The Crisis of Modernity

Readings: Keddie, 183-230
Jalal Al-e Ahmad, Gharbzadegi (Selected Readings)
'Alī Shari'atī, Essays (Selected Readings)

Oct. 14 The Clergy: World-View and Ethos (1)

Readings: Mottahedeh, Prologue and chs. 1-3 (pp. 11-109)

Oct. 21 The Clergy: World-View and Ethos (2)

Readings: Mottahedeh, chs. 4-6 (pp. 110-247)

Oct. 28 The Clergy: World-View and Ethos (3)

Readings: Mottahedeh, chs. 7-Epilogue (pp. 248-390)

Nov. 4 The Coming of the Revolution

Readings: Bakhash, chs. 1-2 (pp. 3-51)
Khomeini, Sermons and Writings (Selected Readings)

Nov. 11 The Clergy's Seizure of Power

Readings: Bakhash, chs. 3-6 (pp. 52-165)

Nov. 18 The Islamic Republic

Readings: Bakhash, chs. 7-10 (pp. 166-250)
The 1979 Constitution (Selected Readings)

Nov. 25 The United States and Iran: The Shah and the Satan

Readings: Sick, chs. 1-5 (pp. 3-101)

Dec. 2 The United States and Iran: The Year of Revolution

Readings: Sick, chs. 6-10 (pp. 102-216)

Dec. 9 The United States and Iran: The Hostage Crisis

Readings: Sick, chs. 11-16 (pp. 217-342)

DUE DATES

Essay 1	Sept. 30
Essay 2	Oct. 28
Essay 3	Nov. 25
Final Essay	Dec. 12

SYLLABUS

History 4015
Iranian Revolution
in Historical Perspective

Dr. Hooglund
Spring, 1986

This course will examine the 20th century political, social and economic developments in which the Iranian Revolution of 1978-79 is rooted. The focus will be on the ideological divisions that have persisted in Iranian society for the past 80 years. The impact of major events in 20th century Iranian history will be analyized: the Constitutional Revolution of 1905-06; the foreign interventions and occupations of 1911-21; the secularizing and economic development policies of Reza Shah, 1921-41;the emergence of political movements in the 1941-53 period; and the socioeconomic transformations of the 1960s and 1970s. These analyses will provide the background for understanding the politicalization of the Shi'i Islamic clergy and their use of religious symbols to challenge the regime, overthrow the monarchy, and establish a theocratic government.

The course will follow a lecture/discussion format. Students are expected to have completed the assigned readings by the dates indicated below so that they may participate in the discussions. Class participation will be part of each student's grade for the course.

Each student will also be required to write a paper of approximately 1500 to 2000 words on a topic selected in consultation with Prof. Hooglund. Topics may be in any subject area related to contemporary Iran: art, economic development, foreign policy, history, land reform, literature, philosophy, politics, religion, technology, etc. Students will present 5 to 10 minute oral summaries of their papers to the whole class during the last weeks of the quarter. All papers are due on June 3.

Other requirements of the course include a map quizz--it may sound third gradish, but this seems to be the most effective way to get students to recognize many unfamiliar place names that will be recurring in the readings!--, a mid-term exam and a final exam.

The following texts will be used for the course and should be purchased. All are paperbacks. All assigned readings from other books and periodicals will be on reserve.

Ervand Abrahamian, IRAN BETWEEN TWO REVOLUTIONS

Samad Behrangi, THE LITTLE BLACK FISH AND OTHER STORIES

Nikki Keddie, ROOTS OF REVOLUTION

MERIP REPORTS #87, "Iran's Revolution: The Rural Dimension"

MERIP REPORTS #104, "Khomeini and the Opposition"

MERIP REPORTS #125/126, "The Strange War in the Gulf"

The class schedule and reading assignments are:

April 3: Intodductory Overview

History 4015 Dr. Hooglund

Apr. 8 - 10: The Constitutional Revolution

Abrahamian, IRAN BETWEEN TWO REVOLUTIONS, Chapters I & II.

Keddie, ROOTS OF REVOLUTION, Chapters 1, 2, 3, 4 (pp. 1-78).

Apr.15 - 17: World War I Disintegration and the Rise of Reza Shah

Abrahamian, Chapter Three

Keddie,Chapter 5

Knapp, "1921-1941: The Period of Reza Shah" (on reserve).

MAP QUIZZ!

Apr.22 - 24: World War II and aftermath: Occupation, political liberalization, and the emergence of the Tudeh

Abrahamian, Chapter Four ; Chapter Five, pp. 225-250; Chapter Six, pp. 281-318; and Chapter Seven.

Keddie, Chapter 6, pp. 113-132.

Apr. 29 - May 1 : The Mossadegh Era and Oil Nationalization Crisis

Abrahamian, Chapter Five, pp. 250-280; Chapter Six, pp. 318-325; and Chapter Eight.

Keddie, Chapter 6, pp. 132-141.

Zabih,"The Mossadegh Era", pp. 20-126

May 6 : MID-TERM EXAM!

Last Date for all students to have paper topics approved.

May 8-13-15: The Royal Dicatorship of Mohammad Reza Shah (1953-1979)

Abrahamian, Chapter Nine

Behrangi, read the following short stories for class discussion on May 15: "The Little Black Fish"; "24 Restless Hours"; "One Peach, A Thousand Peaches"; and "The Little Sugar Beet Vendor."

Keddie, Chapters 7 and 8.

May 20 - 22: The Iranian Revolution of 1978-79

Abrahamian, Chapters Ten and Eleven

Keddie, Chapter 9, pp. 231-258.

MERIP REPORTS, #87, "Iran's Revolution", pp. 3-26.

Hooglund, TRIUMPH OF THE TURBAN, Chapter II.

May 27 - 29: Consolidating Theocracy

Keddie, ROOTS OF REVOLUTION, Chapter 9, pp. 258-272

Keddie and Hooglund, eds., THE ISLAMIC REVOLUTION AND THE ISLAMIC REPUBLIC, Read the following papers:
Akhavi, pp. 17-28
Hooglund, pp. 29-37
Loffler, pp. 59-66
Ferdows, pp. 75-82
Keddie, pp. 88-100
Sick, pp. 127-131
Miller, pp. 132-139
Atkin, pp. 140-150
Cottam, pp. 169-178

Bill, "Power and Religion in Revolutionary Iran", in MIDDLE EAST JOURNAL, vol. 36, Winter 1982, pp. 22-47.

Presentations of papers will be scheduled for both classes.

June 3 : The Iran/Iraq War and the Future of the Revolution

MERIP REPORTS, #125/126 "The Strange War in the Gulf"

Gary Sick essay from IRAN TIMES (on reserve)

Final oral presentations

All papers due by end of class

Review for final exam

June 7 : Final Examination

MUHAMMAD AND THE QUR'AN

Winter Quarter, 1986

Fred Donner
305 Oriental Institute

I. Week of Jan. 6 **Organizational Meeting**

II. Week of Jan. 13 **Pre-Islamic Arabia**

Reading: Maxime Rodinson, Mohammed, pp. 1-37.
W. Montgomery Watt, Muhammad at Mecca, pp. 1-29.
I. Goldziher, "Muruwwa and Dīn," in Muslim Studies 1, pp. 11-44.
R. B. Serjeant, "Haram and Hawtah, the Sacred Enclave in Arabia," in Abdurrahman Badawi, Ilā Tāhā Husayn, pp. 41-58.

III. Week of Jan. 20 **The Traditional View of Muhammad**

Reading: W. Montgomery Watt, Muhammad, Prophet & Statesman.
W. Montgomery Watt, Bell's Introduction to the Qur'ān, pp. 30-56.
Familiarize yourself with Ibn Hishām, The Life of Muhammed (Sīra) (transl. Alfred Guillaume).

IV. Week of Jan. 27 **History and Interpolation in Qur'ān and Sira**

Reading: Q. 8, entire (Badr?) and relevant parts of Ibn Hishām.
Q. 3, vv. 118-185 (Uḥud?) and Ibn Hishām.
Q. 33, vv. 9-27 (Trench, Qurayẓa?) and Ibn Hishām.
Q. 48, entire (Ḥudaybiya?) and Ibn Hishām.
Q. 9, vv. 38-64 (Tabūk?) and Ibn Hishām.
Ibn Hishām, on al-'Abbās b. 'Abd al-Muṭṭalib
Abū Ṭālib
'Alī b. Abī Ṭālib
Abū Sufyān b. Ḥarb
Mu'āwiya b. Abī Sufyān
'Uthmān b. 'Affān
Patricia Crone & Michael Cook, Hagarism, pp. 3-34.
A. Rippin, "Literary Analysis of Qur'ān, Tafsīr, and Sīra. The Methodologies of John Wansbrough," in Richard Martin (ed.), Approaches to Islam in Religious Studies, pp. 151-163.

[recommended for those who have not had Islamic Civilization I:
Bernard Lewis, The Arabs in History, pp. 49-98; OR
Cambridge History of Islam, vol. I, chapters 3 & 4: OR
M.A. Shaban, Islamic History, vol. I]

V. Week of Feb. 3 **Basic Doctrines as presented in Qur'ān and Sīra**

Reading: Q. 2, vv. 1-39, 72-82.
Q. 6, vv. 1-58, 89-118.
Q. 7, vv. 1-58.
Q. 13, entire.
Q. 23, vv. 1-22.
Q. 36, entire.
Q. 39, vv. 22-end.
Q. 41, vv. 1-6.
Q. 69, 75, 76, 77, entire.
Ibn Hishām, pp. 146-155.
Toshihiku Izutzu, Ethico-Religious Concepts in the Qur'ān, pp. 45-116.

VI. Week of Feb. 10 **Islam and the Judaeo-Christian Tradition**

Reading: Q. 2, vv. 40-71, 83-136, 246-253.
Q. 3, vv. 33-115.
Q. 4, vv. 46-50, 153-end
Genesis 4:1-16, compare Q. 5, vv. 12-32, 57-86, 110-120.
Genesis 2-3, compare Q. 7, vv. 10-29, 59-174.
Q. 9, vv. 29-35.
Genesis 37-50, compare with Q. 12, entire.
Q. 18, entire.
Q. 19, vv. 1-40, 88-98.
Q. 20, vv. 1-99.
Q. 28, vv. 1-50.
Q. 29, vv. 14-40.
Ibn Hishām, pp. 270-277.
A. S. Yahuda, "A Contribution to Qur'ān and Hadīth Interpretation," Ignaz Goldziher Memorial Volume 1, pp. 280-308, esp. pp. 292-298.

VII. Week of Feb. 17 **Pagan Opposition and the Notion of umma (community)**

Reading: Q. 2, vv. 83-86, 190-194.
Q. 4, vv. 59-122, 135-149.
Q. 5, vv. 51-58.
Q. 8, vv. 38-46, 72-75.
Q. 9, vv. 1-29, 60-129.
Q. 23, vv. 57-70, 81-94.
Q. 60, entire
R. B. Serjeant, "The Constitution of Medina," Islamic Quarterly 8 (1964), pp. 1-16.

NEHist 211-Muhammad and the Qur'an   Winter 1986

VIII. Week of Feb. 24 Ritual Law

Reading: Q. 2, vv. 142-177, 184-189, 195-203, 215, 261-274.
Q. 4, v. 43.
Q. 5, vv. 87-97.
Q. 6, vv. 136-154.
Q. 22, vv. 25-41.
*Q. 2, v. 255.
*Q. 1, entire.
*Q. 24, vv. 35-41.
G. R. Hawting, "The Origins of the Muslim Sanctuary at Mecca," in G. H. A. Juynboll (ed.), Studies on the First Century of Islamic Society, pp. 23-47.
M. J. Kister, "You shall only set out for 3 mosques. A Study of an early Tradition," Le Muséon 82 (1969), pp. 173-196.

IX. Week of Mar. 3 Social and Family Law

Reading: Q. 2, vv. 178-182, 219-245, 275-286.
Q. 4, vv. 1-42, 127-130.
Q. 5, vv. 38-47.
Q. 24, vv. 1-34, 56-64.
Q. 33, vv. 28-73.
Q. 58, vv. 1-4.
Q. 65, vv. 1-7.
Richard Bell, "Muhammad and Divorce in the Qur'ān," Muslim World 29 (1939), pp. 55-62.

X. Week of Mar. 10 The Problem of Muhammad

Reading: J. E. Royster, "The Study of Muhammad," Muslim World 62 (1972), pp. 48-70.
Maxime Rodinson, "A Critical Survey of Modern Studies of Muhammad," in Merlin L. Swartz, Studies on Islam, pp. 23-85.
J. Fueck, "The Originality of the Arabian Prophet," in Swartz, Studies on Islam, pp. 86-98.

COURSE REQUIREMENTS

1. You must do the reading, and be prepared to discuss it in class. Speak up!--a significant part of your grade will depend upon class participation. Periodically you will be asked to do special preparation for the next class discussion.

2. You must submit a paper (about 15 pages, typed, double-spaced) at the end of the course. Papers are due the first day of the examination period; if your paper is received later, you may be required to take an incomplete (I) until the paper is submitted. You should make an appointment to discuss your paper topic early in the quarter--sometime in the first 3 weeks. Make sure to keep a xerox of your paper when you submit it. You are encouraged to submit a rough draft of your paper in advance.

3. You are required to make an oral presentation, of about 20 minutes' duration, toward the end of the quarter. Its purpose will be to familiarize others with your paper research.

Core Curriculum **Harvard University** **Fall Term 1986-87**

Foreign Cultures 28
The Religion and Culture of Islam

Instructors:

William A. Graham (Near Eastern Languages and Civilizations and The Committee on the Study of Religion). Office: Phillips Brooks House 304. Tel.: 495-7884.

Ali S. Asani (Sanskrit and Indian Studies and Near Eastern Languages and Civilizations). Office: 6 Divinity Avenue (Semitic Museum), Rm. 307. Tel.: 495-5755.

Teaching Fellows:

John Flanagan (Doctoral candidate, Near Eastern Languages and Civilizations)
Linda Kern (Doctoral candidate, Near Eastern Languages and Civilizations)
Victor Ostapchuk (Doctoral candidate, Inner Asian and Altaic Studies)
Najwa al-Qattan (Doctoral candidate, History and Middle Eastern Studies)
Susan van de Ven (Doctoral candidate, School of Education)

This course seeks to introduce the world of Islam. No previous work is presupposed. Emphasis will be given to the development of common classical Islamic institutions and ideas as well as diverse forms of Islamic culture over the past fourteen centuries, with a view to understanding better the Islamic world today. The work is arranged topically and the topics are treated, in general, chronologically. While this is not a history course, anyone taking it should come away with a broad understanding of the basic historical framework within which Islamic civilization has developed.

The focus of the course's work is the weekly section meeting. Each week's discussion will center on selections from Islamic primary sources in English translation. There will be seven sections meeting either on Thursday or Friday of each week, beginning with 2/3 October. Sections will be assigned in the second week of the course. The course will meet as a whole at noon on Monday and Wednesday, and on three occasions on Friday (see schedule of meetings). Evening film showings will be held as indicated on the schedule. In addition to the required primary readings, there will be weekly assigned readings to accompany the lectures. Many of the lectures will presuppose familiarity with the week's assigned readings.

Core Curriculum **Harvard University** **Fall Term 1986-87**

Foreign Cultures 28: The Religion and Culture of Islam
Revised Schedule of Class Meetings and Topics
(as of 20 October)

Week:			
1:	Mo 22 Sep	"Islam": An Introduction (Graham)	
	We 24	Islamic Lands and Peoples (Asani)	
	We 24	Film: "In the Name of Allah"	
	Fr 26	Islam: Outsider and Insider Views (Graham)	
2:	Mo 29 Sep	The Qur'ān (Graham)	
	Tu 30 Sep	Films: "The Empty Quarter", "Grass"	
	We 01 Oct	Muhammad (Graham)	<[Map Exercise Distributed]
	Sections:	Qur'ān: The Joseph Story	
3:	Mo 06 Oct	Successors of the Prophet: the Caliphate (Graham)	
	We 08	Successors of the Prophet: the 'Ulamā'/Fuqahā' (Graham)	
	Sections:	Ṭabarī, "Murder of 'Uthmān	[Map exercise due]
4:	Mo 13 Oct	COLUMBUS DAY HOLIDAY	
	We 15	The Golden Age of Islamic Culture (Graham)	
	Th 16	Film: "Mecca, the Forbidden City"	
	Fr 17	Successors of the Prophet: the Shī'ī Imāms (Asani)	
	Sections:	'Abbasid prose writings	[Essay *1 due (1st option)]
5:	Mo 20 Oct	Sunnī Piety and Practice (Graham)	
	We 22	Shī'ī piety and practice (Asani)	
	Th 23	Films: "O Protecteur des Gazelles", "Saints and Sufis"	
	Sections:	Devotional literature	[Essay *1 due (2nd option)]
6:	Mo 27 Oct	Theological and Philosophical Speculation (Graham)	
	We 29	The Sufis: Origins and Classic Themes (Asani)	
	Fr 31	The Sufis: Music and Dance (Asani)	
	Sections:	Ash'arī, Farabī, Ibn Sīnā	
7:	Mo 03 Nov	HOUR EXAM (MIDTERM)	
	We 05	The Islamic City (Graham)	
	Th 06	Films: 3 films from "The World of Islam" Series	
	Sections:	Ṣūfī literature	[Essay *2 due (1st option)]

8:	Mo 10 Nov	Aspects of Medieval Islamic Civilization, 900-1500 (Graham)
	We 12 Nov	Literature: Arabic and Persian Poetry (Asani)
	Sections:	Arabic and Persian poetry [Essay #2 due (2nd option)]
9:	Mo 17	Mosque and Madrasah (Asani)
	We 19	The Steppe Peoples: Mongols and Turks to ca. 1500 (Graham)
	Th 20	Films: "Art of the Book...Shah Nameh", "Isfahan of Shah Abbas"
	Sections:	Ghazali [Essay #2 due (3rd option)]
10:	Mo 24 Nov	Persian Culture: Extent and Influence (Asani)
	We 26	The Indo-Muslim World: Syncretism and Synthesis (Asani)
	[THANKSGIVING HOLIDAYS]	No Sections (Reading: "Era of the 3 Empires")
11:	Mo 01 Dec	Islamic Identity: Regionalism after 1500 (Graham)
	We 03	Regional Identity: The Swahili Case (Asani)
	Th 04	Films: "Asian Insight: Indonesia", "Asian Insight: Malaysia"
	Sections:	Hussein, An Egyptian Childhood [Essay #3 due (1st option)]
12:	Mo 08 Dec	Religious Identity: Iconoclasm and Imagery (Graham)
	Tu 09	Film: "There is No God but God"
	We 10	Cultural Identity: The Problem of the West (Graham)
	Sections:	Salih, The Wedding of Zein [Essay #3 due (2nd option)]
13:	Mo 15 Dec	Fundamentalist and Modernist Reform (Graham)
	We 17	Islam in the Modern World (Graham and Asani)
	Sections:	Modern Islamic Crisis [Essay #3 due (3rd option)]

Core Curriculum **Harvard University** **Fall Term 1986-87**

Foreign Cultures 28
Course Requirements

The basic work of the course is done in and for section discussion meetings. Section participation is required for successful completion of the course. As indicated on the Course Syllabus, three short essays are due during the term. Each is to be submitted to your section leader at the beginning of the section meeting on the appropriate due-date. In addition, there is a Map Exercise which will be collected by Section leaders at the beginning of section on 9 or 10 October. There is a Midterm and a Final Examination.

The three essays are all short (4-6 pp., typed, double-spaced) and are to be based on one or more of the required primary texts assigned for discussion in the week in which the essay is due. Students may choose one of two or three topics (and hence one of two or three due dates) for each of the three papers, as noted on the course syllabus and repeated here as follows:

Essay * 1 (two options): Due 16/17 Oct. ('Abbasid prose writings) **or** 23/24 Oct. (Devotional literature).

Essay * 2 (three options): Due 6/7 Nov. (Sufi texts) **or** 13/14 Nov. (Poetry) **or** 20/21 Nov. (Ghazali).

Essay * 3 (three options): Due 4/5 Dec. (Taha Hussein) **or** 11/12 Dec. (Tayeb Salih) **or** 18/19 Dec. (Modern writings)

Because everyone has the right to choose from alternative due dates and topics on each of the essays, there will be no extensions granted on any of the papers except in highly unusual circumstances and by written petition to the Head of Course in advance of the due date. The page limitation on each essay can be deviated from only with prior permission of the section leader.

Section leaders will give further guidance and advice on particular topics, but in general the purpose of each essay is to offer a chance to think about the source material for the week's discussion at some length, both in the light of one's own interests and ideas and in the light of secondary readings, lectures, or any other information that helps one elucidate a particular selection or idea in the reading(s) under discussion. Attention will be given to style and form as well as content, and section leaders will both comment on each essay in writing and discuss problems in individual consultation for those who need or desire this. Please use a manual of style and be consistent in the style and format you choose. Ask about recommended manuals if you are in doubt.

The map exercise is self-explanatory and will be handed out in lecture on the first of October. It is due in section on the 9th or 10th of October. Its purpose is to familiarize everyone with the vast Islamic world and the many new place names that will be encountered in the reading.

The midterm examination will be held in the lecture hour on Friday, 31 October. It will cover all material to date and is intended not only as a check on progress, but as a "sample" of the kind of preparation needed for **the final examination**, which will be given at the regularly scheduled time for MWF @ 12 courses. Both will focus on comprehension and understanding of the material of the course rather than sheer memorization of detail. Essay questions will predominate.

For purposes of grading, the different elements of the work of the course will be valued roughly as follows (Note that the Midterm grade will be figured as a part of the Section grade, but in no case will it count more than 12.5%, or 1/8th of the final course grade):

Section Participation (including Midterm and Map Exercise)	25.0 % (1/4th)
Essays #1, #2, #3 (combined)	37.5 % (3/8th)
Final Examination	37.5 % (3/8th)

Foreign Cultures 28
Books Recommended for Purchase

The following paperback books have been ordered in quantity at the Bookstore of the Harvard Divinity School (Basement level, 45 Francis Avenue: call 5-5789 for hours), where a price discount is available on almost all titles. A limited number of copies of some titles in the second category of books have also been ordered for optional purchase. (NB: Two Qur'an translations, marked with an asterisk [*], have been ordered in reduced quantities, so that a choice is available. The Arberry is a better translation but much more expensive than the Pickthall version.)

All these titles--required and recommended--have been placed on reserve at Hilles, Lamont, and Andover libraries. Note that a set of additional primary readings for the course will be available for purchase in photocopy form (ca. $3.00 total) beginning with the second or third lecture meeting. This material will <u>not</u> be available in the libraries.

Recommended for Purchase:

Arberry, Arthur J., ed. *Aspects of Islamic Civilization.* Ann Arbor: University of Michigan, Ann Arbor Paperbacks, 1967.

Denny, Frederick M. *An Introduction to Islam.* (New York: Macmillan; London: Collier Macmillan, 1985).

Hodgson, Marshall G. S. *The Venture of Islam.* Vols. 1 and 2 [of 3] (Chicago: University of Chicago Press, 1964).

Hussein, Taha. *An Egyptian Childhood.* Trans. E. H. Paxton. London: Heinemann; Washington D.C.: Three Contintents Press, 1981.

McNeill, William H., and Marilyn R. Waldman, eds. *The Islâmic World.* (New York, London, Toronto: Oxford University Press, 1973).

Salih, Tayeb. *The Wedding of Zein and Other Stories.* Trans. Denys Johnson-Davies (London, Ibadan, Nairobi: Heinemann).

Smith, Wilfred Cantwell. *Islam in Modern History* (Princeton: Princeton University Press, 1957).

(continued on next page)

Other Books Ordered in Limited Quantities (Optional):

*Arberry, Arthur J., trans. *The Koran Interpreted.* Orig. ed., 2 vols., 1955. Paperback, 2 vols. in 1 (London: Allen and Unwin; New York: Macmillan).

Craig, Albert M., William A. Graham, Donald Kagan, Steven Ozment, and Frank M. Turner. *The Heritage of World Civilizations.* (New York: Macmillan, 1986).

Gibb, H. A. R. *Mohammedanism* (1949. 2nd ed. London, Oxford, and New York: Oxford University Press, Galaxy Books, 1970).

Grabar, Oleg. *The Formation of Islamic Art.* (New Haven and London: Yale University Press, 1973).

Hodgson, Marshall G. S. *The Venture of Islam.* Vol. 3 (Chicago: University of Chicago Press, 1964).

*Pickthall, Mohammed M., trans. *The Meaning of the Glorious Koran* (1938. New York: Mentor Books, n. d.).

Voll, John Obert. *Islam: Continuity and Change in the Modern World* (Boulder, Colorado: Westview Press; Essex, England: Longman, 1982).

Foreign Cultures 28
Weekly Assigned Readings

Under each week, required secondary readings are listed first, followed by primary-source readings (including indication of readings for section discussion that week). The required readings are followed by recommended but wholly optional suggested further readings. "Source Readings" refers to the packet of photocopied selections available for the course. Full bibliographical data on the books cited are available on the "List of Books for Purchase and Reserve".

Week 1 (22-26 Sept.): Required Reading: c. 110 pp.

Craig, Graham, Kagan, Ozment, and Turner, *The Heritage of World Civilizations*, ch. 12 ("Formation of Islamic Civilization"), pp. 363-387

Hodgson, *The Venture of Islam*, **1**: 71-90 ("The Islamic Vision"), 146-186 ("Muḥammad's Challenge")

Arberry, *Aspects of Islamic Civilization*, pp. 19-31 ("Arabia Deserta")

McNeill and Waldman, *The Islamic World*, pp. 3-27 ("Pre-Islamic Arabia")

Source readings, selection 1, Ode of Imru' l-Qays (cf. Arberry trans., above)

Also Recommended:

Gibb, *Mohammedanism*, ch. 1, "Expansion of Islam" (pp. 1-15)

Hodgson, **1**: 1-22 (Introductory), 103-145 ("The World before Islam")

Denny, *Introduction to Islam*, chs. 2 ("Hebrews"), 3 ("Christians"), 4 (Pre-Islamic Arabia), pp. 17-61

Week 2 (29 Sept.-3 Oct.): Required Reading: c. 140 pp.

Hodgson, **1**: 48-66 (on terminology), 71-90 ("The Islamic Vision")

Denny, ch. 5 ("Muhammad and the Early Muslim Community"), pp. 65-91; chs. 8 (Qur'ān), 9 (Ḥadīth), pp. 153-189

Arberry, pp. 30-51 (Qur'ān selections)

Source readings, selections 2 (Sūrah 12, "Joseph"), 3 (Ḥadīth)

Genesis 37-50 (preferably in the Revised Standard Version

For Section Discussion: The Joseph story in the Qur'ān (Sūrah 12) and the Genesis account of Joseph and his brothers (Gen. 37-50)

Also Recommended:

Gibb, chs. 2-5, "Mohammed", "Koran", "Doctrine and Ritual in the Koran", "Tradition of the Prophet" (pp. 16-59)

Hodgson, **1**: 90-99 (on civilization), 146-186 ("Muhammad's Challenge")

Week 3 (6-10 Oct.): Required Reading: c. 171 pp.

Denny, ch. 11 ("Law and State"), pp. 216-238

Hodgson, **1**: 194-279 (Caliphate, "Islamic Opposition"), 352-357 (Ṭabarī)

McNeill & Waldman, pp. 67-74, 79-81 (Balādhurī, Ziyād b. Abīhi, al-Baṣrī)

Source readings, selection 4: Ṭabarī, "The Murder of 'Uthmān"

For Section Discussion: "The Murder of 'Uthmān"

Also Recommended:

Gibb, ch. 6, "Sharī'a" (pp. 60-72)

Week 4 (13-17 Oct.): Required Reading: c. 199 pp.

Hodgson, **1**: 280-315 ("Absolutism in Flower"), 444-472 ("Adab"); **2**: 159-165 ("Arabic Letters")

McNeill & Waldman, pp. 85-134, 142-150 (Tanūkhī, Jāḥiẓ, Ṭabarī)

Arberry, pp. 72-118 (Kalīlah wa-Dimnah); 164-190 (Ibn Hazm, Ring of the Dove), 191-199 (Ibn Hazm, sermon)

For Section Discussion: Selections from Tanūkhī, Jāḥiẓ, Ṭabarī, et al.

Week 5 (20-24 Oct.): Required Reading: c. 210 pp.

Denny, ch. 6 ("Basic Beliefs and Duties"), pp. 92-124; pp. 335-343 (praxis); ch. 14 (Life Cycle and Family), pp. 295-321; 343-346 (Shī'ī rituals)

Hodgson, **1**: 315-358 ("Shar'ī Vision"), 359-392 (Kerygmatic Piety); **2**: 445-455 ("Sunnī and Shī'ī Images of History")

Source readings, selections 5 (Shī'ī drama), 6 (Burdah), 7 (Ismā'īlī sermons)

For Section Discussion: Sunnī and Shī'ī selections

Also Recommended:

Gibb, ch. 7, "Orthodoxy and Schism" (pp. 73-85)

Week 6 (27-31 Oct.): Required Reading: c. 203 pp.

Craig, Graham, etc., ch. 15 (Islamic Heartlands), pp. 455-483

Hodgson, **1**: 410-443 ("Falsafah and Kalam"); **2**: 165-179 (Science and Falsafah), 315-328 (Ibn Tufayl etc.), 467-476 (Falsafah)

McNeill & Waldman, pp. 151-171 (Ash'arī, Farābī)

Arberry, pp. 119-130 (Rāzī), 136-154 (Ibn Sīnā), 279-289 (creeds), 289-299 (Umar al-Khayyām)

Ira Lapidus, "The Evolution of Muslim Urban Society", in *Comparative Studies in Society and History*, 15 (1973): 21-50

O. Grabar, "Cities and Citizens", ch. 3 of B. Lewis, ed., *Islam and the Arab World*, pp. 89-100

For Section Discussion: Selections from Ash'arī, Farābī, Ibn Sīnā, etc.

Also Recommended:

Hodgson, **2**: 152-165, 437-445, 455-467 (intellectual traditions)

A. I. Sabra, "The Scientific Enterprise", ch. 7 of B. Lewis, ed., *Islam and the Arab World* (pp. 181-192)

Week 7 (3-7 Nov.): Required Reading: c. 185 pp.

Denny, part 4 ("The Sufi Way"), pp. 241-292

Hodgson, **1**: 392-409 ("Mystical Orientations"); **2**: 201-254 (Tariqahs)

Arberry, pp. 52-71 ("The Sunna and Its Successors"), 218-255 ("Mystical Moments"), 199-217 (ṣūfī selections), 327-334 (Masnavi selections)

McNeill & Waldman, pp. 239-247 (Rūmī)

For Section Discussion: Ṣūfī writings

Also Recommended:

Gibb, ch. 8, "Sufism" (pp. 86-99); ch. 9, "Sufi Orders" (pp. 100-112)

Grabar, pp. 104-139

Week 8 (10-14 Nov.): Required Reading: c. 148 pp.

Hodgson, **1**: 473-495 ("Dissipation of Absolutist Tradition"); **2**: 293-328 ("Persian Literary Culture"); 152-165 (Firdawsi, etc.), 293-315 (Persian literature), 484-90 (Persian literature)

McNeill & Waldman, pp. 171-177 (Mutanabbī)

Arberry, pp. 19-31 (see week #1 above), 256-258, 273-278 (Spanish Arabic poetry), 334-339 (Sa'dī), 344-358 ("The Art of Ḥāfiẓ")

Sourcebook, selection 8: Firdawsī, Shāhnāmah ("Zāl and Rudābah")

For Section Discussion: Arabic and Persian poetry selections

Also Recommended:

Hodgson, **2**: 3-61 ("Formation of International Political Order")

Week 9 (17-21 Nov.): Required Reading: c. 158 pp.

Craig, Graham, etc., ch. 23 ("Dominance and Decline"), pp. 743-770

Hodgson, **2**: 62-151 ("The Social Order"), 180-200 (Ghazālī, Intellectual traditions)

McNeill & Waldman, pp. 207-239 (Ghazālī, That Which Delivers...)

For Section Discussion: Ghazālī, That Which Delivers from Error

Also Recommended:

Hodgson, **2**: 255-292 ("Victory of New Sunni Internationalism"), 371-385 (Prologue to Book IV);

Week 10 (24-26 Nov.): Required Reading: c. 166 pp.

Hodgson, **2**: 386-436 ("After the Mongol Irruption"), 478-484 (Ibn Khaldun), 501-531 ("Visual Arts")

McNeill & Waldman, pp. 311-391 (Three Empires)

[No Sections (Thanksgiving Holidays)**]**

Also Recommended:

Hodgson, **3**: 333-357 ("Muslim India")

"The Indian Subcontinent", Part V of *The Cambridge History of Islam*, vol. 2: 1-119

Week 11 (1-5 Dec.): Required Reading: c. 217 pp.

Craig-Graham, ch. 31 ("India, Islamic Heartlands, Africa"), pp. 979-1008

W. C. Smith, *Islam in Modern History*, ch. 1, "Islam and History" (pp. 3-40); ch. 2, "Islam in Recent History" (41-92)

For Section Discussion: Ṭāhā Ḥusayn, An Egyptian Childhood

Also Recommended:

J. Voll, *Islam: Continuity and Change . . .*, ch. 3, "Foundations of Modern Experience [18th cent.]" (pp. 33-86), ch. 4, "European Domination, etc." (pp. 87-147)

Hodgson, 3: 1-161 ("Empires of Gunpowder Times"), 176-248 ("Great Western Transmutation", "European World Hegemony")

"Southeast Asia", Part VI of *Ibid.*, vol. 2: 123-207

Week 12 (8-12 Dec.): Required Reading: c. 205 pp.

Denny, pp. 351-359 (Intro to ch. 16, Wahhabi and other movements)

Smith, ch. 3 ("Arabs"), pp. 93-122, 156-160; ch. 4, "Turkey" (pp. 161-205)

Tayeb Saleh, *The Wedding of Zein and Other Stories* (entire)

For Section Discussion: Tayeb Saleh stories

Also Recommended:

Voll, chs. 5, 6, "Twentieth-Century Islam" (pp. 149-274)

"Africa and the Muslim West", Part VII of *The Cambridge History of Islam*, vol. 2: 211-405

Week 13 (15-19 Dec.): Required Reading: c. 186 pp.

Voll, ch. 7, "Resurgence of Islam" (pp. 275-348)

Arberry, pp. 359-378 (Ḥāfiẓ Ibrāhīm, Aḥmad Shawqī), 379-403 (Iqbāl, Nu'aymah, et al.)

McNeill & Waldman, pp. 395-407, 412-468 ("Crisis of Modernization")

For Section Discussion: Selections from Iqbal, Hussein, Afghani, et al.

Also Recommended:

Smith, chs. 5-7 ("Pakistan", "India", "Other Areas") pp. 206-308

Hodgson, 3: 249-332 ("Modernism in Turkey", "Egypt, East Arab Lands",), "Iran and Russia"), 357-441 ("Drive for Independence", "Epilogue")

Yann Richard, "Contemporary Shi'i Thought", in Nikki Keddi, *Roots of Revolution*, pp. 202-229

Keddi, *Roots of Revolution*, ch. 8, "Modern Iranian Political Thought" (pp. 183-202); ch. 9, "The Revolution" (pp. 231-276)

Rel. 679 - Fall 1986
Tamara Sonn
Fridays: 9AM-Noon

Islam in Modern Times

Description:

In this course, we will examine the development of modern Islamic political thought in light of the experiences of similar development in Europe. The 16th and 17th centuries of European history are referred to as the "Age of Religious Wars," characterized as they were by incessant warfare among various religious and political groups throughout Europe and England. The era followed upon the rise of Protestant sects and the breakdown of central Christian religious and political authority, and closed with the consolidation of power in the various political entities which emerged in its wake (the French, British and Spanish empires; the principalities of Italy and Germany; the various smaller principalities in northern and central Europe). Succeeding generations saw the rise of individual nation states on the foundations thus established, but again, not without a considerable amount of both intellectual exertion and military maneuvers to justify and stabilize the new political reality.

In the process, Christian thought -- facing new challenges and articulating responses -- developed significantly. From questions of religious authenticity emerged conflicitng interpretations which served as the bases for competing state governments. Eventually the split between religious legitimacy and political authority was accepted in the emergence of non-sectarian political philosophies which remain the foundation of modern national states.

We will analyze the writings major Islamic political thinkers, from Afghani and Abduh to Shariatr and Mawdudi, in an effort to determine the applicabiltiy of this European model to Islamic studies. Particular attention will be paid to such recurrent themes as the relationship between religion and politics, and the criticism of western "secularism" and "materialism" as alien to Islam but somehow endemic to Christianity. The goal of the course is to place 20th century Islamic political thought in philosophical and historical context.

Texts:

Fouad Ajami, **The Arab Predicament.**
Mangol Bayat, **Mysticism and Dissent: Socioreligious Thought in Qajar Iran.**
Albert Hourani, **Arab Thought in the Liberal Age.**
Fazlur Rahman, **Islamic Methodology in History.**

Outline:

1. Survey of European History
2. Survey of Islamic History
   Discussion Paper (handout): Similarities of 16th-17th Century European History and 19th-20th Century Islamic Hisotry.
3. The Nature of the Rise of Nationalism: Theories of Revolution and Leadership
   Read: Abdal Raziq, etc. (Hourani)

4. Phases of the Struggle for Arab Liberty (Progressive Radicalization)
   Read: Ajami
5. Religious Response: Current Phase of Liberation Struggle (Religious Conservatism)
6. Integrated Model -- Development of Methodology
   Read: Rahman's **Methodology**
7. Discussion of Islamic Reformers in Light of Methodology
   (Afghani, Abduh, al-Banna, Qutb, Mawdudi)
8. Persian Model -- Discussion Paper on Relationship Between Socio-Political Conditions and Religious Response
   Read: Bayat
9. Islamic Theories of Leadership
10. Islamic Theories of Revolution

Instructor: Dr. G. Nashat Spring 1987
Office: SEO 700
Office Hours: Th. :10-11 and 12-1 or by appointment

History 114

Women in thew Middle East: Past and Present

The aim of this elementary course is to provide an understanding of the role of women in Middle Eastern society. This will be attempted through a historical overview of the development of the role of women in the region. We will draw on a diverse body of sources, both primary and secondary, to reconstruct the past and to shed light on developments that are affecting the role of women in the present.

Course responsibilities:

All of the reading materials for this course have been placed on reserve at the library. Due to the absence of satisfactory text book, I will provide you with some of the essential readings in memiographed form from time to time. You are advised to keept up with the readings and to comeplete the assigned reading for every week at the beginning of that week.

Assigned Books:

1. Abbott, N., AISHAH-THE BELOVED OF MOHAMMED
2. Beck, L., and Keddie, N. , WOMEN IN THE MIDDLE EAST
3. Blau, F.D., and Ferber, M.A., THE ECONOMICS OF WOMEN, MEN, AND WORK
4. Bizergan, B., Fernea, E., MIDDLE EASTERN MUSLIM WOMEN SPEAK
5. Fernea, E., GUESTS OF THE SHEIK
6. Nashat, G., WOMEN AND REVOLUTION IN IRAN
7. Savory, R., INTRODUCTION TO ISLAMIC CIVILIZATION
8. Smith, M., RABI'A THE MYSTIC

Weekly Schedule:

Week One Introduction

March 31: Organizational Meeting
April 1: General Introduction to the Middle East , Savory, 1-37
April 2: Can We Study "the Invisible Half" of Midddle Eastern Society?

Week Two Theoretical Discussion

April 7: What Factors Determine Women's Role? Blau, 14-37

April 9: Women in the Ancient Middle East: Inanna Queen of Heaven and Earth; Beck, 1-32

April 10: Sasanian and Byzantine Women, selections from "Arda Viraf" and "The Martrydom of Three Christian Women"

Week Three Women Before Islam

April 14: Arabian Women On the Eve of Islam, Smith, 111-137

April 15: Topic Cont., selections Ibn Ishaq, "Hind b. Utba"; Bizergan, 3-7

April 16: Women in Early Islam, Abbott, 1-177

Week Four Women's Legal Status

April 20: Women in the Qur'an, Nashat, 37-55; Selections from the Qur'an

April 21: Women in the Shari'a, Selections from the Shari'a, Beck, 52-69

April 22: The Laws of marriage and Divorce

Week Five Medieval Women

April 28: Women in Medieval Society, Beck, 227- 245; Smith, 1-47 and137-176;

April 29: The Image of Women in Literature

April 30: Women Sainsts, Smith,137-165

Week Six Women in Transitionional Society: the 19th and 20th Centuries

May 5: Mid-term

May 6: The Causes of Change: Women and Politics, Beck, 261-309 Bizergan, 167-201; Nashat, 97-109

May 7: The Causes of Change: Social and Economic Factors, Beck 261-295

Week Seven The Unwritten Code

May 12: Birth and Education, Beck, 69-122 and 189-227; selection from "Nazik al-Mala'ika"

May 13: Betrothal and Marriage, Fernea, Part 1

May 14: Polygamy: How Does It Work? Fernea, Part 2; Nashat,231-253

Week Eight Urban Women:

May 19: The Women's Movements Beck, 124-141

May 20: Women in the Workforce, Nashat, 69-87

May 21: Professional Women, Beck, 124-158

Week Nine Rural Women

May 28: Village life, Fernea, Part 3

May 29: Tribal Women, Beck, 351-431

May 30: Rural Women in Transition, Beck, 416-541; Bizergan, 201-231; Nashat, 141-195, and 217-261

Week Ten

June 2: Women and Revolution: Algerian Women, Beck 251-261; Bizergan, 251-263; 319-359

June 3: Women' Role in the Iranian Revolution, Nashat, 87-141

June 4: Women's Prospects, Bizergan,373-401; Nashat, 285-289

Week Eleven

June 9 :Final Examination

Department of History
Georgetown University

WOMEN IN THE MIDDLE EAST

144-588-01
W. 11:15-1:05

Prof. Tucker
ICC 622
Office hours:
M. 11-12, W. 1:30-2:30
and by appointment

The colloquium surveys the major developments in women's history in the Middle East from the rise of Islam to the present with particular emphasis on the nineteenth and twentieth centuries. We cover women's economic activities, their relation to political institutions and movements, social and familial life, and cultural contributions. We are concerned with woman's reciprocal relationship with society: with the ways in which women have been viewed and treated as well as the ways in which they have shaped history the history of the region. We try, whenever possible, to hear the woman's voice through the reading of first-hand accounts. Throughout, we address the problem of, and changes in, the gender-based organization of society.

The colloquium revolves around student discussion. It is essential that all students come to class prepared to discuss the assigned reading. Such preparation and participation is a requirement of the course and counts for 25% of the final grade. There is no examination, but two written assignments are required:

1) Bibliographical essay

Each student should choose one of the following topics and prepare a bibliographical essay in which you discuss the major books and articles relevant to the topic in essay form, focusing on the approaches used, the major themes in analysis, the debates or disagreements, etc., among the authors who have contributed to the question. Your own evaluation of the work should be included. Please discuss a preliminary bibliography with the instructor before submitting the final essay, typed and 10 to 12 pages in length, on October 28. Students will be asked to give brief oral presentations of their findings at appropriate class sessions. The essay should cover one of the following areas:

1) Women and production, the 19th century
2) Women and production, the 20th century
3) Women and politics, the 19th century
4) Women and politics, the 20th century
5) Women and social life (includes family), the 19th century
6) Women and social life (includes family), the 20th century
) Women and religion, the 19th century
Women and religion, the 20th century

Ess constitutes 25% of grade.

2) Final Paper

A research paper of 20-25 pages on a relevant topic of your choice is due on December 9. The paper may examine in depth any aspect of women's history in the Middle East, but should be typewritten and adhere to proper academic form for a research paper. Paper constitutes 50% of grade.

BOOKS

The following books are available for sale at the bookstore:
Lois Beck and Nikki Keddie, Women in the Muslim World.
Berenice Carroll, Liberating Women's History.
Elizabeth Fernea, Women and the Family in the Middle East.
E. W. Fernea and B. Bezirgan, Middle Eastern Muslim Women Speak.
Fatima Mernissi, Beyond the Veil.
Nawal El-Saadawi, Woman at Point Zero.

These books, and all other assigned readings, are also on reserve at Lauinger Library.

READINGS AND CLASS SCHEDULE

Sept. 9: Approaches to Women's History

Reading: Frederick Engels, The Origins of the Family, Private Property, and the State, Leascock ed., chapt.2, "The Family", pp.94-146.
Karen Sacks, "Engels Revisited: Women, and Organization of Production, and Private Property," in Rayna Reiter, ed., Toward an Anthropology of Women, pp.211-234.
Ann J. Lane, "Women in Society: A Critique of Frederick Engels," in Berenice Carroll, Liberating Women's History, pp.4-25.
Ann D. Gordon, Mary Jo Buhle, and Nancy Schrom Dye, "The Problem of Women's History," in Carroll, Liberating, pp.4-25.
Gerda Lerner, "Placing Women in History: A 1975 Perspective," in Carroll, Liberating, pp.357-367.

Sept. 16: Approaches to Women's History, the Middle East

Reading: Rosemary Sayigh, "Roles and Functions of Arab Women," Arab Studies Quarterly, III,3 (1981).
Judith Tucker, "Problems in the Historiography of Women in the Middle East," International Journal of Middle East Studies (IJMES), 15 (1983), 321-336.
Lois Beck and Nikki Keddie, Women in the Muslim World, introduction, pp.1-34.
Mervat Hatem, "Class and Patriarchy as Competing Paradigms," Comparative Studies in Society and History, forthcoming (ms. on reserve in Library).

Sept. 23: Early Islam

Reading: Charis Waddy, _Women in Muslim History_, chapts. 1-2, pp.10-56.
E.W. Fernea and B. Bezirgan, _Middle Eastern Muslim Women Speak_, Part I. sections 2,3, pp.7-36.
Fatima Mernissi, _Beyond the Veil_, Part I, pp.1-41.

Sept. 30: The Classical Period

Reading: Waddy, _Women_, chapts.6-9, pp.69-108.
S.D. Goitein, _Mediterranean Society_, vol.III, pp.312-359.
Basim Musallam, _Sex and Society in Islam_, chapts. 1,2,6, pp.10-38, 105-121.
Fernea and Bezirgan, _Middle Eastern_, Part I, sections 4,5, pp.37-76.

Oct. 7: The Ottoman Period

Reading: Fanny Davis, _The Ottoman Lady_, chapts. 1,3,10,13, pp.1-32, 45-60, 171-186, 217-244.
Gabriel Baer, "Women and Waqf: An Analysis of the Istanbul Tahrir of 1546," _Asian and African Studies_, XVII, 1-3, 9-28
Ulku Bates, "Women as Patrons of Architecture in Turkey," in Beck and Keddie, _Muslim Women_, pp.245-260.
R.C. Jennings, "Women in the Early 17th century Ottoman Judicial Records: The Sharia Court of Anatolian Kayseri," _Journal of the Economic and Social History of the Orient_ (JESHO), 28, 1975.

Nineteenth and Twentieth Century Themes

Oct. 14: Women and Production, the 19th Century

Reading: Margot Badran, "Women and Production in the Middle East and North Africa," _Trend in History_, II,3, 1982.
Judith Tucker, _Women in 19th Century Egypt_, chapts. 1,2, pp.16-101.
Abraham Marcus, "Men, Women, and Property: Dealers in Real Estate in 18th Century Aleppo," JESHO, XXVI,2,1983, 137-163.

Oct. 21: Women and Production, the 20th Century

Reading: _MERIP Reports_, #95, "Women and Work in the Middle East," 3-23.

Susan Schaefer Davis, "Working Women in a Moroccan Village," in Beck and Keddie, Women, pp. 416-433.
Andrea Rugh, "Women and Work, Strategies and Choices in a Lower-Class Quarter of Cairo," in Fernea, Women and the Family in the Middle East, pp.273-288.
Fernea and Bezirgan, Middle Eastern, Part III, section 14, pp.219-230, Part IV, section 21, pp.359-371.

Oct. 28: Women and Politics, the 19th Century

Reading: Judith Tucker, Women, chapts. 3,4, pp.102-163.
Thomas Phillip, "Feminism and Nationalist Politics in Egypt," in Beck and Keddie, Women, pp.277-294.
Juan Ricardo Cole, "Feminism, Class and Islam in Turn-of-the-Century Egypt," IJMES, XIII,1981, 384-407.
Shireen Mahdevi, "Women and Ideas in Qajar Iran," Asian and African Studies, XIX, 1985, 187-197.

Nov. 4: Women and Politics, the 20th Century

Reading: Earl Sullivan, Women in Egyptian Public Life, Intro., chapts. 1,2,4,6, pp.1-78, 103-124, 151-170.
Nora Benallegue, "Algerian Women in the Struggle for Independence and Reconstruction," International Social Science Journal, XXXV,4, 1983, 703-717.
Suad Joseph, "Women and the Neighborhood Street in Borj Hammoud, Lebanon," in Beck and Keddie, Women, pp.541-557.
Rosemary Sayigh,"Encounters with Palestinian Women under Occupation," in E.W. Fernea, Women and the Family, pp.191-208.

Nov.11: Society and Culture, the 19th Century

Reading: Afaf Lutfi al-Sayyid Marsot, "The Revolutionary Gentlewoman in Egypt," in Beck and Keddie, Women, pp.261-276.
Leila Ahmed, "Western Ethnocentricism and Perceptions of the Harem," Feminist Studies, VIII,3 (Fall, 1982), 521-524.
Byron D. Cannon, "Nineteenth Century Arabic Writings on Women and Society," IJMES, XVII, 4, 436-484.
Erel Sonmez, "Turkish Women in the Literature of the XIXth Century," Hacettepe Bulletin of Social Science and the Humanities, 1, 17-42, and 2, 123-157.

Nov. 18: Society and Culture, the 20th Century

Reading: Emrys L. Peters, "The Status of Women in Four Middle East Communities," in Beck and Keddie, Women, pp.311-

350.
Nermin Abadan-Unat, "Social Change and Turkish Women," in Abadan-Unat, ed., Women in Turkish Society, pp.5-36.
Mustafa O. Attir, "Ideology, Value Changes, and Women's Social Position in Libyan Society," in Fernea, Women and the Family, pp.121-133.
Fatima Aheb and Malika Abdelaziz, "Algerian Women Discuss the Need for Change," in Fernea, Women and the Family, pp.8-23.
Aminah al-Sa[c]id, "The Arab Woman and the Challenge of Society," in Fernea and Bezirgan, Middle Eastern, Part IV, section 22, pp.373-390.

Nov. 25: Women and Religion

Reading: Valerie J. Hoffman, "An Islamic Activist: Zaynab al-Ghazali," in Fernea, Women and the Family, pp.233-254.
Valerie J. Hoffman-Ladd, "Polemics on the Modesty and Segregation of Women in Contempoary Egypt," IJMES, XIX), 1987, 23-50.
Shireen Mahdavi, "The Position of Women in Shi[c]a Islam: Views of the Ulama," in Fernea, Women and the Family, pp.255-268.
Fatna A. Sabbah, Women in the Muslim Unconscious, chapts.1-3, 9-13, pp.3-22, 63-118.

Dec. 2: Social and Psychological Costs

Reading: Nawal El-Saadawi, Woman at Point Zero, entire.

Dec. 9: Conclusion; PAPERS DUE

ABOUT THE EDITOR

Guity Nashat received her Ph.D from the University of Chicago. She is associate professor of History at the University of Illinois, Chicago. Nashat is the author of *The Origins of Modern Reformation in Iran* (1982) and editor of *Women and Revolution in Iran* (1983), and has published numerous articles about Women's and Iranian history.